ENGLISH PORCELAIN AND BONE CHINA

PLATE 1

Water-colour painted by Thomas Baxter in about 1810, showing the interior of his father's china-decorating workshop at No. 1 Goldsmith Street, Gough Square, Clerkenwell, London. On the wall is a printed bill headed "New Price List, Coalport White China". Thomas Baxter was a celebrated decorator at Swansea and Worcester in the style of the finished plate seen in the foreground.

BERNARD AND THERLE HUGHES

ENGLISH
PORCELAIN
AND
BONE CHINA
1743–1850

LUTTERWORTH PRESS
LONDON

To
L. E. M. P.
and
C. C. P.

7188 1392 8

CONTENTS

CONTENTS

6

LIST OF ILLUSTRATIONS

7

9

FOREWORD

ANTIQUE porcelain is one of England's most fascinating but tantalizing treasures. For its collector, even more than for the connoisseur of many other antiques, a major delight is the limitless range of his subject. Potter, chemist, art authority and social historian are always liable to bring to light new facts, or new evaluations or interpretations of long-established data, that may combine to give a treasured specimen in the china cabinet a new, and sounder, attribution of place or date. It is the purpose of this book to present the collector, in brief but straightforward outline, with an up-to-date appraisal of the position regarding England's valuable heritage of porcelains.

Here, then, is a volume that aims to be something rather different from a mere compilation of facts taken from the overwhelming list of earlier publications on the subject. It has been the constant aim throughout to reject as far as humanly possible the inaccuracies that have constituted so large a part of oft-repeated porcelain lore, and a certain amount of new material has been put in its place. Some of the accompanying conjectures are included with the full realization that they contradict other writers, their justification being that they are made from a strictly technical, factual basis and after wide discussion with leading potters. Perpetuated errors, no doubt, will be found, nevertheless: that is inevitable in such a complex field. Moreover, the more thorough collector is likely to find his pieces showing considerable individual variations from the commonly accepted descriptions, for no porcelain factory could afford to be static. Technicians were always experimenting with processes, and modifying pastes and glazes to secure either better or cheaper porcelains or to meet any of the innumerable crises, such as a supply failure of an essential material.

It cannot be expected, therefore, that the brief descriptions of various pastes given here cover exhaustively the output of any pottery throughout its career.

So few examples of several minor soft-paste porcelain factories have as yet come to light that very little can usefully be said about them. We can only remind the reader of their existence: perhaps to-morrow their turn for recognition will come. These are: Torksey (1803–08), Wirksworth (*c.* 1800), Pinxton (1796–1818) and Church Gresley (1794–1808).

We are indebted to the Secretary and Librarian of the Royal Society of Arts for putting at our disposal contemporary documents and letters with reference to cobalt. A number of the photographs acknowledged to the Victoria and Albert Museum are from the Museum publication *Catalogue of the Schreiber Collection, Vol. I, Porcelain*, 1928, now unfortunately out of print. We are grateful to Mr Gresham Copeland, great-grandson of the first William Copeland, for advice concerning the chapter on Spode.

1

THE STORY OF PORCELAIN

WHEN some unknown Italian shell worker chanced to liken the shape of one lustrous variety to *porcellana* or "little pig", he can scarcely have foreseen that its glistening beauty would prompt the application of the name porcelain to the most exquisite of man-made ceramics—smooth, glistening, above all translucent.

The whole story of porcelain is intimately concerned with that delicate translucence. Even in the Orient there was no sudden discovery of porcelain. Kaolin was being used by the fourth century. But the application of the right natural earths had to be followed by the gradual development of adequate manufacturing methods before the ware could be distinguished from pottery by the perfect fusion of body and glaze into a single, translucent entity. In Europe, the direct copying of oriental ware was rivalled by the composition of substitutes with a translucent delicacy that earned lasting admiration for such manufactories as Chelsea, Worcester and Bow.

Throughout the century most immediately and prolifically the concern of the antiques collector to-day, England contributed some of the loveliest wares and some of the most notable techniques associated with the whole craft of ceramics. But it is essential from the outset that the collector should recognize the range of ceramics termed "porcelain" or, still more vaguely, "china", but distinct from all the other forms of solid, opaque earthenware.

The porcelain of the Orient—true porcelain, or hard-paste porcelain—is a blend of two natural earths which fuse with the overlying glaze into a single hard, translucent

15

substance by firing at a very high temperature. In the eighteenth century, when Europe began serious porcelain manufacture, England produced some hard porcelain (see Chapters 18 to 20), but very much more of what is known as soft-paste or frit porcelain, in which a range of substitute materials were given translucence by the introduction of a glassy frit. And even before the end of the century both hard and soft porcelains were being rivalled by another group of ceramics—the stronger yet still translucent bone china.

Only when fully aware of these divisions, and of the varying limitations and problems they set the potter, can the collector appreciate the craftsmanship of his specimens, and give them their rightful places in the story of porcelain.

This story begins as early as the Tang dynasty (A.D. 618–907), when potters in the Kiangsi province of China, where vast deposits of china-clay had been discovered, were making a ware known as "artificial jade". In the year 621 Ho Chung-Chu, celebrated for his thin, jade-like ware, was appointed purveyor of ceramics to the Imperial Court.

Not until early in the Ming dynasty (1368–1644) did the Chinese potters exploit the technical possibilities of porcelain, with underglaze blue-and-white, and overglaze polychrome enamel decoration. Its manufacture then centred in Ching-tê Chên and in 1369 it came under Imperial control. Statuettes and other decorative pieces were made, as well as useful wares, but many technical improvements were required before it became the superb product associated with the reign of the Emperor K'ang-hsi (1662–1722) and his two successors of the Ch'ing dynasty—pure white, translucent, exquisitely shaped and brilliantly enamelled. Lustrous over-glaze colours were the delight of the K'ang-hsi period, the most prominent being green; delicate opaque enamels dominated by rose-pink shades were favoured later.

Porcelain, the true, hard-paste porcelain of China, is made from two main ingredients, the fusible natural silicate of alumina, a brilliantly white, fine-grained material soft to the touch, known variously as petuntse, china-stone and felspar, and the china-clay or kaolin, which gives the paste its plastic quality, named after the Pass of Kaoling, Kiangsi, where it was originally found, and occasionally called "plastic stone". These two natural earths blended together and fired at great heat produce a vitreous white substance of extreme hardness, ringing with a sonorous metallic note when lightly struck, and breaking with a clean smooth fracture disclosing a fine sparkling grain of compact texture.

As a preliminary the Chinese weathered their kaolin for twenty or thirty years before use to increase the strength of their paste, a process reduced in English manufacture to seven or eight months in a damp cellar. The petuntse was cut from the quarry in brick-sized blocks, dried, and ground to a fine powder. The quality of porcelain is dependent upon the purity of its ingredients, and both petuntse and kaolin were cleaned by complicated and prolonged washing processes. The final sediment was dried and sold to the potters in the form of tile-shaped blocks.

The best Chinese porcelain contained equal parts of these two ingredients: a greater proportion of kaolin made harder porcelain and the paste was easier to handle, but the greatly increased firing temperature required was almost an impossibility in China until early in the nineteenth century. The technical difficulties of hard-porcelain manufacture can be appreciated when it is realized that the unfired clay is difficult to mould and, since it softens at one period during firing, tends to collapse beneath its own weight. To prevent this a varying thickness is desirable; but at the same time, because of shrinkage during firing, the porcelain tends to become misshapen when the piece is not of uniform thickness.

The Chinese potter crushed the blocks of petuntse and kaolin to fine powder, which was carefully rewashed. The necessary proportions were then kneaded together to form a homogeneous paste which was shaped on a potter's wheel, or, from the Ming period, might be pressed in moulds. The ware was then air-dried and decorated. A glaze was applied over the surface with a brush, or sprayed by blowing it through a hollow cane covered with silk. The porcelain was then fired in kilns heated by wood fuel to a temperature of no more than 800 degrees centigrade, with the result that Chinese porcelain is less hard than the comparable European hard porcelain of the eighteenth century.

Chinese porcelain was imported into England during the fifteenth century, luxury ware only for the very rich, under the term "china-metall", defined in a work of reference dated 1599 as "fine dishes of earth painted". During the Tudor and early Stuart régimes it was usually styled "purslane", although Ellis in his *Letters* written during 1530 refers to "iij potts of Erthe payntid, callyd Porceland".

Little Chinese porcelain came to Europe until after 1577 when the Portuguese East India Company founded a trading settlement at Macau near Canton. The Dutch soon competed for this profitable monopoly, and by the end of the sixteenth century large quantities of Chinese porcelain were being unloaded at Amsterdam: in 1615 a single ship brough 70,000 pieces. Not until 1631 did the British East India Company begin importing porcelain on a grand scale.

Spasmodic endeavours were made in Europe from the middle of the fifteenth century to reproduce Chinese porcelain. All these attempts were concerned with alchemy rather than chemistry, for the mysterious "earth" reported by travellers in the East was believed to be associated with the philosopher's stone, magical infusion, and arcana.

An attempt to reproduce oriental porcelain in England during 1506 resulted in failure, materials being unsuitable and casualties in the kiln far too costly for the experiment to continue. A further attempt was made in 1587, and during the following year gifts of English porcelain were received by Queen Elizabeth I: nothing more is known of the venture. John Dwight of Fulham, famous for his fine stoneware, was granted a patent in 1671 for making a material described in the specification as "transparent earthenware commonly known by the names of porcelain or china". None of this has come to light, although a considerable amount of Dwight's stoneware has been identified: his porcelain was probably nothing beyond a thin, good quality stoneware. Francis Place of York and John Clifton of Pontefract may have produced negligible quantities of porcelain.

The growing popularity of *chinoiseries* coincided with

increased economic activity, and the successful reproduction of Chinese porcelain became a matter of importance. The country first to acquire the secret of making true porcelain was certain of an enormous profit-making monopoly. European potters believed that porcelain clay was obtained from beds of natural paste buried in the earth, congealed into porcelain by exposure to the sun and then glazed. Hakluyt in 1599 and Bacon in 1615 refer to this. The theory was disproved in March 1709 when Johann Friedrich Böttger made the first European porcelain in Saxony. This ware was in fact superior to the Chinese in one respect: it was fired at a higher temperature and in consequence was harder.

In the following year the Elector Augustus the Strong of Saxony founded a porcelain factory in Meissen near Dresden, but unexpected technical difficulties arose and not until 1713 was Meissen porcelain sold at Leipzig Fair: a further two years passed before flaws of firing and glaze were sufficiently reduced to make the venture successful. Even then the prosperous development of the porcelain was delayed until the 1720s, after the death of Böttger. Augustus III of Saxony between 1733 and 1753 added a million and a half thalers to his income, as well as acquiring porcelain worth half a million thalers. In eighteenth-century England hard-paste porcelain was made only at Plymouth, Bristol and New Hall in Staffordshire.

Meanwhile, experiments had been made in other continental countries to find possible substitute formulæ, the basic requirement being merely translucence. These were based on the assumption that this essential was analogous with the translucence of glass, and were really mixtures of glass and clay fired at comparatively low temperatures. They contained a vitreous frit—a mixture of white sand, gypsum, soda, alum, salt and nitre melted together in a mass, then broken and pulverized—together with clay and lime. The result was a thoroughly vitrified substance, possessing at its best a creamy or ivory white tint, to which glazing gave a waxy surface. But imperfect blending of the materials often resulted in defects known as grease spots or mooning—small discs of greater translucence visible against a strong light. Decoration was mainly applied over the soft lead glaze, into which the colours sank slightly.

Soft-paste or frit porcelain was made at Florence in 1568 by Francesco de Medici, but it was the celebrated physicist and naturalist René-Antoine-Ferchault de Réamur (1683–1757) who succeeded in producing the first commercially profitable soft-paste frit porcelain, known as Réamur porcelain. This was fired at low temperatures, the frit giving it translucency. The paste had a decidedly yellowish hue and a fine regular grain, and was given a clear brilliant glaze.

This frit porcelain was made at St. Cloud, the factory at which Thomas Briand, one of the founders of Chelsea, possibly learned the technique of porcelain manufacture. No hard-paste porcelain was made in France until after 1768, when a deposit of fine kaolin was discovered at Limoges and production started at Sèvres and elsewhere from 1770. In spite of all efforts, however, soft-paste porcelain remained the mainstay of the French porcelain industry until the nineteenth century.

All the English soft-paste porcelains of the eighteenth century followed Réamur's method, although there was wide variation in ingredients. Notably different in appearance, although still classed as a soft-paste porcelain, was the bone porcelain—not to be confused with the later non-frit bone china, also an English invention—first made by Thomas Frye at Bow from 1749. In this bone ash was introduced to produce greater plasticity.

A comprehensive description of soft-paste or frit porcelain making in England is given in *The Complete Dictionary of Arts and Sciences*, 1764, under the heading of "Chinaware". The writer repeats Robert Dossie's reference in 1762 to the factory employing eleven mills in grinding china wasters for use as "grog" (see Chapter 7). The *Dictionary* refers also to another factory which would appear to be Chelsea. In this interesting contemporary comment the ware is described as being of "great whiteness, and a texture that admits of its being modelled or cast in the most delicate manner; but it is formed of a composition so vitrescent as to have almost the texture of glass: and consequently to break or crack if boiling water be suddenly poured upon it;

which quality renders it unfit for any uses but the making of ornamental pieces. The works at Dresden and St. Vincennes in France may, therefore, be esteemed the only manufactories in Europe advanced as yet to any degree of perfection".

The fragility of the soft porcelains, and their liability to become misshapen in firing and to crack at the touch of hot liquids, was overcome to some extent by the introduction of soapstone instead of china-clay. But a new sturdiness was introduced by Josiah Spode during the early 1790s when non-frit bone china appeared, combining the materials of hard-paste porcelain with bone ash made from the burnt bones of cattle. For the first time a white paste of even translucency could be marketed at a reasonable price, chiefly owing to a great reduction in the number of wasters. This bone china is really a porcelain intermediate between hard porcelain and soft porcelain, its translucency being due to the formation of a glassy material by combination of bone ash and silica.

Experts recognize soft-paste porcelain by the feel of its surface. To the finger-tip it somewhat resembles the surface of new toilet soap. Where chipped or broken a piece of Georgian soft-paste porcelain will feel roughish and granular; but if the porcelain is hard the surface of the fracture will be flint-like, curving off from the point of percussion. If the edge of the fracture is drawn across the finger-nail a hard porcelain will mark the nail; a soft porcelain will leave no mark. Soft-paste porcelains vary in degree of hardness, but all except those made with soapstone can be scratched by steel. They are also susceptible to acids.

Somewhere on every piece of eighteenth-century porcelain will be found a small unglazed area. If this can be marked when scratched by the finger-nail or with a pen-knife blade, then the porcelain is soft. While scraping with the nail it is almost possible to feel the paste crumbling away. If the paste is hard, scratching will merely roughen the finger-nail.

In the case of hard-paste porcelain, decorations were usually applied direct to the biscuit ware. Before thin pieces were decorated the ware was painted with a solution of sugar to prevent colours sinking into the paste. The colours curded slightly during the firing, baking on to the biscuit rather than into it. The piece was then dipped into glaze and again fired at a much higher temperature. This vitrified both body and glaze, making the porcelain appear as though covered with a heavy coating of varnish.

This underglaze decoration was more difficult to fire than that applied over the glaze because the intense heat of the glazing oven tended to spoil nearly all colours with the exception of cobalt blue. Black, brown, yellow and green are also found, while copper oxide fired in a reducing atmosphere produced brilliant reds. Overglaze decoration was applied above a coating of fired glaze without the addition of a further protective glaze. The range of colours possible with this method was unlimited.

Georgian hard-paste porcelain was fired at a low temperature in the unglazed state to produce biscuit ware. Then, after the application of a thin, transparent glaze, it was re-fired at a higher temperature. Soft-paste porcelain was first fired at a temperature higher than that required for glazing, but not by any means so high as for hard-paste porcelain or porosity would have been lessened, making the ware incapable of retaining the glaze. Colours applied under glaze slightly sank into the soft biscuit, which was then glazed and fired. In overglaze decoration the colours were fixed by re-firing at a lesser heat than the glazing temperature. English colours were less transparent, less brilliant and applied in thinner washes than the oriental.

An excellent test to distinguish hard from soft pastes is to hold the porcelain at a slant to the light. On hard porcelain the glaze is rather dull and light is not reflected; on soft-paste porcelain both glaze and colour gleam together. In Georgian soft-paste porcelain the paste, colours and glaze blended into a tender brightness. So soft was the glaze on the early soft-paste porcelains that cups were scratched inside merely by the stirring of spoons. To the collector all these details are far more important than the factory marks beneath some pieces. Many of these have been reproduced on modern copies. Other marks are liable to mislead the beginner-collector. For instance, there was the mid-nineteenth-century vogue for including in the mark the date of a factory's original foundation, often long before porcelain or china was made there. Coalport, for instance, might add to its mark the date "A.D. 1750", a period a full quarter of a century earlier than the first manufacture of porcelain at Caughley. The addition of the word ENGLAND to a mark indicates manufacture after 1894.

2

THE surface brilliance of porcelain and bone china is brought about by coating the paste with glaze. This is essentially a transparent, vitreous substance, and when it was applied to porcelains it sealed their slight porosity, making them impervious to liquids; it produced smooth, glossy surfaces; and it acted as an ideal foundation for enamel ornament painted over the glaze, and as protection for ornament under the glaze.

Early glazes contained a considerable amount of lead oxide, and are now termed "lead glazes", although they were known contemporaneously as "varnishes", a name that continued in use throughout the eighteenth century. For several decades lead glaze was notable for its softness, and could be scratched easily, even by a spoon stirred in a cup or by the cutting edge of a knife upon a plate.

English potters for centuries glazed their earthenware by a process known as leading, a method which continued into the early years of soft porcelain. They used a fine-quality natural sulphide of lead known as smithum, more recently as galena. This was prepared for use by melting the lead in a crucible, throwing charcoal dust upon the liquid, then stirring for a long period. After separation by washing, the resulting lead was dried and ground to a fine powder.

The green ware, leather hard and unfired, was dusted with this and fired at a moderate temperature, baking the clay and melting the lead so that it spread into a thick, smooth coating over the ware. Hardening of the clay and glazing were done in a single operation: no second firing was needed. The finished ware had a high gloss and the glaze should have been colourless. The presence of impurities such as iron, however, produced a rich yellow or brownish tinge, and sometimes the glaze had a bubbly appearance.

The early porcelain makers improved upon this by dusting their green ware with calcined lead ground to a flour-like powder. This produced a smoother, colourless glaze which penetrated farther into the paste than the glaze prepared from smithum and finished with a higher gloss. When applied over blue underglaze ornamentation this glaze gave to the colour a delicate sheen.

This was quickly superseded by transparent frit glazes applied over the biscuit with a brush, or, in the case of decoration in relief, with pencil brushes. Care was taken to ensure even distribution and prevent accumulation in hollow parts. Embossing on fine porcelain was given two or three coatings of this glaze, each being allowed to become almost dry before another was applied.

Every potter had his own formula for frit glazes, but according to Robert Dossie writing in 1764 they were all subject to crazing after manufacture. This crazing was visible to the naked eye and not only did it "impair the polish, but gave moreover a coat of greyness to the colour".

The method of glazing porcelain by dipping the biscuit into a prepared liquid, and refiring to fuse it on the porcelain, was introduced to England by the Frye-Heylin patent of 1744 (see Chapter 7). This method of glazing was therefore a legally protected process until 1758, the monopoly being further extended to 1763 by a patent in 1749. Any other firm employing liquid glaze would require therefore to be licensed by the patentees. There is no evidence that licences were issued, but it seems highly probable that Frye took this course after leaving Bow.

An improved version of glazing was incorporated into Thomas Frye's patent of 1749, the specification reading: "take salt petre one part, red lead two parts, sand, flint or other white stones [calcined and ground to flour fineness] three parts. To make a glass [frit] melt this well and afterwards grind it. To every twenty pounds of this add six pounds of white lead, adding a small portion of smalt to clean the colour."

This was finely ground in water until of a suitable consistency for applying to the biscuit porcelain by dipping. The porcelain was then dried in a warm room, "put into cases [saggars] and burned with a clear wood fire until the surface of the ware was clear and shining". A further advantage of this method of glazing was that the glaze was fully transparent and the glossy surface reliably uniform. These two firings, in the biscuit oven and the glost oven, have been standard glazing practices ever since. The glaze is always inclined to be thick and obviously lies on the surface of the porcelain, a feature overcome by some potters during the 1770s. The individual glazes used by the different potteries are discussed under their chapter headings.

Frye's patent did not extend to earthenware, with the result that liquid glaze was introduced to the Potteries in about 1750 by Enoch Booth who had established a factory at Tunstall five years earlier. It was this transparent liquid lead glaze that gave Whieldon a new decorative medium for his earthenware. He took this glaze and coloured it with various metallic oxides, intermingling his shades to produce the tortoiseshell effects for which he was celebrated.

Frye's method of glazing was taken up eventually by all makers of soft porcelain and continued in use throughout the eighteenth century. The basic materials for producing transparent glazes remained unaltered, but each potter possessed a favourite formula. Until the 1770s the frit was melted in uncovered pots, and the contents might become discoloured by black drops falling from the roof of the furnace. This accounts for specks and flaws and the tendency for some early glazes to display a greyish hue. "Caped" or covered pots were introduced by Robert Sherbourne during the early 1770s.

Glazing on soft-paste porcelain has often become crazed: that is, it has cracked in a network of thin, irregular lines crossing each other in all directions. This defect is due to constant changes in atmospheric conditions, body and glaze expanding and contracting in response to these changes at different rates. When the glaze contracted to a greater extent than the body, crazing was inevitable. Crazed porcelain that has been stored for a long period in a damp place sometimes displays extensive brown stains due to the penetration of moisture into the porous paste beneath.

In a large collection of authenticated pieces it has been observed that where the porcelain has stood upon its base the protected underside has retained its original brilliance. The remainder of the glazed surface, having been exposed to light and atmospheric pollution, is invariably slightly discoloured.

As porcelain potters became more familiar with the capabilities of their materials, and processes were improved, crazing was virtually overcome, and little made after about 1780 displays this defect.

Felspathic glaze was used on the hard porcelains of Plymouth, Bristol and New Hall, as lead glaze failed to adhere to the surface of such porcelain. English felspathic glaze consisted of the same constituents as the body of the porcelain, but in different proportions, containing more felspar and less kaolin. Felspathic glazes, viscous and slightly milky, have a velvety, richer appearance than calcareous glazes and were applied more thickly. Calcareous glazes, with the addition of limestone flux, were also used on hard porcelain, being more transparent than the felspathic and penetrating farther into the paste. The processes associated with the glazing of hard-paste porcelains are dealt with in Chapter 18.

By the end of the century glazing technique had been standardized to some extent and was brought into use for the new bone china. The glaze for this ware was composed chiefly of Cornish stone, powdered calcined flint, white lead, flint-glass cullet, whiting and other fusible materials. These were ground together in suitable proportions with water until of a fine creamy consistency.

The glazing was carried out in dipping houses fitted with large tubs containing glaze. Stages were erected for the reception of the dipped ware, upon which it was dried. Heating was achieved by means of a large iron stove, known as a "cockle", from which iron pipes extended in various directions so that there was an equable heat throughout the houses.

Each dipper stood at a tub of liquid glaze. A boy handed him the biscuit ware, one piece at a time, which he held so that as small an area as possible was protected by the fingers. He then plunged it into the glaze, and by a skilful jerk coated the entire surface. The biscuit being porous imbibed the water, leaving an even coating of fusible material upon its surface. An able workman could glaze as many as seven hundred dozen plates in a twelve-hour day.

The piece was then handed to a boy who carried it to the "hot house" for drying. The glaze was opaque until fired, so that any underglaze painting or printing was hidden from view. Upon removal from the glost oven the glaze was transparent with a brilliant surface through which any underglaze decoration was clearly visible.

Glaze dippers notoriously died after a few years at work, because of lead poisoning. Attempts were long made to produce a smooth, hard leadless glaze for bone china. Josiah Wedgwood invented a hard leadless glaze, but so rough was its surface that it was no competitor with lead glaze. Although glaze made from unfritted lead was virtually innocuous, so exact was the firing needed to produce a transparent glaze with a smooth hard surface, in a day when rule-of-thumb methods necessarily predominated, that it was never used.

A hard highly lustrous glaze was evolved by John Rose of Coalport in 1820, however, in an effort to avoid hazards to health. The Society of Arts reported Rose's glaze to be the finest that had come under their observation and awarded him the Isis gold medal. Rose's leadless glaze had the advantage of fusing at a lower temperature than lead glaze and without specks and flaws. Enamels incorporated solidly with it, brilliance and tint being unaffected, resulting in more radiant colours. Lead glaze caused off-tinting of coloured enamels, particularly those containing gold or chrome.

The published recipe, which remained unpatented, was "27 felspar, 18 borax, 4 Lynn sand, 3 Cornwall china clay. This was melted to a frit, ground to a fine powder with three parts of calcined borax added before grinding." Owing to the high cost of borax, leadless glaze was used only on expensively decorated bone china requiring repeated firings, until after the development of the Etruscan borax deposits in 1828.

During the 1840s borax glaze came into general use as a flux in glaze for bone china, partially displacing lead glaze, which continued to be used, however, on most domestic ware. A non-frit borax glaze was also used: this always produced a surface full of imperfections and was much less glossy than lead glaze.

3

TECHNICALLY the most successful, æsthetically the most satisfying, blue has always been the colour especially associated with porcelain decoration. For long it was almost the only colour that could endure the heat of the glost oven and thus be used for the more enduring underglaze form of ornament. Yet even among those who specialize in the collection of lovely "blue and white" porcelains there appear to be few who have any exact knowledge of the terms zaffre, smalt, and the rest. In this chapter it is proposed to outline the story of this important metal in relation to porcelain decoration.

Chinese potters long decorated with a blue that they knew as Mohammedan blue, imported by them from Persia. But this was ultramarine, a colour prepared from the azure stone lapis lazuli, and not from cobalt ore as so often suggested. Blue manufactured from indigenous cobalt does not appear to have been used by the Chinese until late in the Ming period (1403–1619) although there is evidence of supplies being shipped from Amsterdam to Canton by the Dutch East India Company in the late sixteenth century. The beauty and technical perfection demanded in porcelain by the Emperor K'ang-hsi (1662–1722) brought about the creation of an intense, luminous cobalt blue which the Chinese decorators skilfully applied in exquisite tone gradations envied by contemporary potters and connoisseurs alike.

The making of this superlative blue was highly extravagant in time: the final pulverizing, for instance, might occupy more than a year of continuous hand-labour with pestle and mortar. The Chinese potters painted directly on the unfired, air-dried paste. This was subsequently coated with transparent glaze and fired in the kiln. Painting in cobalt blue was in the hands of a highly specialized group of artists, for once it was applied to the absorbent body no corrections were possible.

Cobalt blue does not appear to have been known to either Chinese or Europeans earlier than the 1540s. Suggestions that it was used for decorating pre-Elizabethan earthenware may therefore be disregarded. Cobalt, a greyish-hued metal faintly tinged with red, brittle, slightly magnetic, was first found in Saxony, a state long-celebrated for its richness in minerals.

Christopher Schürer, a glassmaker of Neudeck, discovered during the 1540s that cobalt oxide, produced by roasting cobalt at a great heat, was capable of tinging glass an attractive transparent blue, and, when suitably prepared, could be used for decorating earthenware. This substance he named zaffre. By 1550 production was being carried out on a commercial scale and a new industry was founded. This zaffre contained many impurities. A century passed before it was discovered that insoluble matter could be removed from cobalt oxide by dissolving it in hydrochloric acid and then recovering the cleansed zaffre. This process was several times repeated. Further purifying treatments were evolved in the nineteenth century which removed all traces of copper, lead, iron, bismuth and nickel, but the blue produced by the resultant zaffre gave a less attractive tint to glass and ceramic ornamentation.

The earthenware potters of Holland and elsewhere, exploiting tin-enamelled ware, found in zaffre an ideal colour capable of being fired beneath the glaze and so protected from wear. The pigment consisted of one part of zaffre mixed with four to five parts of calcined flint, both ground to an impalpable powder. This was brush-painted upon the unfired enamel, oil of spike lavender being used as a medium. When applied it was dirty brown in colour: firing at a suitable, equable temperature converted it into the celebrated cobalt blue.

Schürer, primarily interested in glass, continued his

experiments and discovered that more delicate, smoother, bluer blues could be obtained by colouring potassium silicate glass with from 2 to 10 per cent of fine-quality zaffre. While molten this was poured into cold water and then pulverized. Melting, cooling and grinding were repeated ten or a dozen times, making the glass exceedingly hard. The resulting fragments were finally ground in a series of mullers until of flour fineness, and this powder, termed smalt, was stored in small bags of white leather.

Smalt was preferred for ceramic decoration, but its high cost limited its use to expensive ware. Added to molten transparent glass, the metal still remained transparent, but displayed a strong blue tint. One part of fine smalt to ten thousand parts of mid-eighteenth-century flint-glass produced an effective blue.

Dutch colour makers of the seventeenth century improved the quality of cobalt oxide, removing to some extent the indigo tone associated with zaffre. They purified the Saxon cobalt oxide, pulverizing it and the calcined flints by means of windmill-operated granite grindstones. This Dutch smalt, often termed Dutch ultramarine because of its ultimate colour brilliance, was ten times as costly as the Saxon product.

English miniaturists, even by 1573, were already using Saxon smalt for the brilliant blue backgrounds then so fashionable in portraiture. *Treatise concerning the Arte of Limning* by Nicholas Hilliard, *c.* 1600, states that "smalte or florrey being tempered in a shell with gum water maketh a blewe", and in 1612 Peacham noted that the principal blues used by miniaturists were "Blewe bice and Smalt".

Nevertheless, when Augustus the Strong, Elector of Saxony and King of Poland, was organizing the manufacture of hard-paste porcelain at Meissen during the 1720s, he was dismayed to discover Saxon-made smalt incapable of producing the exquisite effects obtained by the Chinese. He therefore offered a premium of one thousand thalers to anyone, no matter of what nationality, who would instruct him in making smalt equal in colour brilliance to the Chinese and capable of being applied in similar delicate gradations of tint. The premium had been claimed and

PLATE 2

Chelsea porcelain sweetmeat stands with figures dressed in pseudo-Turkish costumes, each supporting a large scallop shell, copied from Meissen figures of the Kändler period. Mark, red anchor.

Chelsea porcelain figures adapted from Meissen originals.

PLATE 3

Chelsea porcelain. *Top left:* Madonna and Child group, the Madonna wearing a flowing yellow cloak and the Child, draped with a red cloth, standing on a globe around which is entwined a serpent; red anchor mark; *c.* 1755. *Top right:* actor in Roman costume; red anchor mark; *c.* 1755. *Lower left:* female hen-harrier perched on a tree stump with leaves and flowers. Mark: anchor in relief painted in red on an applied oval medallion; *c.* 1755. *Lower right:* goat-and-bee jug, moulded in relief. The jug is supported on the backs of two goats lying down, and has a twig handle, and there is a bee in relief on the flowers below the spout. Mark: a triangle incised; *c.* 1745.

awarded by 1723 when Augustus established the Royal Saxon smalt works near Dresden. So precious was the monopoly of this superfine smalt to the Royal Saxon Porcelain Manufactory at Meissen that export was forbidden: penalties for smuggling were severe. Smalt had always been costly owing to the labour involved in the continual refining of the ore essential in the production of the basic superfine zaffre: in 1733 a medium quality was exported at £11 an ounce.

Zaffre importations into England had long been substantial, but from the late 1730s there arose a progressively increasing demand for colourful table-wares in blue-painted delft, blue-coloured stoneware, and English porcelain. White salt-glazed stoneware, for instance, was given a surface hue somewhat resembling the later *bleu de roi* of Sèvres, by dipping into a cobalt-stained clay slip before firing. Zaffre and smalt imported in 1748 weighed 180,000 lb., rising to 286,000 lb. by 1754. Supplies ceased early in 1756 when Saxony became involved in war with Prussia.

Cobalt deposits were known to exist in England, and in the spring of 1755 the Society for the Encouragement of the Arts offered a premium of £30 for its discovery in quantities large enough to warrant development. The *Gentleman's Magazine* owned and edited by Edward Cave, a partner in the Worcester Tonquin Manufactory, with a personal interest in cobalt production, published a long essay on cobalt in the issue of May 1755. In the course of this he stated "that large quantities of Cobalt have lately been discovered in England . . . the ore is richer in the metal than the Saxon and disposes of it in fusion much more readily".

The Transactions of the Society record that large cobalt deposits were discovered near the lead mines of Truro early in 1755 by Francis Beauchamp, of Longreed, Givondon, near Helston. After demonstrating to the Society that zaffre and smalt could be made profitably from this cobalt, Beauchamp was awarded the £30 premium. Reports of rich deposits of cobalt ore came also from the Duke of Ancaster's estate in North Wales, and from the lead areas of Derbyshire, Yorkshire and Cumberland.

3*+

Contemporary opinion decided that English cobalt oxide was superior to that formerly made in Saxony. S. More in a letter dated February 11, 1756, now preserved in the Society's Library, wrote: "Some of this [Cornish] zaffre was given to Mr. Stephen Hall, partner with Mr. Hughes, Glass Maker, at the Faulkon Glass House, Southwark, who a few days later gave me a small piece of glass of a most excellent Blew Colour and which had been coloured with this Zaffre, and he told me that two parts of this Zaffre would colour as much glass as three parts of that usually sold. A considerable quantity of this glass was made and a vase sent to the Society of Arts."

A manuscript *Treatise Upon Cobalt*, written by J. B. [randonburgh], M.D., in March 1758, also preserved in the Society's Library, outlined the method of making English smalt. "Melt in a covered crucible two or three parts of sand of flints [ground calcined flint], one part zaffre, and three or four parts of white potash. The molten glass is drawn into slender filaments and then ground to dust in a mortar of glass with a glass pestle." The zaffre is specified as consisting of one part calcined cobalt and one to two parts of calcined flint, both finely ground and thoroughly mixed together. The author also described a water-powered grinding mill designed for commercial production.

English zaffre, however, was not comparable in beauty of colour with the Saxon product. It is recognized on ceramics by its deep hue strongly tinged with indigo, violet or purple, a defect inherent in the basic cobalt and never overcome. This was used by all decorators unable to draw on the fast-dwindling pre-war stocks. Worcester under Dr. Wall and his associates appears to have received supplies from the Beauchamp cobalt mines and to have used English-made smalt for dark powder blue. The dry, finely powdered smalt was blown through a tube, covered at the end with a piece of fine muslin, on to an oiled surface before glazing, thus producing a powdered sprinkled effect.

The Prussians under Frederick the Great were victors when the war ended in February 1763. A group of merchants trading in goods seized from Saxony acquired stocks of superfine smalt removed from the Royal Saxon smalt works.

A considerable quantity of this was disposed of to a Bristol warehouse, believed to have been owned by the wholesale druggist William Cookworthy of Plymouth. He sold it to potters, glass-makers, paper-mills and others at 15*s.* an ounce, far less than the pre-war price of the poorest quality Saxon smalt.

The porcelain painters of England were now able, for the first time, to enrich their work with the superfine ultramarine blues of cobalt silicate, so long a distinguishing feature of fine Meissen porcelain, and which even France had only obtained in small quantity in the late 1740s, following personal requests from the king. A comparable blue had been used in England, but very rarely. This was a preparation of lapis lazuli, a paler and more delicate sky blue than the Meissen smalt, applied sparingly and carefully at great cost.

Variations of tint were secured by altering the proportions of smalt used with the medium: Sèvres blue, mazarine blue and *bleu du roi* were all fine smalt under different names. It has been suggested that Sir Everard Fawkener, secretary to the Duke of Cumberland, obtained a supply of fine smalt from the Prussians before Cumberland's recall in 1758 and sent it to Sprimont at Chelsea. Dr. Wall used the Bristol smalt to such excellent advantage at Worcester that his decorations in this colour more nearly approached K'ang-hsi blue and white than did the work of Meissen: not until the late 1820s, when the Spode firm reproduced Dr. Wall's blue-and-white porcelain in bone china, was this colour ever equalled.

Robert Dossie in his *Handmaid to the Arts*, 1764, suggested that the Saxon cobalt industry was being revived. He recorded that "parcels of fine smalt or vitrified oxide of cobalt brought from Saxony has not long been available in England and is sometimes sold at higher prices as ultramarine [prepared from lapis lazuli], but more usually under its own name". He referred to its "extremely strong body of colour" and noted that "its goodness lies in being dark, bright, and cool although always verging towards purple, but the less so the better". The ceramic and other industries using cobalt products appear to have disliked the violet

35

tinge of the English material, particularly as the hue appeared unexpectedly in varying strengths making standardization impossible. The English cobalt industry could not contend against Saxon reliability and mining was discontinued during the early 1770s. Refiners established in Bristol, Liverpool and Staffordshire continued operating, however, importing Saxon cobalt ore, washed cobalt ore in various strengths, and zaffre containing uniform strengths of cobalt, packed in one-hundredweight casks. Not until the 1790s did the newly equipped cobalt mines and mills of Saxony experience renewed competition, and then from Scandinavia.

The deep-blue tint of cobalt products was known throughout the eighteenth century as "Saxon blue", although from the mid-1750s the term "smalt blue" distinguished the English product. The potters continued using the term "smalt blue": only since the nineteenth century has it been known as "cobalt blue". Ure's *Dictionary of the Arts*, 1853, noted that the darkest coloured smalts were then known as "king's blue" or "azure".

A process for making artificial ultramarine was discovered in about 1802 by a French chemist and named "*bleu de Thenard*". It was little known until the patent had expired, but by the late 1840s had superseded cobalt products for nearly all industrial work. Its colour resembled the bright blue of genuine ultramarine, then only obtainable in quantity from Siberia. Genuine ultramarine cost £20 an ounce in 1848 and was used by jewellers and silversmiths for enamelling precious metals.

Artificial ultramarine at 1s. 3d. a pound, at a time when poor-quality zaffre cost 6s. a pound, was cheap enough to be applied plentifully to bone china and formed the basis of that lovely hue so fashionable from about 1840 to the 1870s and now known to collectors as "Staffordshire blue". Artificial ultramarine was made largely in Birmingham by the nickel refiners, but also in London and Manchester. In Germany its manufacture was monopolized by the Royal Saxon smalt works.

PLATE 4

Chelsea porcelain. *Top row:* cream jug, tea-pot and basin with reeded sides and scalloped rims, painted in colours; *c.* 1755. *Middle row:* plain white porcelain (*a*) figure; (*b*) cup moulded in relief, decorated with fluting over which are curved sprays of flowers in relief, *c.* 1745; (*c*) goat-and-bee cream jug marked with incised triangle, *c.* 1745; (*d*) scent bottle in the form of a woman nursing a child, *c.* 1755. *Bottom row:* (*a*) scent bottle in form of a lady dancing, mounted in gold, *c.* 1755; (*b*) bonbonnière, figure of Cupid playing on a pair of drums, *c.* 1765; (*c*) scent bottle in the form of two boys at a distilling furnace, *c.* 1760; (*d*) scent bottle in the form of Cupid and a woman with clock, *c.* 1760.

PLATE 5

Chelsea porcelain. *Top row:* (*a* and *c*) figures of shepherd and shepherdess on rococo-scrolled bases. The shepherd wears black hat, turquoise-blue coat, pink-lined yellow cloak, red breeches; the shepherdess red drapery, crimson bodice, turquoise-blue skirt and flowered petticoat. Slight gilding. Mark: anchor in gold. *c.* 1765. (*b*) vase enamelled with three panels of exotic birds, and with single bird motifs on foot, *c.* 1765. *Lower row:* (*a* and *c*) a pair of candlestick *bocages* each containing an Æsop's *Fables* group, the "Cock and the Jewel" and "The Vain Jackdaw", *c.* 1768; (*b*) the smallest of a set of three vases moulded in relief and decorated with gilding on a dark mazarine ground. A lizard is coiled around the foot; *c.* 1765.

4

OVERGLAZE ENAMELS

THE radiant enamel colours glowing against the glaze of fine English porcelain and china beguile every collector. Unfortunately, however, technical difficulties long prevented accurate matching of colours, so that some early enamel colours emerged from the muffle distinctly dull and inclined to flake from the glaze. Because of impurities in the ingredients and rule-of-thumb methods of firing in the muffle, no two colour preparations could be guaranteed to produce the same shining tint. The glaze itself might tend to display a greyish hue. Enamelling was regarded as a mysterious craft, processes savouring of magic. Even the most proficient master-enameller on ceramics was compelled to prepare the full range of colours before starting work on a matching service.

This chapter is primarily intended to assist beginner-collectors to realize that there are visible and progressive differences between the enamels painted on soft-paste porcelain, on the hard porcelains of Plymouth, Bristol and New Hall, on the early bone china of Staffordshire, and on ware from about 1820 following the general adoption of Walker's improved muffle. It must also be realized that certain bone china copied the form and decoration of earlier soft-paste porcelains.

Enamels are really coloured glazes used as decoration on ware previously coated with a harder glaze, and then fired at a lower temperature, between 700 and 750 degrees centigrade. The pioneer porcelain potters of England for nearly two decades were faced with the difficulty of finding: (a) chemists capable of supervising preparation of the

37

colours; (*b*) artists skilled in fine enamel painting willing to exchange studio work for purely commercial ceramic decoration; (*c*) firemen experienced at the muffle furnace.

Enamel colours already prepared for the painter were at that time virtually a Venetian monopoly and costly. Robert Dossie recorded in 1764 that such enamels "are now prepared at Meissen since the establishment of the china factories there". Augustus the Strong, Elector of Saxony, had attracted to Dresden men experienced in all departments of enamel painting from Nuremburg, where the art had been highly developed on metal during the preceding half-century. These enamellers adapted their processes to the new medium so successfully that smuggling prepared enamels was made a penal offence and absconding colourmen and foremen risked the headsman's block.

Instructions for making metallic oxides and converting them into enamels had already been published in 1699 by H. Blanchard, and in *Dictionarium Polygraphicum*, 1735. These recipes were of little practical value, however, impure ingredients making them hit-or-miss affairs when prepared without skilled supervision.

Dossie also reported in 1764 that no Englishman was adequately experienced in the preparation and firing of enamels on ceramics, because there had been no opportunity to learn the craft. This suggests knowledge that at Chelsea, Bow and elsewhere enamel preparation and firing of the resultant decoration were under the supervision of foreigners, and that independent enamellers such as Duesbury and Giles used Venetian enamels. Bow did in fact advertise that Meissen enamellers were employed from about 1757. Thomas Craft, who painted a Bow bowl, now in the British Museum, has recorded in an accompanying document that nearly a hundred painters were in continuous employment at Bow. These were, of course, English men and women, and included a numerous group working on blue underglaze decoration.

There is reason to believe that Chelsea obtained supplies of prepared enamels from Meissen through the good offices of Sir Everard Fawkener. These consignments failed upon the outbreak of the Seven Years War in 1756 when

Dresden was occupied by the Prussians. This might have been the underlying reason for the temporary closure of Chelsea from 1756 to 1758.

Dossie collected and published recipes for preparing a range of forty-one tints of enamels in red, blue, yellow and green. These appear to have been adapted from earlier printed sources. Under the firing conditions then available none could have produced a clear brilliant surface, nor be relied upon to fuse permanently to the soft lead glazes then in use. This meant ever-present danger of flaking. For instance, the well-known red of early Bow, although not to be identified with any of Dossie's recipes, lacked high gloss and tended to blister or peel from the glaze. This was not entirely the result of applying the enamel in thick coatings as has so often been suggested. Even when Bow employed experienced enamel-makers from Meissen many years passed before their colours approached the brilliance of Chelsea work.

It must be acknowledged, however, that Bow catered for a less wealthy group of customers than Chelsea. Mrs. Papendiek, maid of honour to Queen Charlotte, wrote in her *Diary* at the time of her marriage in 1763: "Our tea and coffee set were of common Indian china, to which for our rank there was nothing superior; Chelsea porcelain, and fine Indian china being only for the wealthy. Pewter and Delft could also be had, but were inferior."

In 1765 the newly formed Society of Arts, concerned at the poor quality of enamels available to English potters and their inability to master the technique of firing, offered a prize of £50 to "the person who shall make the finest true Red colour for the use of Enamel painters, which shall bear repeated and sufficiently strong firing without change; the quantity to be produced not less than two ounces, from which a quarter of an ounce will be token trials. Preference will be given to the colour which approaches nearest to fine vermilion. No regard will be had to any that verges at all towards the purple."

William Duesbury, the proprietor of Derby, had worked in London during the early 1750s as an independent enameller. When he established the porcelain factory at

Derby he personally supervised the enamelling department, the result being that his porcelain figures were celebrated for their beauty and range of colours. Apart from Derby the porcelain men of England did little to improve the quality of their enamel colours, contenting themselves with Venetian and, from the late 1760s, German supplies. Domestic ware, however, was decorated in the main with enamels made in the workshops, often by a skilled chemist.

Competition between the established porcelain makers was negligible from about 1775, proprietors being fully aware that newcomers were unlikely to appear in the field until after the expiry of the Cookworthy-Champion patent (see Chapter 18) by which the use of china-clay was monopolized. Each porcelain potter appears to have kept rigidly within well-defined limits, until the introduction of bone china brought with it devastating competition from Staffordshire, survived only by Worcester and Derby.

Enamellers working independently of any factory flourished for a century after the introduction of English-made porcelain. At first they used Venetian colours, employed decorators, and operated their own muffle furnaces. These decorators enamelled porcelain bought in the white, china-sellers being their customers. William Duesbury, in his work-book for the period 1751–53, preserved in the British Museum, has recorded porcelain described as "Bogh", "Chelsey", and "Darbey".

China-sellers' trade cards from the 1760s to the 1830s occasionally announce "Enamelling done on the Premises". Customers selected their porcelain in the white from the dealer's stock and decoration was chosen from hand-painted pattern books. The many newspaper advertisements and other contemporary references to these enamellers show them also to have ornamented flint-glass in coloured enamels. These announcements particularly emphasized the advertisers' skill in painting armorial designs.

Coalport from its inception in 1795 was a source of bone china in the white for independent enamellers. Even as late as the 1850s large consignments of undecorated ware were supplied to Mortlock of Oxford Street, London, who decorated it to his customers' requirements. During the same period A. B. and R. P. Daniel of Wigmore Street, London, were sending designs to Coalport because the colour intricacies were so involved that they could only be entrusted to highly experienced factory enamellers.

The basic materials for manufacturing enamel colours suitable for porcelain decoration were not in themselves costly, but their preparation was long and arduous. To such a degree of fineness was it essential to reduce each ingredient and the final colour and flux together that "the labour of half a day was employed in grinding a drachm"—eight working days, then totalling more than one hundred hours, being required for the final grinding of one ounce of enamel colour.

A steam-driven mechanical device was invented in 1806 for grinding certain enamel colours used on bone china table-ware. Fine enamelling still called for colours produced by meticulous hand-preparation. These two methods continued side by side until the 1840s when the specialist colour-makers provided a wide range of excellent enamel colours in varying qualities at lower cost. The finer and more exclusive colours continued to be made by individual enamellers.

Enamelling paints are colours mixed with flint-glass— from the 1830s borax glass might be used. During firing they fuse into the glaze and become fast. Standardization of quality in the metallic oxides and other ingredients was not accomplished until the 1820s. Robert Wynn, Wellington Place, Vauxhall, London, an enamel-maker of nearly twenty-five years' experience, noted this in his treatise on the subject communicated to the Society of Arts in March 1817. In this he gave "a concise and compleat method of composing enamel colours". The Society placed such value upon the information that they voted Wynn an *ex gratia* payment of 20 guineas, and specimens of the twenty colours concerned were placed in the Repository.

In an introductory note Wynn emphasized that enamel colours for painting over the glaze must mature at a temperature well below that which the ware could withstand without fracture. In the case of several applications of enamel and their firings, the first colours were required to be considerably harder than those used in subsequent firings, fusing temperatures progressively decreasing. Soft enamels could be hardened by the addition of more colour or made softer and more brilliant with more flux. The colours for which Wynn supplied recipes were various tints of yellow, orange, red, brown, black, green, blue, purple and rose.

Transparent fluxes were essential accompaniments to the prepared colours. By mixing a colour with a flux rich in lead oxide, a coloured glaze was produced, becoming liquefied at a low melting point in the muffle. This flux not only caused the colour to adhere to the glaze on the ware, but also produced a glassy surface. Great skill was essential in the adjustment of quantity and quality. If too little flux were used the enamel was inclined to have a matt surface, and if too much, the colour was altered.

Wynn's eight recipes for fluxes consisted mainly of flint-glass and red lead. Typical was his flux No. 1: red lead, 8 parts by weight; borax calcined to a fine oxide, 1½ parts; flint powder, 2 parts; flint-glass 6 parts. No. 2 flux was composed of: flint-glass, 10 parts by weight; white arsenic, 1 part; nitre, 1 part. For a very soft flux, to give a brilliant gloss to the enamel after firing, he recommended his No. 8: red lead, 6 parts by weight; borax not calcined, 4 parts; flint powder, 2 parts. The method of making flint powder differed little throughout the porcelain and bone-china periods. The flints were burnt until white, cleaned with hot water and a brush, again heated until red hot, and thrown into cold water. After two or three such treatments they were pulverized and then finely ground in a biscuit mortar. In some of the finest enamel colours, too, Wynn recorded the introduction of powdered flint.

With similar thoroughness Wynn described the preparation of various metallic oxides to be incorporated in enamels. Light red and orange, for instance, were made from sulphate of iron bought from the manufacturing chemist. The sulphate of iron was pounded and placed in an earthenware muffle until all moisture evaporated, leaving a grey powder. This was placed in a crucible over a charcoal fire and stirred with a steel bar until it became red in colour.

It was then poured into a pan of cold water and placed under a chimney to disperse the fumes into the outer air. When it had settled at the bottom of the pan it was washed several times in hot water and then dried for use. The more it was burnt, the darker red it became.

Orange enamel consisted of red lead, 12 parts; red sulphate of iron, 1 part; oxide of antimony, 4 parts; flint powder, 3 parts. These were mixed well, and calcined sufficiently to form a cohesive mass without melting. One part of this was mixed with $2\frac{1}{2}$ parts of a suitable flux and ground for use. Light red was composed by grinding together: red sulphate of iron, 1 part by weight; No. 1 flux, 3 parts; white lead, $1\frac{1}{2}$ parts.

These flour-fine powders were stored in labelled bottles and when required for use mixed with an oily medium which enabled the colour to be conveyed by brush to the ware and adhere to the glaze. It was allowed to dry out by exposure to the air before firing. Spike oil of lavender was used on the finer work: on less costly table-ware spirits of turpentine stiffened with thick oil of turpentine was generally used. The colour tempered with the oil was mixed on a china tile and applied to the glaze with a camel-hair or sable brush. So volatile were these oils, however, that only small quantities of colour could be mixed at a time.

Ceramic enamellers were under the great disadvantage of painting with drab-coloured mixtures bearing no resemblance to the attractive colours finally brought out in the firing. This was particularly disconcerting when a complex picture was painted on porcelain or bone china, possibly requiring delicate hues such as flesh tints. The enameller's skill did not end here, however. It was also necessary to apply each colour separately and fire it in the muffle furnace to a dull red heat, allowing it to become cold before applying a further colour, for each needed a prescribed temperature to bring out the final tint to perfection. Seven or more firings were not unusual for such work. Throughout the various stages of gradually increasing temperature, the hue of an enamel changed progressively towards its final radiance. The heat also partially softened the glaze, thus permanently fixing the colours.

When the decorator painted rose or crimson to the ware it was a dirty violet in colour. During firing it changed with the rising temperature to brown, then to a dull reddish tint, continuing towards its proper colour. If the heat exceeded the point of perfection, however, the pattern became blurred and the colour changed to a dull purple, impossible to restore. This was a frequent occurrence: the advertisement announcing the sale of Chelsea in 1764 included imperfectly enamelled porcelain in the list of goods; when Derby closed in 1848 considerable stocks of imperfectly enamelled bone china were sold.

Fire cracks and breakages in the biscuit kiln might occur during firing if the temperature were suddenly raised, large pieces being particularly liable to this risk. Small defects of this kind were effectively concealed by the enameller judiciously extending his pattern to cover them.

The firing of enamelled porcelain was carried out at first in small charcoal-heated square muffle furnaces of iron, so designed as to protect the ware from direct contact with fumes. Very fine paintings were treated individually, but usually a number of articles were enclosed in an air-tight box known as a "coffin". The enamelled decoration was fired for a period ranging between five and twelve hours at temperatures varying from 700 to 950 degrees centigrade, according to the type of ware and the metallic oxide involved. It was then allowed to cool gradually for eight to twenty hours. Unless cooling was carefully controlled the ware would quickly fracture when taken into use.

A more efficient enamelling furnace was the muffle-kiln designed in 1812 by Samuel Walker, then employed by Barr, Flight and Barr at Worcester. This produced far finer results than were formerly achieved and made enamel painting a less hazardous process. Walker's enamelling furnace quickly made Worcester china celebrated for the brilliance of its fine colouring. Its use became widespread from about 1820.

A considerable amount of ware could be fired at one time in these muffle-kilns heated by coal fires without tinging glaze or enamels with smoke fumes. The small circular-topped kiln, measuring about 42 inches wide, 54 inches

PLATE 6

Chelsea porcelain. *Top:* figures of a parrot and a pair of white partridges, (*a*) marked with raised anchor at back of base; (*c*) marked with raised anchor outlined in red at back of base. *Below:* two bowls with oval handles decorated with pastoral scenes, their bases in mazarine blue and gilded. Mark: gold anchor. Tall vase with grounds of mazarine blue enriched with gilded trellis-work, and two panels of pastoral scenes in colour.

PLATE 7

Bow porcelain. *Top:* bowl and cover with lion finial; decorated in colours and gold with floral motifs in imitation of the Japanese; *c.* 1755. *Below:* a pair of candlesticks modelled as standing figures of a girl and youth beside flowering tree stumps, supporting the foliage nozzles, the girl holding a bird's nest, the youth a goblet and a bunch of grapes; and a single candlestick modelled as a bird with a bird's nest on a flowering tree stump supporting the nozzle, and with a lamb and dog at the base.

high, and 78 inches long, was built with an inner lining of fired marl slabs of uniform thickness. Flues were constructed beneath and around them in such a way that the draught drew the flames through them with a continual subdued roar.

Decorated ware was stored in an adjoining room, and from this the fireman selected pieces most suited to the temperatures of varying kiln positions. The articles were arranged on stages constructed of "slabs" or "bats" supported on props of fireclay. The entrance to the kiln was sealed with iron doors fitted with small apertures through which the fireman drew periodic "trials" of colour made upon small pieces of work, thus ascertaining the progress of the firing. Trials could be drawn from one part of the oven only, the remainder being left to the skilled experience and personal judgment of the fireman. The time of firing bone china in such a kiln was between six and seven hours. After each firing the interior walls were washed to remove any accumulation of acids from fumes given off by the ware, glaze or enamels.

Overglaze enamelling has one disadvantage: it can be removed from the glaze by frequent or prolonged rubbing, and certain food acids are liable to attack the colours and free them from the glaze. It was customary, therefore, for both soft-porcelain and bone-china potters to class their finer productions as "for the cabinet". In some instances overglaze decoration on bone china table-ware was protected by a thin coating of transparent glaze.

5

PRINTED designs applied to ceramics by means of paper transfers form the basis of virtually all the decoration on present-day table-ware. The development of this craft brought unprecedented prosperity to the Potteries and has left us with a magnificent range of eminently collectable porcelain and bone china, including the world-famous Staffordshire blue-and-white. Yet this wholly English discovery, originating in the mid-eighteenth century, was applied in this country for half a century before its possibilities were appreciated elsewhere. The collector displaying a chronological sequence of transfer-printed porcelain and china dating from 1753 onwards may present every technical advance in the process, concluding with the invention of ceramic lithography in 1839.

For three centuries designs engraved on copper had been reproduced in quantity on paper, but not until the 1750s was this method further developed and such designs quantitatively reproduced on ceramics with similar saving of time and cost. This development was incalculably important to the Staffordshire Potteries. Yet the men who may be considered to have introduced the idea in a practical way remain strangely elusive.

The possibility of transferring clear-cut impressions from copper plates direct to flat earthenware such as tiles had already been considered and rejected by the London potters. The men who converted the idea into a working proposition were Stephen Theodore Janssen, a leading patron of the arts and a prominent merchant-stationer in the City of London, John Brooks, a notable mezzotint engraver with a studio in the Strand, and Henry Delamain, a Dublin potter and manufacturer of delftware tiles. Together they solved the various technical difficulties associated with the transfer-paper, evolving a process by which imprints from engraved copper could be transferred to an enamel or glazed ceramic surface. It is doubtful, however, if any of the three fully appreciated the importance of the discovery. At any rate, the immediate result was its application to little enamelled snuff-boxes and similar charming trifles decorated at the celebrated Battersea enamels manufactory.

This brilliant but short-lived establishment was founded in 1753 under the partnership of Janssen, Delamain and Brooks. Janssen's contact with paper-makers enabled him to gain their interest in devising paper suitable for transfer-work, for none had existed hitherto. This paper needed to be strong, faultlessly hairless, and with a smooth surface free from pinholes. It was made non-absorbent by vigorous calendering, thus ensuring that the oil colour would be completely transferred from the paper to the enamel or ceramic surface. White linen rags were used exclusively in making the pulp for this paper, and the process was costly in time and labour.

It is possible that John Brooks initiated the transfer process, and while experimenting would contact London's leading paper merchant in his search for suitable paper. There is no doubt that his was the hand that first cut the copper plates for this purpose, applying the particular technique required for this specialized work, with deep incisions shaped to hold the enamel-oil ink firmly yet permit it to be printed with clarity on paper when copper plate and ink were warmed to an equal temperature. Henry Delamain no doubt was responsible for preparing the finely ground enamels with printer's ink in such a way that, when fired overglaze at a temperature of about 550 degrees centigrade, the oil was burned away, leaving the lines of enamel fused to the surface.

Among the elusive figures associated with ceramic transfer-printing is Robert Hancock, who was probably one of the engravers working for Janssen, then being fresh from his apprenticeship with George Anderson, a minor engraver of Birmingham. The Battersea works operated for less than three years, however, compelling young Hancock to seek work elsewhere. It is considered virtually certain that, to the good fortune of English ceramic manufacturers, he met the situation by introducing the transfer-printing process to Bow, then under the management of Thomas Frye. As a mezzotint engraver, Frye was already in possession of the tools and facilities required for engraving, including the essential printing press. This association must have begun early in 1756, for the memorandum books of the Bow traveller, John Bowcocke, show that on May 28 and June 18 he received orders for "printed teas" and "a pint printed mug" and "half-pint ditto". This is the earliest reference yet noted in connection with printed porcelain.

Bow porcelain of the transfer period (1756–60), although technically a soft-paste porcelain, was extremely hard, and the lavishly applied glaze was faintly blue or slightly greenish yellow in tint. Bow is known to have printed in four colours: brick red, black, a dull, dark purple and brown, and these might be overpainted with transparent washes of coloured enamels. Battersea worked in brick red, near black, crimson and mauve. An early stage in the application of transfer-printing on Bow porcelain consisted in ornamenting the centre of a piece of flat-ware with a transfer pattern enclosed by a hand-painted cartouche within a hand-painted rim border. Hancock is represented by the "Tea Party" signed "R. Hancock *fecit*". A Bow plate bearing this print is in the British Museum. The same pattern with the signature "R.H.*f*" occurs on South Staffordshire enamels of the 1770s, and also on Worcester porcelain. Several prints of children at play decorating Bow mugs are attributed to Hancock, and these also have been noted on enamels. Several examples of an oval dish with a wavy rim display in their centres a purplish black transfer design showing a group of five figures adapted from Watteau's painting " Le Bosquet de Bacchus ". Later in the same year Hancock introduced transfer-printing to the Worcester Porcelain Company. He was thus the vital link between the pioneer enamellers and the porcelain factory.

Hancock's copper plates were beautifully engraved, every

PLATE 8

ow porcelain, *c.* 1755. *Top:* porringer and cover painted in enamel colours and gilded, the cover
ith pug-dog finial; sides decorated with sprays of flowers in imitation of Japanese Kakiemon
ork. *Below:* sauce-boat with scroll edge on high spreading foot with moulded festoons; painted
ith oriental flowers in colours. This piece contains 48 per cent bone ash.

PLATE 9

A collection of plain white Bow porcelain in the Victoria and Albert Museum. *Top row:* (*a* and *e*) pair of sphinxes on scrolled bases, with portrait heads of Peg Woffington after the painting b Arthur Pond, *c.* 1750; (*b*) spaniel with a dead bird, *c.* 1755; (*c*) one of a pair of lions seated on oblon base, *c.* 1750. *Middle row:* (*a*) cream-stoup resembling a wooden piggin, with spoon, *c.* 1755; (*b* Chelsea jar and cover, *c.* 1750; (*c*) pheasant on rocky base, *c.* 1750; (*d*) tea-cup, 1½ inches high, an saucer, both with wavy rims and decorated with applied sprays of prunus-blossom in relief, *c.* 1755 *Bottom row:* (*a*) sweetmeat dish in form of shell encrusted with three murex shells, a limpet, an other shells; (*b*) salt-cellar in form of large shell resting on heap of smaller shells, *c.* 1750; (*c*) cran in imitation of Chinese porcelain, *c.* 1750; (*d*) pug-dog marked with sign of planet Mercury incisee *c.* 1750; (*e*) tea-pot and cover moulded in relief with rose sprays, *c.* 1755.

line delicate, yet firm and clear. On a few examples the monogram "RH" and the name Worcester were incorporated into the pattern. Hancock's best-known transfers were "Garden Scenes", "Ruins", "Courtship", "Milkmaid in a Farm", "Birds" and "The Hunt", all adapted from contemporary engravings. All manner of pictures were transferred to Worcester porcelain at this period, following the current vogues—pastoral scenes with shepherds and milkmaids, romantic ruins in classical landscapes and subjects from sporting prints. Many of the designs were copied from such pattern books as that by Jean Pillement and others, entitled *The Ladies Amusement, or Whole Art of Japanning*, published in about 1760. Black, which produced prints described at the time as jet enamelled, and deep red gave the clearest impressions; blue, lilac, brown and dull purple were also used. Transfers might be clumsily overpainted with washes of enamel, and from about 1775 black transfers might be associated with gilding.

A partner of the Worcester firm, Richard Holdship, appears to have been in charge of the printing department until his bankruptcy in 1762. His initials and rebus, "RH" and an anchor, sign several copper-plate designs decorating early Worcester porcelain. By 1764 he was at Derby under an agreement with the proprietors "for the making and printing of China or porcelain ware", the process being described as "printing in enamel and blew". Here he stayed until 1769, but it appears that his work was not greatly appreciated for he complained that his presses were often standing. Derby transfer-work might be marked with Holdship's rebus, the anchor, and the name Derby.

Meanwhile, financial misfortune had overtaken Janssen in 1756 and he was declared bankrupt, plant and stock of his enamel works being sold by auction on June 8, 1756. This might account for the fact that, on the following July 27, John Sadler, a Liverpool printer and engraver, was able to give a display of transfer-printing, decorating 1,200 earthenware tiles during a six-hour period. He had long experimented in this direction, and it seems extremely probable that his success at this time was due to the fact that he attended the sale at Battersea and acquired a supply of transfer-paper—Janssen's monopoly. He may also have seized the opportunity to secure and study prepared enamels and copper plates. With his partner Guy Green, Sadler attempted to patent the process, no doubt in its application to ceramics. But the officials concerned were apparently aware that his process differed in no way from that already developed by Janssen and his associates.

Sadler and Green established themselves as transfer-printers to the porcelain and pottery trade, however, their customers including most of the local firms as well as Littler of Longton Hall. Early Liverpool prints on porcelain have blotchy, uneven lines, and the red printing is in a distinctive dark shade.

The actual process of printing appears to have been little used at the porcelain factories, with the exception of Worcester; Derby was responsible for a little between 1764 and 1769; Lowestoft decorated in underglaze blue. It was found commercially impracticable to apply transfer-printed designs to the thinly glazed hard porcelains of Plymouth and Bristol.

This early overglaze printing called for fine engraving to ensure sharpness and clarity of design. A wider range of tints could be used than was then possible with underglaze printing, which could only be carried out in blue pigment prepared from cobalt. This called for a fluxing temperature about 50 per cent higher than was used for overglaze enamel colours, which could not survive a kiln temperature exceeding about 750 degrees centigrade. In some early nineteenth-century examples both dark- and light-blue transfer-printing appear on a single piece of ware.

Printing in underglaze blue appears to have originated at Worcester under the control of Robert Hancock, whose assistant from March 1772 was Thomas Turner. In October 1774 they both resigned from the firm, Hancock at that time being a director. Turner established the Salopian works at Caughley with the fixed intention of developing blue underglaze transfer-printing on table-ware. At first he printed in black, sepia and blue underglaze. Meanwhile, and possibly with Robert Hancock's assistance, technical improvements were made in the underglaze printing technique:

lines became vigorous and hard compared with the coarse, blotchy, blue printing so far produced. Engravers and printers worked under lock and key to prevent intrusion— Llewellyn Jewitt says this was also the case at Worcester— and the colours were prepared by Turner in a private laboratory: during his frequent absences from the works his sister deputized for him in preparing colours. So successful was the venture that eventually Turner possessed four printing presses, each operating a seventy-hour week in transfer production.

Among the early copper plates supplied by Hancock were Gainsborough's "Milkmaid", various classic ruins after Pannini, and a design including parrots, trees and fruit. Several plates signed by Hancock still remain, and others were illustrated by Jewitt. In the Victoria and Albert Museum, London, is a collection of seventeen impressions taken from original plates engraved by Thomas Turner. Compared with nineteenth-century blue printing, the lines were thickly cut, to facilitate printing and the process of transferring the colour to the biscuit. Characteristic of these impressions and of Caughley productions generally is the uncommon type of shading in strong parallel lines, almost as if drawn with a ruler. Each transfer includes the mark "S" in various sizes, and the plate number accompanied by the initials "T.T." Two are dated 1779, and some name the article that the design was intended to decorate, such as "P. Bason", "Tea Pot N° 308", "Tea Cup", "Ewer N° 47".

The "Fisherman" design, highly popular for nearly twenty-five years, is marked "Plate N° 1", dated 1779, and signed "T.T." The right of the pattern shows a boat with half-spread sails and a fisherman, standing in the stern, holding up a fish. In the foreground a duck rises on outstretched wings, and on the left sits another fisherman with his line in mid-stream. The original Caughley willow pattern, dated 1779, designed for a tea-pot, has no man on the bridge; the succeeding impression shows one man crossing the bridge. This design, the forerunner of blue-and-white all-over patterns, was known as "blue willow" for more than a century. The original copper plate is in the

British Museum. A third impression shows two men on the bridge, one riding a donkey, and a parasol-bearer following on foot. On each version the tree bears twenty-nine apples. Not until the late 1780s did Turner develop the better-known version, also with twenty-nine apples.

Josiah Spode in the early 1780s became aware of the immense potentialities of decorating earthenware with transferred designs. He developed the technique, acquiring it from Caughley by introducing into his own workshops one of their engravers and a transfer-printer. The firm subsequently applied transfer-printing to bone china with notable effect.

The success of Spode's transfer-printing caused dissatisfaction among the enamellers until Spode increased their output—and so lowered prices—by painting overglaze colour decoration over underglaze transfer-printed outlines. These transfer outlines—they are found too on the productions of others—remained visible through the applied enamels. Then Spode began printing the outlines in colours to harmonize with the design, eight varieties of blue, brown and black being available. From about 1820 it became customary to leave portions of the transfer pattern undecorated, confining brushwork to outstanding features of the design. The fine wearing qualities of this blue underglaze printing, in which the decoration was protected from the friction of daily use and washing, secured a wide market.

This early work, until 1805, followed the long-established convention for designs derived from the Chinese. Then the romantic mood of the late eighteenth century reached the Potteries and was quickly adapted to meet nineteenth-century requirements. Cleverly derived from engravings of the period, many of these pictures in blue-printed Staffordshire are now extremely rare.

Not until about 1800 was it found possible to overcome the slightly smudgy effect of cross-hatching associated with eighteenth-century blue printing. Engraved lines were thinned, making possible a variation in tone gradation, thus introducing dark shades and high-lights into transfer pictures. By 1810 even finer tone variations were secured by combining line and stipple engraving on the one plate.

Even then, decoration was of course limited to a single colour from one impression of a copper plate. Exceptional skill was required to make the best use of light and shade effects and achieve a well-balanced picture, clear in detail, yet covering every part of its allotted space. This accounts for the frequent introduction of figures and water in the foreground and massive cloud effects to fill the sky.

The process of transfer-printing is little different to-day from when it originated, apart from improvements in materials and minor details. At first designs were engraved upon copper plates which had been produced by the battery process and consequently were very close-textured. These were tougher than plates made from the rolled copper general after about 1790. Sharp steel gravers incised deep lines into the flat polished surface of the metal: the quality of the pattern displayed upon the finished ware was dependent largely upon the engraver's skill. To maintain their sharp clear-cut lines rolled plates required occasional re-cutting.

In the printing shop the engraved plate was kept sufficiently warm upon a stove to facilitate working the colour into the lines. The colour was mixed with printer's oil and raised to approximately the same temperature. This soft colour mixture was pressed into the incised lines with the aid of a wooden rubber. Excess colour was scraped away with a steel knife and the copper surface cleaned by wiping with a beaver-skin cushion—corduroy has been used since the mid-nineteenth century. The copper plate was then ready for printing a single impression, after which the plate was again warmed and the remaining ink removed.

The transfer-paper, saturated with a solution of soft soap, was then laid upon the copper plate and printed in an engraver's press. Several thicknesses of flannel placed over the paper absorbed its moisture and thus drew out the colour from the incised lines. When the paper was peeled from the copper it bore a perfect imprint of the pattern. A cutter then trimmed superfluous paper from the transfer, and separated border design from central pattern.

The pattern was transferred to the biscuit by laying it face downward on the ware and rubbing the back with a roll of soaped flannel called a burnisher, the worker resting one end against his shoulder while he rubbed the other upon the paper. This forced the colour evenly from the print into the surface of the biscuit. The transfer paper was left in position for a few hours, then immersed in cold water and sponged away. The ware was then fired in the hardening kiln. This fixed the colour and burned away all trace of the printer's oil, which would have prevented the glaze from adhering.

The printed ware was dipped by hand into liquid glaze of cream soup consistency, and for a time the pattern was obscured. The ware was then dried and put in a saggar. This was placed in the kiln and fired at a temperature of about 1050 degrees centigrade. This melted and matured the glaze into a glassy coating over the ware. When the oven was suddenly opened at the end of about thirty-six hours the inrush of cold air gave added brilliance to the glaze.

Underglaze transfer-printing on ceramics was carried out solely in various shades of dark blue until 1828, when it was discovered that certain crushed enamel colours mixed with Barbados tar could be used without distortion. Underglaze transfer-prints in black and various shades of green, yellow and red were issued, but they failed to oust the ever-popular blue. The collector will find that examples are not yet rare, although uncommon.

Two or more colours might now be printed on a single piece of ware, but the demand was negligible and did not justify the increased cost of applying each colour individually and treating it to a separate firing. Examples are to be found, however, some bearing the impressed mark of Wedgwood. But in 1848 F. W. Collins and A. Reynolds invented a process by which three colours, blue, red and yellow, could be fixed from a single transfer with one firing. The colours, applied separately to the transfer paper, were arranged to fix at the same temperature.

Transfer gilding was invented in 1835 by Godwin Embrey, who sold his productions to most of the leading potters under the name of gold lustre transfers. According to the patent the lustre consisted of potter's varnish together with a complicated and unlikely concoction including gold, nitrate of mercury, grain tin, nitro-muriatic acid, balsam of sulphur, boiled oil, and gum. A transfer was made with this in the usual way, applied to the ware and then dusted with gold. After firing the resulting gold design was burnished. Examples of this transfer gilding are uncommon, but they remain as brilliant as when made.

Stock patterns made by specialists in the design, engraving and production of transfers account for the appearance of similar designs on ware bearing the marks of factories far apart. In 1841 John Lamb of Newcastle-under-Lyme speeded up the process of transfer production by using engraved copper rollers to print reels of transfers. The resulting decorations, however, lacked the fine finish of those made individually in the press and were indirectly responsible for the decline of Staffordshire blue.

Lithography was first used as a medium for decorating bone china and earthenware in 1839 when the process was patented by A. Ducote. The design from which the transfers were taken was drawn on the stone in acid-resistant wax and the background then removed with dilute nitric acid, so that every detail to appear in the decoration stood out in relief. The stone was then inked with potter's varnish and impressed upon transfer-paper coated with lithographic size. The paper transferred the size to the surface of the glazed ware where it was dusted with colour in the form of powdered metallic oxide. Transfers used for underglaze printing were made in the same manner, but vegetable gluten replaced the size.

Great skill was required at first, or the lithographed decoration would emerge from the kiln dull and uninteresting owing to the infinitesimal amount of colour used. At first only light-blue lithography was possible, carried out with artificial ultramarine, but from 1845 such decoration was produced in pink, green, purple, mulberry, grey and black.

Collectors of bat-printed ware should note that the *Technical Repository*, 1823, recorded a revival of the bat-printing process, thus confounding those who would like to ascribe all ware so decorated to the eighteenth century.

The advantage of the process, which was introduced in 1761 by William Wynn Ryland, was the extreme fineness of the engraved line. Although little use appears to have been made of bat-printing until the mid-1770s, it proved especially successful for small motifs such as flowers, foliage, fruits, shells, inscriptions, and the outlines of richly painted coats of arms and crests.

The design was stippled on a copper plate with a special graver: short lines were also incorporated, but these were subsidiary to the stipple work. The plate was then cleaned and thinly coated with linseed oil, the worker passing his hand across the plate to remove superfluous oil, leaving it only on the stippled spots. The design was transferred in oil to the glazed ware not by means of a transfer paper but on a flexible bat, a quarter of an inch thick, composed of glue, treacle and whiting. This design in transferred oil was dusted with finely powdered enamel ground with Barbados tar. This adhered to the ware, which was then fired in the usual way.

6

BRILLIANT continental notions, modified and restrained to suit the tastes of early Georgian England, achieved a European reputation for the treasures which emerged from the Chelsea Porcelain Manufactory. To-day Chelsea porcelains enriched with exquisite floral decorations, lively figures full of grace and fun, richly lustrous colouring and magnificent design, still make them the supreme joy of many a collector.

Some authorities believe the Chelsea factory to have been established in 1745 by Charles Gouyn, who in 1750 advertised himself as "late Proprietor and Chief Manager of the Chelsea House". It is more probable, however, that the factory was founded by Thomas Briand late in 1742: a goat-and-bee jug is known incised with the name Chelsea, a triangle, and the date 1743. On February 11, 1743, Briand displayed before the Royal Society "several specimens of a fine white ware made here [in London] by himself from native materials of our own country, which appeared to be as good as any of the finest porcelain or China Ware . . . when broken it appeared like broken sugar and not like glass as the Dresden ware does". It must be admitted, however, that the known examples of early Chelsea paste are soft and glassy.

Whether in fact Briand made this ware at Chelsea or at some unrecorded pottery, it was the Huguenot silversmith Nicholas Sprimont (1716–71) who became Chelsea's dominant personality. He arrived in London late in 1741 and in the following January was registered at Goldsmiths' Hall. Then, in partnership with Charles Gouyn, he began trading as a silversmith in Hanover Square. A few months later Sprimont made the acquaintance of Thomas Briand and apparently induced Gouyn to finance the porcelain project. Workshops were acquired in Chelsea and a small kiln erected.

So closely does early Chelsea resemble the soft-paste porcelain developed in France by Réamur that it is conceivable that Briand was formerly employed at St. Cloud, and left for England when he had familiarized himself with the details of the materials used and the manufacturing processes. Unlike other contemporary porcelain Chelsea ware displays none of the uncertainties of an infant industry, although paste, glaze, modelling and decoration progressively improved and had reached a high standard by 1750.

Nicholas Sprimont, a flamboyant personality of Falstaffian proportions, appears to have become directly associated with the management of Chelsea late in 1746: a few months later skilled potters from Staffordshire were being attracted to Chelsea by the lure of high wages. Advertisements issued at this time suggest that production consisted mainly of table-ware. In 1749 it was announced that orders would be accepted for "Plates, Dishes and all Table Utensils, as well as for Tea, Coffee and Chocolate Services". Within a year the scope of production had widened to: "Tea, Coffee, Chocolate Services, Sauce-boats, Basons and Ewers, Ice-pails, Terreens, Dishes and Plates, of different Forms and Patterns, and a great Variety of Pieces for Ornament." It may be assumed, and the number of known pieces confirms this, that few Chelsea figures were issued earlier than 1750.

The patronage of George II and the Duke of Cumberland, followed by a highly influential court, enabled Chelsea to overcome some of the financial difficulties which faced English porcelain factories during their early days. It has long been conjectured that the Duke of Cumberland and his secretary Sir Everard Fawkener financed Sprimont in his project, and documents in the Royal collection indicate that the duke invested sums of money in the firm. The duke's brother, George II, whose influence brought experienced porcelain artists and workmen from Saxony and

Brunswick, delighted in the possession of Chelsea figures and toys, he and Cumberland leading the fashionable world as collectors of these charming trifles. In 1763 the king commissioned from Sprimont a magnificent combined dinner and dessert service at a cost of £1,200. Because such patronage influenced lavish magnificence, the firm was able to indulge in ambitious projects far beyond the means of its competitors, who to a great extent relied upon their sales of table-ware.

Even at Chelsea table-ware was bound to be the mainstay of production. Although orders for ornamental porcelain were never scarce, ever-increasing competition—coupled with Sprimont's own ill-health and also, in all probability, the illness of Sir Everard Fawkener, who died in 1758—led to the temporary cessation of potting in 1756. Many of the workmen thereupon transferred their services to Bow where a tougher porcelain containing bone ash as an ingredient was being made.

When Chelsea restarted in 1758, it was with Nicholas Sprimont outwardly as sole proprietor, using a paste strengthened by the addition of bone ash to the frit. The use of bone ash as an ingredient of porcelain was monopolized until 1763 by Thomas Frye's patent of 1749. It must be assumed, therefore, that Frye licensed his process to Chelsea.

The Chelsea Porcelain Manufactory under the proprietorship of Nicholas Sprimont appears to have been no more financially sound than formerly. As early as the spring of 1761 Sprimont announced in the *Public Advertiser* that owing to ill-health he would not continue production at Chelsea much longer. Several advertisements to similar effect followed until the *Public Advertiser* dated January 2, 1764, announced that "every Thing in general belonging to the Porcelaine Manufactory at Chelsea, and all the remaining unfinished Pieces, glaz'd and unglaz'd; some imperfect enameled ditto, the useful and the ornamental; all the Materials, the valuable and extensive Variety of fine Models in Wax, in Brass, and in Lead; all the Plaister Moulds, and others ditto; the Mills, Kilns, and Iron Presses . . . as Mr. Sprimont, the sole possessor of this rare Porcelaine Secret,

is advised to go to the German Spaw, all his genuine Household Furniture will be sold at the same Time.—N.B. Soon
after, when every Thing is sold belonging to the Manufactory is clear'd, there will be some most beautiful Pieces
of the truly inimitable Mazarine Blue, Crimson, and Gold,
that Mr. Sprimont has thought deserving finishing; that
will be sold at Chelsea, as a Whole remaining, and the last
Produce of that once most magnificent Porcelaine Manufactory."

It is probable that when the Duke of Cumberland visited
the factory on about December 18 of the previous year he
finally withdrew his financial support, thus virtually forcing
Sprimont to sell. A sale was unnecessary, however, for
Sprimont apparently secured a measure of financial support from Francis Thomas, one of London's leading dealers.
But it appears that porcelain was no longer produced in
quantity and no further public sales took place. By the
spring of 1768 production was negligible, and a paragraph
in the *Public Advertiser*, May 1768, stated that "the Chelsea
Porcelain Manufactory is declined and the Porcelain become
scarce". In the following May the plant and stock-in-trade
was again advertised for sale. It was bought by James Cox
for £600, and possibly he intended to run the factory with
Sprimont as director. This did not come about, however,
for on February 5, 1770, he sold it to William Duesbury of
the Derby Porcelain Company who continued the manufacture of porcelain at Chelsea until December 1783, three
years after he had become sole proprietor of the Derby
establishment, following the bankruptcy of his partner
John Heath. The moulds and materials were then sent to
Derby, and Christie's sold "all the remaining finished and
unfinished stock of the Chelsea Porcelain Manufactory,
with all the remaining buildings and fixtures".

Chelsea porcelain is classified according to five major
changes made in the paste during the factory's forty years
of production. Each paste may be distinguished by a different group of marks, but it is essential for the tyro collector
to appreciate that Chelsea marks have been reproduced on
all manner of fakes and imitations.

I. Chelsea porcelain made until 1747 was either unmarked or impressed beneath the glaze with an incised triangle, the alchemist's sign for fire. The soft creamy body was flawed with disfiguring specks. The presence of 10 per cent of lead oxide in its composition suggests that flint-glass cullet constituted one-third of the ingredients. The flint-glass created technical difficulties such as an undue proportion of kiln distortions, pinholes and other flaws. Pinholes are revealed by holding the piece to the light: they take the form of small, irregularly placed flecks, more translucent than the rest of the paste, somewhat resembling floating grease spots, and are the forerunners of the famous "moons" of the two following periods. This early Chelsea paste is suggestive of porcelain made by the Réamur process described in technical books of the period, and appears to have been made as late as 1750. Glaze was thickly applied and age has often invested it with a slightly yellowish tinge. Soft and glassy, with occasional surface bubbles, it has usually crazed.

II. In 1747 a paste was evolved by Sprimont or his technicians by eliminating lead oxide from the formula and substituting a considerable proportion of lime. This resulted in a somewhat sandy body, faintly greyish in tone, but the added weight failed to prevent warping in the kiln, although the percentage of wasters was appreciably decreased. Pinholes were fewer and larger, known to collectors as "moons". Porcelain of this type, somewhat whiter and with fewer specks after 1750, continued in production until 1753. A creamy glaze was used, thick like paraffin wax and inclined to choke the modelling. A characteristic of this glaze was the tendency to shrink, leaving an edge of exposed paste around the base rim. Because of its exceptional thickness, small pools of this glaze tended to accumulate on flat areas. The mark used was an anchor in relief on an applied medallion; from about 1751 the relief anchor was painted in red overglaze (see p. 66).

III. By 1753, when the firm had considerably expanded, Chelsea paste had become finer grained and more translucent, although of a faintly greyish hue and still exhibiting some blemishes. The glaze was highly lustrous with a uniform surface, being applied by brush. The cool white of the glaze appears slightly blue against the white of the body. It is seldom crazed. The fine quality of this paste enabled Chelsea to produce ceramic masterpieces which have seldom been equalled, and formed a fine ground for the enamels. During this period the usual mark was a plain red anchor, painted overglaze in varying forms and sizes.

IV. An important change occurred in the composition of Chelsea paste when the factory recommenced operations in 1758 under the sole proprietorship of Sprimont. Bone ash was now incorporated as a strengthening ingredient to the extent of about 40 per cent of the formula. As a result Chelsea porcelain was denser of texture, harder, more translucent and chalky white, but tended to suffer from a surface cracking visible through the glaze. Warping in the kiln no longer exceeded normal expectations. The limpid, glassy glaze was liable to craze, and where it gathered in angles and hollows showed a faintly green tinge. It was no less soft than formerly, enamels sinking into it with equally rich effect. It now became the standard practice to grind the bases of figures, the paste thus exposed being greasily smooth to the touch. This paste continued in production until the factory was acquired by Duesbury.

Gold anchors, in the same design as the red, marked Chelsea porcelain figures of this period.

V. The porcelain made at Chelsea under Duesbury is known to collectors as Chelsea-Derby, although the firm still operated as the Chelsea Porcelain Manufactory. The paste, strengthened with calcined bone, was little different from that of the former period, milk-white in appearance, of medium translucency perhaps faintly tinged cream or green. The glaze was clear and with a surface smoothness equal to that of glass. At first it was marked with a gold anchor traversing a cursive "D". In 1773 appeared the crowned anchor.

W. Moore Binns in *The First Century of English Porcelain* comments very truly that "no English factory produced a greater variety of articles than Chelsea: simple articles of daily use for the table and for the boudoir; figures and groups both in white undecorated and richly coloured and gilt in a wonderful variety; models of birds, beasts, fishes and, lastly, costly and richly decorated vases, painted and gorgeously gilt."

The catalogue of "the Last Year's Produce of Chelsea Porcelaine Manufactory" sold by auction in 1756 listed "Magnificent Lustres and Epargnes, Services for Desarts, Sets of Dishes and Plates, Tureens and Sauce-Boats, compleat Tea and Coffee Equipages, beautiful Groupes of Figures, Sets of Jars and Beakers, and a great variety of other useful and ornamental PORCELAIN, all exquisitely PAINTED IN ENAMEL, with Flowers, Birds, Insects, India Plants, etc."

It is seldom realized that long before porcelain was made in England enamellers flourished in London, decorating imported white ware. These enamellers painted simple designs in a narrow range of colours. Their services were in great demand by the china sellers after the introduction of English soft-paste porcelain at Chelsea and elsewhere, but they operated independently of any factory. A few decorators, such as William Duesbury, then established themselves as master-enamellers employing enamellers, gilders, colour grinders, mufflemen, and so on.

Associated as it was with Briand, Gouyn and Sprimont, it is not surprising that Chelsea porcelain was far removed from the English tradition in industrial design. Basically, however, the same influences were at work. In England, as in France, oriental styles of decoration were proving vastly popular, and to meet this unwelcome competition English potters were impelled to decorate their wares with westernized Chinese and Japanese motifs. Elegant, florid, exotic, the more continental versions of *chinoiserie* presented by Chelsea were wholly in accord with the other rococo fashions of the mid-eighteenth century.

Some Chelsea porcelain, like the Chinese, was enamelled in reds, blues and greens, relieved by matt gold and panelled in black. The Chinese powdered-blue, mazarine-blue and apple-green grounds, with oriental ornament, were also much copied. Characteristic treatment of birds, flowers and other motifs came to distinguish Chelsea from the oriental. All this magnificence, however, although now regarded as the principal feature of Chelsea, was a gradual development.

The incised triangle period (1743–47) was devoted almost entirely to the production of table-ware such as tea- and coffee-pots, cream-jugs, cups and saucers, salts, and sauce-boats, usually undecorated. Embossed reliefs such as prunus blossom on *blanc de chine* were frequent, characteristic being the tea-cups ornamented with eight overlapping acanthus leaves, their stems extended to form feet. Flowers in relief might be touched with colour. Colour decorations were artless in the extreme, simple motifs, often carefully outlined, such as a butterfly or flower spray, cleverly concealing blemishes in paste and glaze. This covering of flaws continued until the end of the red-anchor period. Handles might be fluted, twig or of the cane variety, and knobs were either in the form of flower and leaf motifs, or shaped as if turned in ivory. Dark-red or chocolate-coloured rims enlivened domestic ware until the introduction of gilding at Chelsea.

Early Chelsea table-ware was adapted from silver models —in fact, the term "silver shape" was later used in various sale catalogues of Chelsea porcelain. The celebrated goat-and-bee jugs were adapted from a silver jug made by Edward Wood in 1737. The workmanship of the several Chelsea goat-and-bee jugs still remaining displays a high standard of excellence even in the example dated 1743, suggesting that the founders were already experienced in porcelain production. This famous design consists of two goats lying head to tail, supporting a body ornamented with raised flowers and an applied bee, ascending or descending according to the whim of the repairer. Sometimes the jug is found in *blanc de chine*; in other examples the raised flowers on the body are touched with colour (plates 3 and 4).

The modelling of Chelsea porcelain during the next phase, known as the raised-anchor period (1747–53), displays many technical advances. Table-ware continued to be the mainstay of production. Tea services were made in hexagonal, octagonal and fluted forms, coloured in delightful pale shades. Spouts were short, straight and tapering,

PLATE 10

collection of Bow enamelled porcelain figures in the Victoria and Albert Museum. *Top row*, 1770: (*a*) a group allegorical of Charity; (*b* and *d*) a pair of dancing peasants; (*c*) boy supporting flower vase on his head; (*e*) bishop with mitre, vestments and cope. *Middle row, c.* 1760: (*a* and *e*) ·gro and negress copied from Meissen figures by Kändler; (*b* and *d*) Columbine and Harlequin on ·und bases; (*c*) Pierrot wearing yellow clothing and standing beside a flowering tree stump. ·ttom row, 1765–70: (*a*) candlestick consisting of an old man and a little boy warming themselves ·a brazier; (*b*) an actor; (*c*) a Red Indian woman; (*d*) Venus with two doves at her feet; (*e*) candle- ·ck in form of a woman and child seated on rococo-scrolled pedestal.

PLATE 11

Chelsea-Derby porcelain. *Top:* pair of figures carrying baskets as sweetmeat containers, *c.* 1770s
Below: cup with cover and saucer, painted with roses in natural colours on a ground of closely s
gilt stripes. Mark, script "D" intersected by an anchor in gold. Early 1780s.

and might be round or square, with their openings cut slightly above the horizontal; handles, usually round or square in section, might have thumb-rests, and the scroll type is also found; knobs resembled those of turned ivory or boxwood on silver. Much ware was decorated after the early Meissen style, the remainder adapted from Chinese and Japanese originals. The well-known "yellow tiger" and "red lion" were copies of Meissen after Kakiemon.

A best seller of this period and later was the Æsop's Fables tea service. The flat pieces are octagonal, their centres painted with different subjects from Æsop and rim borders in pale yellow or brown. Early examples were less colourful than later and without cloud effects, foliage being depicted with a yellowish-green wash over-enamelled with black tendril-like lines to give tree effects. Individual leaves were veined and tended to shade off from dark to light, and not, as later, painted in single washes of colour. Dr. Bellamy Gardner discovered that many of these designs were adapted from Francis Barlow's *Æsop's Fables with his Life,* 1687; others originated as illustrations to John Ogilby's *Fables of Æsop Paraphrased in Verse,* 1651. The second series was issued during the 1770s.

A few figures may be attributed to this period, including a number of original conceptions and models based on contemporary engravings. Even a few of the Italian Comedy figures may be associated with this group, although many early attributions are open to doubt. Figures now began to be coloured with some attempt at realism in the restrained use of a warm opaque brown, translucent blue and green, a yellowish red, and several tints of verdant green. These were applied in flat washes with large areas of white and touches of black. Cheeks might be tinted bright red. Thin square plinths gave way to simple mounds with sparsely applied flowers and a characteristic moss.

Models of small birds when issued by Chelsea quickly became a favourite ornament for the dessert table, occasionally finding a place as the apex of a towering pyramid of sweetmeat glasses, as well as on the cloth. Chelsea birds were often copied from plates in *The Natural History of Uncommon Birds* by George Edwards. Colours were intended

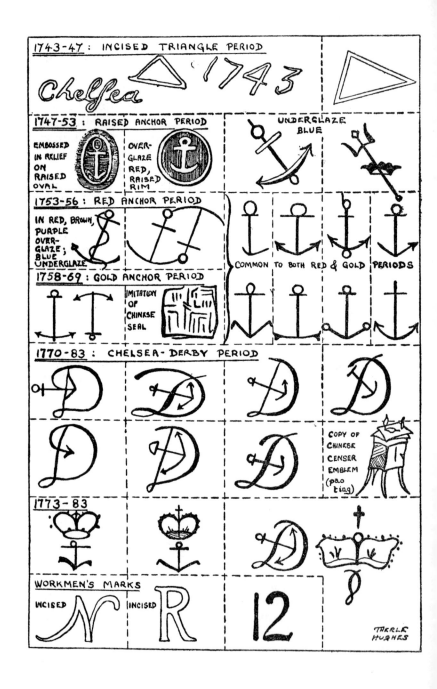

1743-47 : INCISED TRIANGLE PERIOD

Chelsea △ 1743

1747-53 : RAISED ANCHOR PERIOD

EMBOSSED IN RELIEF ON RAISED OVAL

OVER-GLAZE RED, RAISED RIM

UNDERGLAZE BLUE

1753-56 : RED ANCHOR PERIOD

IN RED, BROWN, PURPLE OVER-GLAZE; BLUE UNDERGLAZE

COMMON TO BOTH RED & GOLD PERIODS

1758-69 : GOLD ANCHOR PERIOD

IMITATION OF CHINESE SEAL

1770-83 : CHELSEA - DERBY PERIOD

COPY OF CHINESE CENSER EMBLEM (pao ting)

1773 - 83

WORKMEN'S MARKS

INCISED

INCISED

R

12

THELLE HUGHES

to be naturalistic, but the range of the commercial enamel-ler's palette was not yet wide enough. William Duesbury in his *London Account Book 1751-1753*, published 1931, entered a considerable number of Chelsea bird figures which he received for enamelling. These included "flapwing Birds Chelsay, Boolfinchis Birds, Topnot Birds, Chelsay phesons, King Fishiars, Hostrigsis", among others such as owls, parrots, goldfinches, partridges. Animals formed a less numerous group and included sheep lying on oval mounds with clover leaves and flowers, cows, goats, pug dogs and lions.

The red-anchor period (1753-56) is the most fascinating of all to many collectors. Table-ware, some of it still copied from silver models, was decorated in the oriental manner, finely painted by skilful artists. Fluted hollow-ware and

---

MARKS ON CHELSEA PORCELAIN

The Chelsea mark, until 1747, was a triangle incised or impressed into the base of the piece; on early pieces the name and date might be added.

The raised-anchor mark belongs to the years 1747-53. This was a small anchor embossed in relief on a raised oval medallion applied underglaze. From about 1752 the anchor might be painted in red overglaze. This anchor sometimes appears on a circular pad with a raised edge. Occasionally an elaborate blue anchor is found underglaze: even more rare is the crown and trident in underglaze blue.

The plain red anchor painted overglaze in varying forms and sizes belongs to the years 1753-56. It is usually small and bright red, or may have a brownish tinge. This anchor must not be confused with the red anchors of Bow, Derby and Worcester. The Chelsea anchor of this period is also found in brown and purple overglaze, and in blue underglaze. An anchor with a cable is found painted in red and incised; interlocked twin anchors, one inverted, are also found in red.

Gold anchors, in the same designs as the red, marked Chelsea porcelain from 1758 to 1769. A pair of anchors in gold, one inverted, but not inter-locked, was an occasional mark of this period. Similar marks are found on Derby porcelain and on Chelsea reproductions made at Coalport. The smaller the anchor, either red or gold, the finer is the quality of the piece. These marks are sometimes hidden in crevices and may be so insignificant as to be discovered only after careful search. During this period pieces decorated in the Oriental style might be accompanied by marks resembling Chinese seals painted in red overglaze. Until 1769 there was an inflexible rule that Chelsea porcelain decorated outside the factory should not be marked.

Porcelain of the Chelsea-Derby period was at first marked with a gold anchor traversing a cursive "D." In 1773 appeared the crowned anchor, the anchor being sometimes replaced by a cursive "D." A cursive "N" is sometimes found.

wavy-edged dishes continued: handles might be simple loops of round section, or scrolled, and the slightly tapering spouts dipped at the mouth. The earlier Chinese patterns in blue underglaze gave way to dainty decorations in red and gold. Leaves were painted in light and yellowish greens, side by side, and veined in black. Applied flowers in full relief were introduced: a ring of dots encircling the centre was a characteristic of Chelsea applied flowers. The splendid brocade patterns of Imari porcelain were reproduced, and borders of embossed work copied from Meissen. Detached sprays of flowers and fruit with butterflies and insects interspersed were sparingly applied. Detailed studies of individual flowers were much used, echoing the period's interest in flower prints. Pictures and minor motifs in crimson monochrome also appeared. Gilding enlivened tableware towards the end of the period. White porcelain imported from the East was decorated by Chelsea artists in Chinese and Kakiemon styles.

The excellent quality of the soft paste used during this period, coupled with the fact that fine productions were probably subsidized by Sir Everard Fawkener, enabled Chelsea to produce masterly work forming a superb ground for the enamels, which were usually applied in thin washes covering large areas. After Sir Everard's death in 1758 the *Public Advertiser* announced a sale of his Chelsea porcelain and silver plate. This included a "beautiful Table Set of Dishes and Plates, elegant Epargne, rich blue and gold Perfume Vases, Desart Plates, and Jewel Cabinet with Gold Toilet Furniture; the Tea and Coffee Equipage exquisitely painted in green landscapes".

Some figures of this as of earlier periods were intended to recline upon the dessert table. The most charming figures made during the red-anchor period represented characters from the Italian Comedy, adapted from the celebrated Meissen models. The seriousness of the Doctor, the mirth of the Jester, and the coyness of Columbine are delightfully portrayed in these little figures, full of life and movement. Figure subjects were copied from paintings by Rubens, Teniers, Van Loo, Watteau, Boucher and others. Statuettes of celebrities were modelled after engravings. In the catalogue

PLATE 12

Longton Hall porcelain enamelled in colours and gilded. *Top left:* figure of Britannia wearing a flowered robe and holding a medallion portrait of George II, with lion at side, and flags and trophies on the green and puce scrolled base, *c.* 1755. *Top right:* figure of a goat-herd, *c.* 1755. *Lower left:* vase and cover with applied decoration in high relief. The domed cover has small perforations and is thickly encrusted with large flowers in naturalistic colours; among them are small figures of a cock and hens. *Lower right:* coffee-pot.

PLATE 13

Early Derby figures. *Top:* lady carrying flowers in her apron, and wearing a yellow-flowered puce-lined jacket, and a flowered skirt with a yellow ground; man carrying a basket of fruit and wearing a puce-lined yellow cloak and a turquoise jacket; *c.* 1775. *Below:* pair seated on tree stumps and supporting baskets on their knees, and with lambs at their feet; lady with flowered dress, puce scarf and yellow sleeves; man with flowered coat and puce breeches; *c.* 1770.

of the Chelsea sale which took place in 1755, a copy of which is to be consulted at the British Museum, reference is made to "an exceeding fine figure of a Madonna and a Child standing on a globe, with a Cross in its Hand". This is one of the rare religious groups found in porcelain. Soft pastel shades were used to emphasize the delicacy of the sharp modelling throughout the period (Plate 3).

Chelsea porcelain marked with the gold anchor (1758–69) differs entirely from that of earlier periods. Modelling of figures became less sharp and pastel shades were replaced by a blaze of vivid colour enriched with gilding. The gilding was at first comparatively dull and was applied by the Chinese method: gold leaf was ground in honey and applied with pencil brushes. This was fired at a low temperature, but burnishing failed to increase its lustre. Chelsea quickly switched over to the dangerous mercury method of gilding, in which the gold was thickly laid, and then burnished to complete its splendour.

Gilded scrollwork was now introduced around the decorated panels on the white which formed the central motifs on sets of vases, and tea and dessert services, whose magnificence largely depended upon their rich and deservedly celebrated ground colours. The lovely *gros bleu* or mazarine-blue ground was introduced in 1759; pea-green—often referred to as blue—in the same year; claret and turquoise in 1760; the rare yellow in 1761. These grounds, too, might be enriched with gold and chased. The reserves were filled with bouquets, fruit, figure subjects and pastoral scenes copied from the works of Watteau and others. More often than not there were large-crested pheasants with sweeping tail feathers, and these might be accompanied by other equally colourful birds and insects. Unfired decoration was also frequent, the thick paints obscuring both merits and defects of body.

A four-day sale of "matchless Chelsea Porcelain" announced in the *Public Advertiser*, April 8, 1760, gives an insight into the productions at this time. In addition to table (dinner) and tea services there were included "Baskets, Leaves, Compotiers, Sweetmeat Vases for Desserts, and some small figures for ditto, some large Brackets and

Groups of Figures, Table Cloces, Essence Vases, Urns, Jars, and Beakers, Ewer and Dish, two-handle Cups, with Covers &c. of the inimitable Mazarine Blue, Pea-Green, and Gold, finely painted with History Pieces, Birds, Festoons, and Groups of natural Flowers, and many other Articles in the useful and ornamental Way. There will be likewise in this National Sale, for the Approbation of the Connoisseur, a few pieces of some new Colours which have been found this year by Mr. Sprimont, the Proprietor, at a very large Expence, incredible Labour, and close Application, all highly finished, and heightened with the Gold peculiar to that fine and distinguished Manufactory, which makes this Porcelain the most beautiful and magnificent ever seen, and cannot be made at any Foreign Manufactory."

Sèvres shapes and styles predominated in table-ware, which was exceptionally well potted and its sectional thickness somewhat greater than during former periods. The favourite decoration was in soft purple tones in white reserves on coloured grounds. Elaborate rococo handles were usual. Yet another style copied from Sèvres was a feature of Chelsea work from about 1765: large, elaborate vases were made with pierced bodies and covers, and wildly interlacing handles.

Delightfully decorative sets of figures were modelled, such as the four "Senses", which had been made also during the red-anchor period. The gold-anchor theatrical figures known to collectors as the Vauxhall Masqueraders were a riotous blaze of colour, differing entirely from earlier versions of the same subjects made from the same moulds. Placed side by side they offer fascinating contrasts and display the range of work emanating from a single factory. Some of the finer figures were accompanied by loose pedestals in porcelain. Shepherds and shepherdesses, singly and in pairs, beside flowering tree-stumps rising from rococo scrolled bases, were greatly admired and made in considerable numbers in heights varying from 6 to 15 inches. Both were dressed in radiantly coloured attire, the shepherd usually accompanied by one or two dogs, his companion by lambs (Plate 5). Pairs of groups, two figures in each group, were richly gorgeous affairs.

Shortly before 1765 came the introduction of those leafy, heavily flowered bowers in which small figures were grouped, known to collectors as *bocages*, but referred to by the Chelsea Porcelain Manufactory as "arbours" or "canopies curiously ornamented with flowers". *Bocages* in the form of "candlesticks, girandoles for two lights each, and branched lights" for toilette table use are noted in the sales catalogues. The Æsop's Fables group of these *bocages* have loop handles behind for carrying, and their rococo scrolled bases, supported by three feet, are inscribed with their titles in gold.

Some indication of the renown these figures achieved at the time, and their resemblance in colour and design to continental models, is the fact that during the years around 1760 various French and German porcelain makers petitioned their governments to prohibit the importation of English porcelain figures such as were being made at Chelsea and Bow. The English government replied by placing an import tax of 150 per cent on all continental porcelain.

The so-called Chelsea-Derby porcelain made at Chelsea during the thirteen years under the Duesbury régime (1770-83) naturally displays a marked Derby influence. The fashion for the neo-classic style led Duesbury to abandon Sprimont's rococo forms in favour of severe outlines and restraint in colour and ornament, although gilding was lavish. Table-ware followed the forms made fashionable by Sèvres. Decoration consisted chiefly of centrally placed urns, flower sprays, or cupids, with festoons and swags. The former costly ground colours were discarded in favour of a beautiful though inexpensive red. Edges might be gilt lined or dotted and foot rims were usually encircled with single gold lines. Chelsea-Derby leaves were dark green and twisted: those painted at Derby during the same period were light green and straighter, with ragged edges.

Chelsea-Derby figures are notable for their interpretation of Louis XVI sentimental groups after the manner of paintings by Boucher, Falcourt and others. Their scroll bases were more symmetrical than Sprimont's. Colours were smoothly bright and included a pale turquoise, brilliant crimson, purple, green, orange, yellow and chocolate. Eyes were given pin-point pupils and pale brown outlines: hair was smeared on to the head, and cheeks faintly touched with crimson.

Dainty scent bottles were carried by those Georgian ladies who could afford the luxury. Chelsea made these bottles in a great number of patterns, none of them marked. The typical Chelsea scent bottle had a "kick-up"—that is, a deep concave base. The original intention had been to fit a box-shaped gilt mount to the base, containing a decorated painted enamel in its hinged lid, thus forming a combined scent bottle and patch box. Shallow conical kick-ups belong to the gold-anchor period. Simple pear-shaped scent bottles having flattened sides painted with river scenes or flowers belong to the red-anchor period. These were never gilded, and the body decoration shows an occasional application of black enamel. Later examples were lavishly gilded. *Bonbonnières*, sponge boxes and *étuis* belong to the late gold-anchor and Chelsea-Derby periods. In nearly all instances the box is decorated with small flower sprays and a wavy green-and-blue design encircles the rim.

Chelsea porcelain has been widely reproduced: many reproductions made during the 1830s and 1840s bearing marks are often believed to be original although made from bone china. Many later copies have been made from continental hard-paste porcelain: these are often, but not invariably, marked with the gold anchor. Such reproductions are still being made. The collector will usually be able to discover a chipped spot in both genuine and reproduction Chelsea. Examined with a magnifying glass the hard paste will glitter like sugar: genuine Chelsea will have a chalky appearance. It is no exaggeration to say that the majority of porcelain now known as Chelsea is reproduction ware. A series of highly glazed so-called Chelsea figures prominently displaying gold or red anchors is easily recognized. They are of bone china and were made in the 1920s and 1930s. Colours are cold, dull and harsh, and modelling lacks delicacy.

7

A NOTABLE contemporary commentary on the state of porcelain manufacture was made by Samuel Richardson when, in 1753, he edited Daniel Defoe's *Tour of Great Britain*. In this he described the newly established porcelain factory at Stratford-le-Bow "where they have already made large quantities of Tea-Cups, Saucers, Plates, Dishes, Tureens, and most other Sorts of useful Porcelain; which, though not so fine as some made at Chelsea, or as that brought from Dresden, is much stronger than either and therefore better for common use; and being much cheaper than any other China, there is a greater Demand for it. The Proprietors of this Manufactory have also procured some very good Artists in Painting, who are employed in painting some of their finest Sort of Porcelain, which is so well performed, as to equal Dresden in this Respect. If they can work this so as to undersell the foreign Porcelain, it may become a very profitable Business to the Undertakers, and save great Sums to the Public, which are annually sent abroad for this Commodity."

The first porcelain to be associated with the name of Bow was manufactured in Middlesex, not in the more famous china works at Stratford-le-Bow in Essex. This early porcelain came from Edward Heylyn's glass-house, already well known for its flint-glass table-ware since about 1730. Heylyn, possessing ideal experimental facilities, carried out a lengthy series of trials in association with Thomas Frye (1710–62), the former Dublin mezzotint engraver who, in 1738, had set up a studio in West Ham as a miniaturist and portrait painter. By 1744 they had developed a formula considered worthy of protection by patent, an expensive procedure before 1852.

The specification submitted to the Patent Office gave them a monopoly to make an "earthenware equal to china or porcelain ware imported from abroad". Actually they produced a glassy soft-paste porcelain. The main ingredient was unaker, "a fire-resisting china earth, the produce of the Chirokee nation of America". This substance, described in the patent as being "extremely white, tenacious and glittering with Mica", is still used for making porcelain in South Carolina. Numerous washings in clean running water removed the mica and other impurities from this china-clay, the properties of which closely resembled those of Chinese kaolin.

Like all soft-paste porcelains, the Frye-Heylyn process necessitated the preliminary preparation of a glassy frit. This was made by fusing together equal parts of sand and potash, the resulting glass being ground into a fine powder in the flint-mill. One part of this powdered frit was mixed with two parts of cleansed unaker, but the proportions might vary to one in four. The potter worked these ingredients together until they were blended into a plastic paste of even consistency. The ware, which the specification said might be thrown, cast or moulded, was fired in a wood-burning kiln and allowed to cool. The resulting white biscuit was then painted with simple decorations in blue and dipped into liquid glaze. This glaze was made by grinding to a fine powder ten parts of glass with a frit prepared from four parts of unaker and one of glass, the whole being ground finely with water until of the required consistency.

Bow porcelain made in accordance with the specification must necessarily have had a white glassy body probably flawed by firecracks, specked and slightly warped. It is recorded by Thomas Frye that if properly fired it was white in colour. It is doubtful if many of the pieces now attributed to Middlesex Bow were in fact made there, for those noted are described as cream tinted with a faintly green hue brought about by the addition of cobalt in an effort to correct the yellowish tinge. The smooth-surfaced glaze would be thick in texture, tending to obscure the moulding in relief work and giving a distinct haze to the underglaze blue-painted decoration, carried out with "lapis lazuli, lapis armenus, or zapher".

Production on a commercial scale began in 1745, but the porcelain was too coarse and the ware too ill-shapen to be marketed profitably. In 1748 Heylyn decided to abandon manufacture. Frye continued experimenting towards a more perfect porcelain, his intention being to develop a utility ware that could be sold at prices considerably lower than were those of ware imported from China and Saxony. His researches met with success when he evolved a formula in which calcined bones were a new and important ingredient. The long-term economic value to England of this discovery cannot be over-estimated. Frye was granted a patent for his discovery on November 17, 1749.

Imported unaker was replaced in the formula by fireclay. The frit was composed of two parts bone ash, cleansed by many washings, and one part ground flint with enough moisture for it to be worked into plastic balls. These were burned in a fierce fire and later pulverized. The powdered frit was mixed with one-third its weight in fireclay and enough water to make a plastic paste. The patent claimed that when fired this paste was "superior in strength to the ware brought from the East Indies, and commonly known by the name of China, Japan, or Porcelain Ware". The biscuit was decorated in light or dark tones of blue and later dipped in lead glaze and put aside to dry. The ware was then placed in saggers and fired in a wood-burning kiln "until the surface is clear and shining". The first use of liquid lead glaze has always been attributed to Enoch Booth of Tunstall in 1750. It appears, however, that Thomas Frye owned a fourteen-year monopoly on the use of liquid lead glaze, dating from the previous year (see Chapter 2).

Frye's new porcelain was sponsored by the firm of Weatherby and Crowther, owners of an earthenware pottery in Southwark. A new factory known as "New Canton" was built at Stratford-le-Bow on the Essex side of the River Lea, its architectural features resembling those of the celebrated porcelain warehouses at Canton in China. Frye was appointed works superintendent on a commission basis with, apparently, a seven-year contract. This was the Bow factory that issued some of the elegantly ornamental porcelain now gracing the cabinets of collectors.

Some early publicity for the new English porcelain was secured by distributing to china-sellers and others a series of circular, flat-topped ink-pots decorated with blue flowers and inscribed "Made at New Canton, 1750". A number of these still remain, including several dated 1751: twentieth-century copies have been made.

The mainstay of production throughout the twenty-five-year life of the factory was domestic table-ware. A trade card illustrating a tea-pot, two cups and saucers and a basin in Bow china was issued in 1750 by John Sotro, St. Paul's Churchyard, London. The first year's trading amounted to about £10,000, a figure suggesting that some two hundred thousand pieces of white and blue-and-white porcelain were issued, for no magnificent ware appears to have been made until 1753. Tea-cups and saucers cost 9d. each, small figures on plinths ranged from 6d. to 1s. 6d.

Production was at its finest between 1756 and 1759 when Thomas Frye retired, his health having been undermined through wearying years of constant close application to porcelain manufacturing processes. Either silicosis or lead poisoning may have been responsible for his death three years later, for no protection from these hazards of pottery-making had yet been envisaged. According to a document now in the British Museum and written by Thomas Craft, a former painter at Bow, "the firm of Crowther and Weatherby at this period employed 300 persons; about ninety painters and about 200 turners, throwers, &c., were employed under one roof . . . the whole was heated by two stoves on the outside of the building, and conveyed through flews and pipes and warmed the whole, sometimes to an intense heat".

The departure of Thomas Frye from Bow led to a decline in the quality of the porcelain. It was he who owned the patent which did not expire until 1763, and in consequence held the monopoly of making phosphatic porcelain and using a liquid lead glaze.

PLATE 14

erby porcelain. *Top:* pair of candelabra in form of seated figures of shepherd and shepherdess
ith flower-encrusted backgrounds, the former accompanied by a dog, the latter by a lamb.
low: two dancing groups: that on the right, incised "No 17" and painted with crossed swords
blue.

PLATE 15

Top: Derby porcelain vases with covers, the painted figure subjects possibly by O'Neale; on the reverse are panels painted with birds; royal blue ground. *c.* 1770. *Below:* pair of Derby pierced vases in green and gold, and vase encircled with exotic birds on a claret ground.

At about the time Frye resigned from Bow, bone ash became a constituent of Chelsea porcelain. It is probable that Frye withdrew from Crowther and Weatherby the sole rights for exploiting his formula and assigned an additional licence for the remaining years of the patent to Nicholas Sprimont of Chelsea.

Several authorities have suggested that ground oriental porcelain wasters were introduced into the paste, although they give the period as about 1755. That such a project was in operation at this period is confirmed by the *Handmaid to the Arts*, 1764, which records that "near London" eleven mills were engaged in grinding fragments of oriental porcelain to "remake it by the addition of some fluxing or vitreous substance which might restore the tenacity". There is little reason for associating this with Bow, however. The porcelain so made was described as "grey, full of flaws and bubbles and wrought in a very heavy clumsy manner". This process, which would produce a hard opaque ware, was fully described in *Essays, for the Month of December 1716*, and certain heavy porcelain, difficult to attribute to any of the known factories, could have been made by this method.

Little is known of Bow activities after 1762 when Weatherby died. In the following year John Crowther became bankrupt, and the stocks in factory and warehouse were sold by auction in May 1764. The plant was retained, however, and operated under Crowther's direction until 1775. It appears from contemporary evidence that machines, models and moulds were then bought by William Duesbury and removed to Derby.

So far as paste, glaze and decoration are concerned Bow porcelain can be divided into three main groups: 1750-56; 1756-63; and 1764-75. Even within these dates there might be variation according to the quality of materials available, and manufacturing processes were far from standardized.

The dense-textured, cream-coloured paste made at New Canton until 1755 was notable for its freedom from the grease-spot or moon defects associated with Chelsea porcelain. The thinner areas of Bow porcelain are translucent, but normally the ware is thick in section and appears opaque when held to the light, often to the extent of suggesting earthenware. By transmitted light the translucent areas may appear yellowish-green, but this tinge is in the glaze and not in the paste itself. Other distinctive features are its great weight and surprising strength: Bow porcelain, being hard, compact and vitreous, will chip but seldom crack. It is frequently stated that Bow porcelain would not withstand boiling water and was therefore unsuitable for tea- and coffee-pots. This was the case with all soft-paste porcelains excepting Worcester soapstone porcelain, which rarely broke under boiling liquids. But Richardson in 1753 listed Bow cups and saucers among the strong ware in great demand, and tea services were advertised in 1758.

Two types of lead glaze were used at New Canton, both covering the ware thickly owing to inexperience in applying them by Frye's patented dipping process, which could not be used by other porcelain makers without licence. First came a virtually transparent glaze of the glassy type. This had a faintly bluish tinge and was soft enough to be scratched easily. It was applied to ware bearing blue underglaze decoration, enabling the colour to be revealed to the full. In addition Frye used a thick creamy glaze, either faintly blue or with a slight tinge of greenish yellow: this appeared on *blanc de chine*, and also as a ground over which coloured enamels were painted.

These liquid glazes tended to collect in thick drops at the base of the ware and in crevices of applied ornament, often obliterating its finer reliefs. The later glaze has a distinctly yellowish hue when not cleared by the addition of zaffre. Much is now discoloured owing to excess of lead, displaying brown patches, particularly towards the base of a piece. Surface decomposition of the glaze has caused some Bow porcelain to assume a pinkish iridescence.

An improved, softer paste, creamy yellow in tone, had been evolved by 1756, and this was used until 1763. Transmitted light reveals bright flecks in its texture, explained by W. B. Honey in *Old English Porcelain* as "due to 'tearings' in the paste which are sometimes visible on the surface, resembling the 'parting' of uncooked dough, or of dry non-plastic clay". The more amenable texture of this paste led to the large-scale production of figures and other ornamental porcelain. The glaze was now smooth and slightly tinted, concealing flaws and specks in the paste, and providing a rich ground for enamel colours and gilding. The transparent glaze continued in use with blue and white underglaze ware.

After the disruption of Crowther's bankruptcy in 1763 the reorganized factory produced paste that was harshly white, potted with a thinner section than formerly and displaying a faintly brown tinge when held to the light. The glaze, given a distinctly blue tinge in imitation of the Chinese, was less carefully prepared than formerly and was liable to be flawed with black specks.

A great deal of early Bow porcelain, like that of other factories, was issued in the form of plain, white glazed domestic ware, sometimes decorated with white ornaments stamped in high relief from the plastic paste and applied to the body of the ware in the style of the white porcelain of Fukien. Collectors recognize this sprigged work on unmarked Bow by the sharp edges of each applied ornament: this is apparent only on close examination. Edges are also slightly discoloured as though the glaze has been affected from beneath. Favourite designs included prunus blossom, acorns and oak leaves, and a pair of roses on a single stem. In the Victoria and Albert Museum is an oval mould of porcelain, described in the *Catalogue of the Schreiber Collection*, Volume 1, as "impressed with a spray of Prunus-blossom and foliage, used for moulding sprigs to be applied as relief decoration. Found by Lady Charlotte Schreiber in March 1868, in excavations on the site of Bow porcelain works. Length, 3 in.; width, 2⅛ in."

Plain white Bow porcelain was made throughout the first period, and probably into the second owing to shortage of zaffre for blue decoration. Examples remaining include dishes, plates, tureens, sauce-boats, tea- and chocolate-pots, bowls with covers and stands, sweetmeat dishes, and salt-cellars. In some later pieces oriental flowers in colour might be painted between sprigs, and occasional examples were enriched with gilding. Figures in plain white porcelain were also made.

Blue-and-white domestic ware was intended by Frye to

be the mainstay of New Canton, and until about 1753 little ornament was used apart from this simple colouring which was continued throughout Bow's existence. The blue was painted on the biscuit before glazing, and its fusing temperature was but little higher than that of the glaze into which it was dipped. The result was that the colour tended to blur and spread around the edges of the design.

Frye's patent of 1749 scheduled that blue-and-white underglaze decoration should be carried out with zaffre or smalt, preparations of cobalt oxide which he noted could be applied "deeper or paler as required". The weight of zaffre imported from Saxony during 1750 was 90,000 lb. greater than in the previous year, but was considerably less in 1751. This suggests that Frye was a large purchaser for stock. Frye seldom used smalt owing to its high cost. The early blue was extremely pale as if diluted with calcined flint. From about 1756, however, an almost indigo purple was used. War had caused Saxony to cease the export of cobalt oxide products in 1756, and English cobalt was used almost exclusively from 1756 until the end of the second Bow period. This was much darker in hue than the Saxon product. It was found impossible to standardize English cobalt blue: this resulted in a wide range of tints, often unexpected by the decorator. Because it was much cheaper than the Saxon product it could be applied with a lavish hand.

Decoration covered a wide range of designs adapted from the oriental style with birds and weeping willows predominating. Powdered blue grounds with reserves for designs in underglaze blue became a very popular decoration on domestic ware.

Painting in enamel colours was used comparatively little by the Bow decorators until about 1753, when the Japanese style of Imari chrysanthemum decoration on criss-cross panels came into use. Colours were red, green, blue, yellow and gold applied over the glaze. Similar motifs in adapted forms soon ornamented other English porcelain.

The brownish-red enamel on Imari-Bow porcelain, known to collectors as "sealing wax red", usually lacks gloss owing to inadequate blending of the iron oxide in its composition, and the enamel has a tendency to fall away

PLATE 16

ollection of Derby bone china in the Victoria and Albert Museum. *Top and second rows:* 1820s. *Third row:* 1830s. *Bottom row:* inkstand, bell pulls and plates 1820s; basket 1840.

PLATE 17

Top: Pinxton porcelain cup and saucer painted in colours and gilded. Mark: a script "P"; dated 179
Below: Torksey cup and saucer painted in colours and gilded. Mark: impressed "T". *c.* 1800.

from the glaze. A pale mauve-pink applied in thin washes is a feature of Bow colour work, termed gold-purple by present-day collectors. Blue enamel is notable only for its lifeless opacity.

Diversity of tones in Bow painted enamel colours, particularly in pinks, greens and reds, was the result of attempting to reduce the grinding and other processes in its preparation so as to issue the ware at the lowest prices possible. This haphazard preparation of the enamels is less marked in oriental motifs. It must be conceded that Bow painted enamels never reached a richness comparable with those of Chelsea.

Bow introduced what was perhaps the first daring design to appear on English porcelain. This was the celebrated quail or partridge pattern. The design is simple and consists of a blue-stemmed tree displaying brilliant red and gold blossoms, with two quails or partridges sheltering beneath, sometimes with hedges and wheat sheaves, all on a white ground with a narrow edging of thick foliage in red. It was advertised in 1758 that this design was painted by artists from the Royal Saxon Porcelain Manufactory at Meissen, recently despoiled by the invading Prussians. The Meissen version of the partridge pattern had been adapted from the designs on Japanese porcelain of the school of the potter Kakiemon.

Famille rose designs appear to have been copied by Bow directly from Chinese export porcelain, worked with clear enamels thickly applied. Customers might also send their own original oriental pieces to New Canton for copying. These were noted from time to time in the original Bow account books formerly in the collection of Lady Charlotte Schreiber, such as "Patterns received from Lady Cavendish. A japan octagon cup and saucer, lady pattern." The centres of some plates made during the second period have the slight central kick found in contemporaneous Chinese work. Plate centres might be two or three times as thick as their rims.

Some indication of the increased range of ware is shown in the advertisement of the first public sale of Bow porcelain recorded by Nightingale, and which appeared several times in the *Public Advertiser*, April 1757: "The very extensive and valuable Production of the Manufactory of Bow China and Porcelaine, consisting of Epargnes, Branch Candlesticks, Services for Desserts &c. exquisitely painted in Enamel, and Blue and White. Also a large Assortment of the most useful China in Lots, for the Use of Gentlemen's Kitchens, Private Families, Taverns, &c."

Still further developments were indicated by the advertisement of a sale in February 1758 which included "Perfume Pots, beautiful Groups of Figures, Jars, Beakers, Birds, Beasts, &c. Services of Dishes, Plates, Sauce-boats, complete Tea and Coffee Equipages, both Blue and white and enamelled."

Some elaborate table-ware was made during the third Bow period, decoration including raised vine sprigs, enamelled fruits and birds, and blue underglaze reserves containing colourful birds or paintings in the Boucher or Fragonard manner; later the blue grounds might be diapered in gold.

Porcelain with decoration printed over the glaze was made at Bow from about 1756 until about 1760, but results were seldom pleasing, and impressions might be indistinct. The transfers in black, brick red, brown or the rare dull manganese purple might be enclosed within hand-painted borders. Designs were sometimes printed in outline and painted over by hand with enamel colours (see Chapter 5).

Bow figures made at New Canton may be classified in three main types: the earliest "in the white"; those decorated in blue under the glaze; and the delightful figures, groups and *bocages* in polychrome enamels.

The figures in plain white porcelain usually stand on rectangular bases and are characterized by vigorous though elementary modelling, full of technical imperfections. Supports were almost crude in their simplicity, sometimes little more than lumps of clay moulded to resemble a stump, a coat or a dress. When colour was first applied to figures the result was florid, a dry red and a yellowish green being frequent.

The earliest reference to figure moulding at Bow so far noted appeared in *Aris's Birmingham Gazette*, dated November 5, 1753, which circulated in the Potteries. Here "The China-Works, near Bow" advertised for "Painters in the Blue and White Potting Way, and Enamellers on China-Ware. . . . Likewise painters brought up in the Snuff-Box Way, Japanning, Fan Painting &c. N.B. At the same House, a Person is wanted who can model small Figures in Clay neatly."

The employment of such a modeller suggests that at this period Bow figures were still being shaped entirely by hand. It is probable that figures were a minor production until the introduction of highly experienced craftsmen and decorators who had fled from Meissen.

Copies of Meissen figures began to be made and by 1756 had become important items of production. Until about 1758 they usually stood upon flat, rectangular bases, either lacking all ornament or with almost imperceptible scrolls in low relief. Their height seldom exceeded 11 inches. Colours generally used on these figures included puce, in shades varying from pink to crimson, and an opaque milky blue. These colours might be merged to produce marbling effects on the bases.

By about 1758 a more elaborate stand was evolved, with scrolls so designed that the corners of the base became small supporting feet. Bow was the first factory to make the footed pedestal most characteristic of eighteenth-century English figures. The figures were now modelled with greater delicacy, larger examples being supported by elaborately shaped four-footed bases enlivened with touches of purple and other tints. Small figures generally stood upon round, flat-based pedestals. Additional colours on the enameller's palette included opaque purple, brick red, and pale yellow, all sparingly applied. Another distinguishing feature was the introduction of hand-modelled conventional flowers bordering feminine garments. They were usually coloured in puce-crimson.

Bow figures under the Crowther régime from 1764 displayed more creative individuality: decoration was more elaborate, colours costlier and richer, continental work seldom copied. Pedestals were designed with gracefully pierced scrolls. Frank Hurlbutt, in his invaluable *Bow*

Porcelain, describes figures as being decorated with "resplendent garments patterned with a brilliant *rose à la Pompadour* or rich underglaze cobalt blue, turquoise, or copper red ground, having ornately shaped and scrolled white reserves, delicately pencilled with flowers in one or many colours, the reserves often edged with fringed gold; breeches or waistcoats of a peacock's tail scale pattern, and gorgeous disc patterns, make Bow figures desirable. Dresses of female figures were frequently of blue or crimson with small yellow flowers and miniature gold leaves. Crimson, pale blue, and yellow usually appeared on the bases."

Among Bow figures were Italian Comedy Pantaloons, Harlequins, and Columbines, mythological gods and goddesses, musicians, shepherds and shepherdesses, and male and female cooks, in colourful attire. In 1758 shepherds and shepherdesses, Pierrots and Harlequins were priced at the factory 7s. and 9s. each; boys and girls 12s. a pair; ladies and gentlemen 9s. a pair. Figures might be adapted from contemporary engravings, such as the Marquess of Granby, copied from a print after Reynolds in 1768. Bird and animal models, including the well-known squirrels, were also made.

There is considerable resemblance between many Bow and Chelsea figures. Close examination of the surface of many Bow figures will disclose marks caused by the modeller's use of a flat knife for sharpening the surface, and a pointed tool for accentuating lines before firing. Colours too are conspicuously brighter and more garish. On many a Bow figure a triangular, circular or square hole was cut into the back of the base: this was intended for the attachment of a leafy branch of ormolu or green-enamelled metal with stalks surmounted by porcelain flowers or candle sockets. Crowther sold such figures complete with their metal branches.

Renowned among Bow productions were the little leafy bowers with small cherubs grouped against backgrounds of closely clustered flowers. These *bocages*, with twisted leaves and petals, are smaller than comparable ornaments of Chelsea, in which leaves are flatter and the outer petals of flowers are saucer-shaped. Girandoles, branches and candlesticks "for Chimney Pieces and finely decorated with Flowers and Figures" were advertised, as well as table chandeliers. The stem of such a piece might be in the form of a cherub holding aloft a single socket or a branch of two, three or four; more frequently a splendidly coloured shepherd or shepherdess undertook the task. A group of colourful birds masking a metal stem and candle socket was highly approved, but few of these delicate candle-holders appear to have survived.

Beautifully proportioned vases were made at Bow from about 1756 in sets of three, five or seven: they were advertised as jars, beakers and essence pots. Grounds were in underglaze blue with reserves in which colourful flower, bird or figure motifs were enamelled over the glaze. The central vase in a set might be fitted with a cover surmounted by a bird-shaped knob realistically coloured: this vase would be flanked by a pair of similarly decorated beakers. In some instances the vessel was enhanced by a pair of applied handles in such shapes as a pair of cupid or lion heads. Reserves might be decorated with relief ornament, brightly enamelled flowers and foliage being interspersed with butterflies and other insects.

Those vases ornamented with panels after the "old Japan" style lack the harmony of arrangement notable in the originals, chiefly because Bow decorators tended to fit too many motifs in confined spaces. Panels might be outlined by moulding in low relief, enclosing flowers, figures or landscapes in coloured enamels. Other well-known vase decorations in which the white porcelain formed the background were the *famille rose* patterns, and an archaic Japanese design dominated by the figure of a lady in appropriate court dress.

Perfume vases, advertised as essence pots, were concealed beneath cone-shaped bouquets of tiny clustered flowers. Perfume was introduced by sprinkling these colourful posies with flower essence or by filling the vases with *pot-pourri* so that the scent percolated through finely pierced holes. Other vases were arranged to contain cone-shaped scented pastilles for slow burning. These were ornamented with rococo scrollwork in relief enriched with crimson or

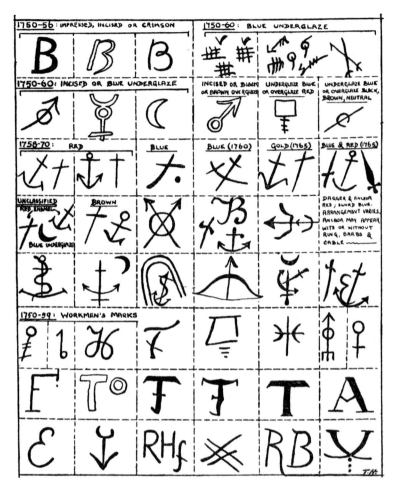

turquoise enamel or gilding, or all three. On such a vessel this decoration would surround two reserves, each painted with a bouquet of flowers, a bird on a branch, or a figure.

The decoration of porcelain marked with an anchor and dagger has been attributed recently to James Giles, entered in *Mortimer's Directory*, 1763, as "China and Enamel Painter, Berwick Street, Soho." It is thought that William Duesbury's decorating shops were in this area and newspaper advertisements show that Giles, like Duesbury, was also a china seller, specializing in Worcester and Derby porcelains. The possibility therefore arises that Giles was Duesbury's successor, but Mr. Stanley Fisher considers it more probable that Giles began by taking over the business of John Bolton, enameller, the Church, Lambeth. Oddly enough, when Giles failed in 1778 his business was acquired by Duesbury, whose London decoration at this time was being carried out at his Bedford Street showrooms.

Giles occupied other premises in addition to those in Berwick Street. He probably prepared his enamels at Kentish Town, and there is evidence that he sold enamel colours to potters such as Philip Christian (see Chapter 14) and to independent enamellers. From Cockspur Street, Charing Cross, between 1767 and 1776 he advertised "elegant dessert services, fine tea services, & curiously enamelled in figures, birds and flowers, and ornamented with mazarine and sky blue and gold." Remaining examples of his work show that during the quarter century he was in

---

MARKS ON BOW PORCELAIN

Bow porcelain was seldom marked, still more rarely after 1764. Only careful study of marked pieces will enable the collector to become familiar with the distinctive features which ensure correct identification. Marks were usually incised in the paste, roughly painted in red, or inscribed in blue underglaze.

Among those used until about 1756 were several versions of the letter "B," incised, impressed or in crimson; three thick vertical lines crossed by three horizontal lines, and similar pseudo-oriental marks in blue underglaze.

Contemporary and until 1760 were a circle crossed by an arrow, sometimes modified to a "C" crossed by a stroke; crossed daggers in blue underglaze; a crescent or the sign of the planet Mercury or in blue underglaze.

From 1758 to 1770, the sword in blue was used. The anchor and dagger found on Bow porcelain is now attributed to the decorator James Giles. Late in the period the anchor might have a cable. Dagger and anchors were used in many variations. One version of the dagger accompanying the anchor mark was borrowed from the coat of arms of the City of London, in which it symbolizes the treacherous slaying of Wat Tyler by Walworth at Smithfield in 1380.

Rebus marks such as a violin bow and a bow and arrow are also known.

Workmen's marks were numerous until about 1760 and included the numerals 1 to 49. Some blue-and-white pieces are marked with "TF," the monogram of Thomas Frye. "R.H.f." is the signature of Robert Hancock, who engraved transfer designs for Frye, probably working as a freelance artist. The mark "To" impressed has not been explained satisfactorily.

Presence of a mark must not be allowed to overshadow more important characteristics of genuineness. Bow marks appear on modern copies from Paris and elsewhere.

business he employed a number of enamellers of outstanding ability, whose names are lost.

Giles often decorated porcelain already ornamented with
blue underglaze bought from Caughley and Worcester. He
also bought overglaze transfer-printed ware in black and
lilac which he enriched with enamels. In 1773 he is recorded
as having bought engraved copper plates from Thomas
Turner of Caughley. This suggests that he might have made
transfers and issued transfer-printed ware from his own
workshops; or he might have made transfers for sale to
potters, probably employing someone familiar with the
technique as carried out at the Battersea enamel works.

Giles also made a feature of decorating Worcester porcelain with coloured grounds and heavy gilding which might
be chased. This was in a quality inferior only in the crudity
of the chasing to similar work issued from the factory. In
addition to the Worcester products, decoration attributed
to Giles has been noted on porcelain made at Bow, Chelsea,
Derby, Longton Hall, Bristol, Caughley and Philip
Christian's pottery at Liverpool.

8

AT most, Longton Hall played a minor part in the history of English porcelain. Nevertheless, it is strange that so few facts have been established regarding its decade of considerable productivity, and that the deductions drawn here appear to have been overlooked by earlier investigators. Much of its output may have been mediocre—although not all is to be dismissed as such—but the firm was of some importance in the early development of the great Derby porcelain establishment, providing early experience for William Duesbury and employing the Meissen-trained father of Derby's manager and technician André Planché. Longton Hall was also one of the very early English porcelain factories, and the earliest in Staffordshire.

Dr. Richard Pococke, visiting Newcastle-under-Lyme in 1750, noted in his diary that there he inspected a porcelain factory, meeting a potter formerly employed at Limehouse "who seemed to promise to make the best china-ware". Although "statues of elephants, lyons and birds" were being produced, difficulty was experienced in the firing, the percentage of wasters being high.

With this rather vague record must be associated the fact that William Littler, successful manufacturer of salt-glaze pottery, established at Longton Hall the only Staffordshire porcelain factory known to have been in operation at the period in question. Longton Hall must therefore be assumed to be the Newcastle-under-Lyme establishment referred to by Dr. Pococke. In corroboration of this is the fact that figures taken from the same moulds have been found in both white porcelain and salt-glazed pottery. In the Victoria and Albert Museum are examples of early Longton Hall figures in the white, so thickly covered with a greenish-hued glaze that modelling details are obscured. Collectors refer to such figures as the "snow-man" family.

As regards Dr. Pococke's "Limehouse potter", all that is known of the porcelain factory at Limehouse is that it was established near Dick's Shore in about 1746, advertising on January 1, 1747, in the *Daily Advertiser* that "the new-invented blue-and-white Limehouse ware" was on sale, and going bankrupt before the middle of 1748. The potter responsible for this small venture appears to have been a technician named Planché who had acquired his knowledge at Meissen and who moved to Staffordshire when the Limehouse factory failed.

More is known of his son André Planché who served his apprenticeship (1740–47) with Edward Mountenay, a London jeweller (see page 95), and who presumably first went to Derby because that town was a centre of the jewellery trade. Like his father, however, the young jeweller appreciated the potential value of the older man's Dresden experience, and it was as a maker of white glazed porcelain figures that he too found employment. While his father worked at Longton Hall, André was engaged at the newly established Derby Porcelain Manufactory, forerunner of the more important Derby Porcelain Company.

Simeon Shaw, writing in 1829, recorded that "William Littler and his brother-in-law Aaron Wedgwood first introduced the use of Cobalt in the manufacture of salt-glazed ware. . . . From his success in this he was led to attempt the production of porcelain. He left Brownhills near Tunstall and removed to Longton Hall where he lost all his money in the venture. The porcelain was a frit body; was fired with wood because it would not bear coals [coal was not yet being used in connection with pottery kilns]; and its defect was its inability to bear sudden or excessive changes of temperature. The specimens which are well calculated to deceive the eye of the spectators are cylindrical cups, with handles, showing some taste, a tolerable glaze, and enamelled with flowers; but there are many specks and the whole has a greenish hue."

William Duesbury appears to have had some association with Littler and Planché senior at Longton Hall before establishing the Derby Porcelain Company in 1755 with André Planché as works manager (see page 95). Duesbury's account book for 1751 shows that he was then decorating ware supplied to him by Littler and Company. In 1754 he joined William Littler, and various legal documents of 1755 describe him as "enameller of Longton Hall".

Several advertisements indicate the scope of Longton Hall productions during the 1750s. *Aris's Birmingham Gazette* announced that Littler and Company, established at Longton Hall, Newcastle, Staffordshire, were prepared to supply ornamental porcelain and china ware in great variety. A London auction sale was announced in the *Public Advertiser* for April 1757: "New and Curious Porcelain or China of the Longton Hall Manufactory—Tureens, Covers and Dishes, large Cups and Covers, Jars and Beakers with beautiful sprigs of Flowers, open-worked Fruit Baskets and Plates, Tea and Coffee Equipages, leaf Basons and Plates, Melons, Colliflowers, elegant Epargnes, and other ornamental and useful porcelain both white and enamell'd." In the following June additional ware was advertised in the *Birmingham Gazette*: "plain *blue and white* tea china, coffee cans, chocolate cups and saucers, punch bowls and mugs". Nevertheless, within three years the venture was abandoned, most probably through lack of sufficient capital, the last record consisting of an advertisement published not in the Potteries but in Salisbury, which throws some doubt on the usually accepted theory that workers and equipment were acquired by Derby. The *Salisbury Journal,* September 1760, announced the sale of "the genuine and valuable stock of the Longton Porcelaine Factory, which as the partnership is dissolved will be sold without Reserve or the least Addition, containing upwards of 90,000 pieces". Shaw has recorded that William Littler became manager of Baddeley and Fletcher's unsuccessful porcelain venture at Shelton.

Longton Hall made soft-paste porcelains of two major types, variations occurring in each. Early porcelain was soft, creamy white, glassy and very translucent, with a small amount of bone ash in its composition. Later the paste became noticeably heavier owing to the introduction of lead oxide, a result of using flint-glass in preparing the frit. This paste is rather grey in colour with a greenish-cream translucency displaying irregularly shaped moons when held to the light. Surface specks are usual. It must be noted, too, that a distinctly uneven surface characterizes Longton Hall porcelain.

Glaze at first was thinly applied and is recognized by its cold glittering surface. Although faintly tinged with cobalt it is whiter than that of Bow or Chelsea. A glaze slightly greyish in tint was used on the later heavier paste, giving the surface an appearance of having been dipped into paraffin wax. This usually ends a fraction of an inch above the base. The exposed biscuit has absorbed two centuries of dust and now appears as a dark line around the base.

Contemporary with the "snow-men", Longton Hall made blue painted flat-ware and small hollow-ware such as sauce-boats, some of which have been recognized as from the same moulds as salt-glaze examples. These were decorated with wide uneven borders or with solid grounds, with reserves enclosing simple oriental motifs, the intention being to revive the *gros bleu* developed at Vincennes in 1749. This underglaze blue ground, characteristic of Longton Hall and lavishly used on decorative porcelain, has little richness or depth. It always has a streaky appearance as if sponge-applied to the biscuit by an amateur, and the glaze is thin. Longton Hall blue is often ornamented with cartouches outlined in raised, opaque white-enamel scrollwork. This feature is not found on other English porcelain although it had been used on Littler's salt-glaze ware and was later very popular with the South Staffordshire enamellers. Longton Hall blue is lighter than that used at Chelsea and is brighter than the blue grounds of Derby and Worcester. In the British Museum is a butter-dish with the Longton Hall mark, its characteristic blue ground and the cartouches in raised white enamel. From 1753 the blue reserves might contain motifs in polychrome enamels such as flowers, exotic birds and figure paintings.

Polychrome decoration was used throughout the period.

At first unfired pigments were used which have tended to flake away with the passing of years, a fact which may account for some of the now white figures. Dresden flower motifs in enamels were painted from 1753 by a single artist whose style is unmistakable, his petals being irregularly outlined with delicate charm. Longton Hall landscapes with buildings and exotic birds are characterized by peculiar-hued brown and yellow enamels; a feature of the foreground is a tuft of rushes with the tips of some leaves bent over. Kakiemon and *famille rose* patterns were adapted in a wide variety, the latter being distinguished by the presence of an opaque lemon yellow. Gilding is always sparse and was never burned into the glaze, with the result that it appears dull and much of it quickly wore away. When present it appears as thick gold leaf.

Longton Hall productions are associated with some clumsy potting and a frequent but not invariable lack of grace. This criticism does not apply to the plates, basins and jugs shaped as overlapping leaves. These are moulded in higher relief and more finely finished than similar pieces made elsewhere. They are, however, decorated with an unattractive yellowish green.

Among the ornamental vases is a series of elaborate *pot-pourri* jars—of which a strangely large number appear to have survived. The design shows a wide, concave neck, handles in the form of volutes, and a high foot spirally fluted above a wide spreading base. On either side of the body is a panel decorated with colourful birds. The domed cover is pierced with small perforations and encrusted with a bouquet of large applied flowers in natural colours.

Longton Hall domestic ware, particularly jugs and mugs, is found with black transfer decorations, sometimes bearing the signature of Sadler and Green of Liverpool. None of this transfer-printed porcelain preceded 1756, and as the Liverpool–Stoke canal had not yet been cut consignments sent from Longton Hall must necessarily have made the double journey by pack-

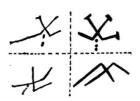

Longton Hall: all in blue; *bottom right*, in the field of the decoration.

horse. It is believed that a large proportion of the 90,000 pieces sold at Salisbury in 1770 were in the white: it is possible therefore that the purchaser sent consignments to Liverpool for transfer-printing. A characteristic of Longton Hall jugs and mugs, not noted on other porcelain, is the handle construction. The design consisted of two sections joined centrally with a curved crosspiece.

Figures, made of a heavy grey paste, tend to lack skill in modelling and artistry in enamelling. They are supported by rococo scrollwork bases unskilfully moulded and decorated with a few lines of enamel applied to the edges of the scrolls. Costumes are decorated with star or diaper patterns, never with flower motifs. Characteristic colours are a harsh crimson, an uneven yellow, a dry yellowish green and a poor red. Some late examples are touched with gilding. Heads are carefully modelled and the faces enlivened with a distinctive red marking the features. The undersides of figure bases have a lumpy appearance and firecracks are frequent.

The Longton Hall mark, rare and found only on early pieces, consists of a monogram of two L's crossed, with a string of two or three dots placed vertically below, in under-glaze blue. The monogram is reasonably assumed to mean Littler, Longton, but some authorities have suggested that it is an adaptation of the crossed L's of Vincennes (later Sèvres).

9

DERBY is famous for its figures and still more for the beauty and range of its colours. The foundations of this celebrated pottery had already been laid by 1741 when the *Derby Mercury* advertised "fine CHINA WARE consisting of completed sets of Tea Table and Table CHINA". This china was possibly imported: it could not have been produced by the Derby Pot Manufactory on Cockpit Hill, then making slipware.

The first name associated with Derby porcelain is that of André Planché, whose father had worked at Meissen and in 1749 was employed by Littler at Longton Hall (see page 90). André no doubt learned the processes of porcelain-making and the art of modelling from his father.

Several authorities perpetuate the tradition that in 1745 the seventeen-year-old André, then working in Derby, was modelling in porcelain simple white glazed figures of cats, dogs, sheep and birds, which he fired in a pipe-maker's oven. Firing in such an oven at that period could not have provided the high temperature necessary for baking porcelain. In any case, the researches of Major William H. Tapp in 1933 proved that Planché was "apprenticed from July 3rd 1740 until July 3rd 1747 to Edward Mountenay, a jeweller of Foster's Lane, London, and consequently could not have started operations in Derby as a china maker before the later of these dates". Major Tapp also discovered that Planché was married to Sarah Stone at St. Pancras Church on September 28, 1747.

Derby at that time was an important centre of the jewellery trade, Simpson employing thirty hands and

Severne and Company nearly one hundred. It is probable that after his marriage Planché found employment in the jewellery trade at Derby, and while following his profession carried out research in the production of porcelain, basing his experiments on formulæ supplied by his father. The resulting models were no doubt taken to the Cockpit Hill Pot Manufactory for firing, and here they attracted the attention of John Heath the financing partner. Heath appears to have taken the young jeweller-potter into his employment, and in 1749 a porcelain department was established under the style of the Derby Porcelain Manufactory. From 1750 a long series of porcelain figures in the white was turned out. Four examples of the plain white glazed porcelain are in the Victoria and Albert Museum, whose technical experts have found them to be non-phosphatic.

Some of these figures were decorated by William Duesbury (1725–86), at that time a porcelain enameller in London. His account book of 1751 establishes the fact that in that year he enamelled 382 pieces of porcelain from Derby, Bow and Chelsea. A man of vigorous personality, Duesbury rose from being an obscure enameller to become proprietor of one of the most prosperous commercial enterprises of the day.

William Duesbury's first venture as a potter was in association with William Littler, whom he joined at Longton Hall in 1754. Littler proved unpractical and unenterprising to the forceful Duesbury, who determined to establish a porcelain factory on his own account. His father, a currier of Cannock in Staffordshire, assisted by making over his small property to his son on condition that he was kept in comfort for the remainder of his life. Supported by a loan from John Heath, Duesbury acquired property in Nottingham Road, Derby, and adapted it to the manufacture of porcelain. The Derby Porcelain Company, a separate establishment from Heath's Derby Porcelain Manufactory, began operations in 1755 with Planché as works manager.

Heath's Derby Porcelain Manufactory at Cockpit Hill thereupon ceased to make porcelain wares. In December

PLATE 18

oalport bone china. *Top: (a* and *c)* a pair of candlesticks modelled as standing figures of a girl and ɔuth before flowering tree stumps supporting vase-shaped nozzles on circular bases modelled ith scrolls and flowers in high relief, enamelled in natural colours and gold; *(b)* figure of a youth ɔside a rustic pedestal on circular base. *Below: (a* and *e)* a pair of vases with painting by Edwin teele, and enriched with gilding; *(b* and *d)* enamelled spill vases; *(c)* vase with blue ground enriched ith gold pencilled work, *c.* 1825.

PLATE 19

Bristol soft-paste porcelain, *c.* 1750. *Top:* bowl painted in colours. *Centre:* pair of sauce-boats, the moulded cartouches characteristically painted with a fine brush in blue underglaze. *Bottom:* pair of hexagonal bottles with bulbous bodies painted in colours in pseudo-Chinese style.

1756 the *Public Advertiser* announced that the proprietors of this establishment were holding a sale of what was termed "a curious collection of fine figures, jars, sauceboats, services for desserts, and a great variety of other useful and ornamental porcelain *after* the finest Dresden Models all exquisitely painted in enamel with flowers, insects, India plants . . . and some of the finest of the Derby Porcelain". This indicates pretty clearly that Planché had proved himself a capable porcelain manufacturer, but he left the town after a few months with Duesbury.

Late in 1757 Duesbury enlarged his premises, enabling double the number of workers to be employed. In the following April he was advertising in the London newspapers "the largest variety of the Derby Porcelain or second Dresden figures". It is generally assumed that at this time he bought the Longton Hall factory, transferring the best workers and the entire stock-in-trade to Derby, but this is not borne out by the fact that the Longton Hall sale was held in Salisbury in 1760 (see page 91) and that some models were apparently acquired by Cookworthy (see page 192).

Little is known of the Derby Porcelain Company until 1770 when Duesbury bought the failing Chelsea factory. He continued operating this as a branch with seldom more than a dozen employees, until 1783, when the models and moulds were removed to Derby. Duesbury had a flair for collecting around him talented artists who brought the art of porcelain decoration to that high degree of excellence which attracted the patronage of the rich. Models of oriental and continental porcelain were at this time lent to Duesbury by the Duke of Newcastle and the Countess Spencer, while Lord Lonsdale lent important sketches. When George III visited the Chelsea factory in 1773 he was so impressed by the beauty of the ware that he gave his patronage, with permission for the royal crown to be incorporated in the trade mark. Assuming his acquisition also of the Bow porcelain factory in 1775 Duesbury controlled the most productive porcelain organization in the kingdom, his only rival of consequence being Worcester.

Duesbury gave his son a partnership early in 1786, the

7*+   97

firm then being styled William Duesbury and Son. A few months later he died, and his son William Duesbury II became sole proprietor and controller of the works until 1795, when, in failing health, he took into partnership Michael Kean, a miniature-painter from London. When Duesbury II died early in the following year Kean managed the business on behalf of Duesbury's widow and nine-year-old son. Shortly afterwards he married the widow.

During the Duesbury régime little domestic ware was made, as Derby soft-paste porcelain could not stand hot water. Kean was quick to remedy this by changing over to bone china which Josiah Spode and John Rose of Coalport were using with such conspicuous success. Kean also followed Spode's success in the use of patterns adapted from the Japanese Imari. At the same time he introduced women copyist painters, the immediate effect being that the finest artists, including Billingsley and Banford, expressed their disapproval by leaving in a group. Only a few years earlier the artists had gone on strike when the widow of a former colleague had been given some decorating work.

Kean retired from the business in 1811, disposing of his shares to William Sheffield, father-in-law of Duesbury III. Business was scarce owing to war-time shortages, and in 1815 the firm of Duesbury and Sheffield was disposed of to Robert Bloor, who for many years had been commercial manager. The price was £5,000, payable by instalments, and certain annuities. Bloor, assisted by his brother Joseph, exerted every effort to save the tottering business from ruin. By following the lead of Josiah Spode II and specializing in inexpensive ware for a wider public than formerly, he was a conspicuous financial success. He also utilized the great stocks of porcelain in the white, the accumulation of decades, by decorating them cheaply and gaudily. Within seven years the purchase price had been paid. Although Bloor was appointed potter to George IV in 1820, Derby under Bloor's management never regained its former reputation for fine porcelain. Bloor ultimately became insane, and three years after his death in 1845 the works were closed and the models and moulds, including those of Bow, Chelsea and Longton Hall, were sold to Samuel Boyle, who later disposed of them to the firm of W. T. Copeland (late Spode).

In 1848 several of Bloor's former employees established a small factory making bone china in King Street, Derby, under the management of William Locker, who was succeeded in 1851 by Stevenson, Sharp and Company, and changed yet again, in 1859, to Stevenson and Hancock. In 1876 yet another Derby company was launched: this was in Osmaston Road, and in 1890 became styled the Royal Crown Derby Porcelain Company. Thus the name Crown Derby has continued to the present day.

Six major changes were made to the paste during the century of Derby porcelain production.

1. Examples belonging to the Planché period 1749-55 are of poor quality and light-weight paste, chalky in appearance. The glaze may have a faintly yellow tinge.

2. The paste used by Duesbury until about 1770 was a glassy frit containing a whitish clay obtained in Derbyshire. Dorset clay was also used. The porcelain, which was rarely marked, is soft, sandy in texture and of creamy translucence often displaying "grease spots" or moons. The white glaze is thick and pellucid. There is little to distinguish Derby paste of the period from other contemporary porcelain, and much Derby is no doubt masquerading as Chelsea or Bow.

3. In about 1760 Richard Holdship, a former partner in the porcelain factory at Worcester, agreed to reveal to Duesbury the steatitic formula used at Worcester, and to supply suitable "soapy rock" necessary for its production. Some Derby porcelain made during the late 1760s has been found to be steatitic.

4. Bone ash was introduced into Derby soft-paste porcelain after Duesbury acquired the Chelsea factory in 1770 and continued in regular use until 1796. The paste during this period was phosphatic, about 40 per cent of bone ash being incorporated in its manufacture. Dorset clay, the finest then available to porcelain manufacturers, was used in this close-grained soft-paste porcelain of remarkable purity and creamy translucency. The soft glaze,

free from crazing and easily scratched, is thick, lustrous and satiny. So deeply might the painting sink into the glaze that it often has the appearance of being under the glaze.

5. During the Duesbury-Kean period, 1796–1811, a hard, white, non-frit bone china was used, more opaque and displaying a greenish translucency when held to the light. The thin hard glaze did not absorb the enamel, which could therefore be applied more thinly than formerly. The beautiful blending of enamel and glaze was lost.

6. Derby china of the Bloor period, 1815–48, has a hard appearance. Its somewhat heavy paste lacks transparency and the thick glaze has usually crazed and become discoloured.

Derby figures of the Duesbury régime have always been admired by collectors. Solon,[1] the great authority on ceramics, wrote of Derby figures: "They show a degree of excellence unapproached by any kindred productions". The artists who supplied the models worked usually from pictures or engravings in vogue at the moment. Consequently, none of their subjects exhibit much invention or originality. It is the careful execution of each copy, and particularly the waxen and mellow appearance of the paste, that constitute their chief merit. A successful model was made in three sizes: the corresponding number 1, 2 or 3 is found scratched in the paste under the article.

The glaze on the rather crudely modelled figures in the white typical of the Planché régime appears to have been brush-applied, and finished an appreciable distance above the lower rim of the base, the underside of which remained unglazed. Specimens in this style are termed by collectors "dry edge" figures.

Duesbury's figures were modelled with a sharpness of outline not found in other contemporary specimens. Folds of garments are thin, almost knife-edged, this distinctive feature being accentuated by the thinness of the glaze which did not accumulate in the slight blobs that may be observed on Chelsea gold-anchor figures. The bases, which are often flat, usually have three or four dark, unglazed patches caused by the pads of clay on which the figures

[1] M. L. Solon, *Old English Porcelain.*

PLATE 20

Worcester porcelain of the Dr. Wall period. *Top left:* dish moulded in relief to resemble wicker-work pattern and coloured canary-yellow with cartouches containing sprays of flowers and bordered in crimson. Mark: crescent in red. *c.* 1770. *Top right:* pear-shaped jug painted with exotic birds in colour in gold-bordered cartouche against green ground, with projecting lip moulded with bearded mask, gilded rim; *c.* 1765. *Lower left:* mug with exotic birds painted in colours on green ground; the rim encircled with white border edged with gilt pencilling; *c.* 1770. *Lower right:* plate painted in colours and gilt, decorated with shaped panels outlined by gilt scrollwork on dark-blue ground.

PLATE 21

Worcester porcelain, 1765 to 1775. *Top:* tea-cups and saucers, and tea-pot, painted in colours an
gilded in the style of Kakiemon ware. *Centre:* tea-pots, left with gilded fret-work; right, with flute
barrel-shaped body. *Below:* covered cup, coffee-pot, and bowl decorated with designs in full colou
with grounds of blue scale pattern.

rested when the glaze was fired. These patches are found on both biscuit and enamelled ware of a later period.

Bases are enriched with painted decoration rather than the more expensive applied flowers used elsewhere. The fabric of petals and the light, yellow-green leaves forming the *bocages* for Derby figures is appreciably thinner than those of other potteries. The tree-stump supports behind some figures are pierced with circular holes for the insertion of ormolu branches.

Drapery may be decorated with flowers in natural colours on a yellow ground and lined with pink of the crushed-strawberry tint, a popular Derby colour. An important feature associated with early Duesbury figures is the reddish-brown colour ringing a darker spot to represent the pupil of the eye. Eyelashes and brows are often picked out in the same tint. Colour appears often to have been applied carelessly. Gilding is sparse, and normally decorates only garment edges and buttons with a touch to enliven the base.

Duesbury's figures of the Chelsea-Derby period indicate that the provincial factory dominated the London branch. Although advertised in flamboyant language, modelling appears to have been less skilful than formerly and productions appear to be mainly copies or adaptations of the sentimental designs made fashionable by Sèvres. Figures of celebrities in the style of the monumental sculpture of the period also found favour with a wide public. Figures of this period are usually only slightly tinted with pale washes of colour, greens and pinks being sometimes particularly uneven. The turquoise enamel used during this period is clear and inclining towards blue, contrasting with the former cloudy effect.

It was the rule throughout the Duesbury period that all figures should be roughed out in the nude and then draped. In this way anatomical accuracy was achieved. When the original figure left the modeller, it was cut into sections by figure-makers, known as repairers, each limb and the head being cast separately in plaster moulds. The castings were later joined together with slip made from the same formula as the paste itself. The figure was then mounted on a base with an animal or flowers all moulded separately and added in the same way.

The catalogue of the Chelsea-Derby sale in 1771 records a biscuit figure. As Duesbury had acquired the factory only a short time earlier it is possible that this was of Chelsea origin, perhaps an experimental piece. There is little doubt that when shrewd William Duesbury took over the business he would have insisted on including Sprimont's book of experiments and formulæ. Here, possibly, he found a method of making biscuit soft-paste porcelain adapted from that of Sèvres. This he appears to have brought into use at Derby under his own supervision, using Trent sand and calling upon the vast deposits of alabaster near at hand.

Derby biscuit figures appear to have been in production by 1773. They never approached the whiteness of Sèvres, but were sculptured in lines cleaner and more distinct than figures made by any other English potter. The surface of the biscuit required to be absolutely flawless, and so few were the perfect examples issued from the oven that prices were necessarily high, costs of manufacturing processes and labour far exceeding those for ordinary porcelain. When imperfections or blemishes disfigured the surface of biscuit ware the figure was white-glazed and might be enamelled, then sold at the considerably lower price-range associated with decorated figures.

Collectors class Derby biscuit figures into three groups: (a) to 1795, unglazed frit biscuit porcelain; (b) 1795–1811, smear-glazed frit biscuit porcelain; (c) 1811–c. 1830, Bloor non-frit biscuit.

The frit formula used at Derby has never been revealed, but until 1811 the paste was close-textured, light ivory-white in tint, and slightly translucent in thin places. When smear-glazed it was slightly velvety to the touch. Smear-glazing was a process introduced to biscuit porcelain in 1795 by Michael Kean, successor to the Duesburys. This delicate surface texture was procured not by applying glaze directly to the figure, but by introducing it into the saggar containing the figure in the firing kiln. Whether placed in a small cup or painted thickly over the walls of the tightly sealed saggar, the glaze melted and volatilized as the temperature rose, its vapour settling as a fine mist upon the surface of the biscuit.

A non-frit biscuit, less costly in manufacturing processes, was introduced early in the Bloor régime dating from 1816. This displayed a dry-looking chalky surface. Even this deteriorated, and by 1820 Derby biscuit resembled merely ordinary unglazed non-frit porcelain. Figures were carelessly modelled, even when Duesbury originals were brought into use. It is doubtful if any biscuit was issued after 1830.

When a renewed demand for sculpture in white marble for interior decoration began during the late 1830s the firms of Copeland and Garrett and Minton experimented in an endeavour to reproduce a biscuit of the early Duesbury type. They were unsuccessful in this, but John Mountford, one of Copeland's technicians, invented a highly vitrified translucent frit porcelain suitable for statuary ware and not at all costly. This became known as parian ware.

Duesbury's biscuit figures were modelled with a sharpness of outline and depth of undercutting bespeaking much hand-modelling. Folds of garments were often knife-edged, a distinctive feature noted on blemished examples glazed and enamelled.

When William Duesbury senior started his experiments in making figures of biscuit porcelain he already had in his employ two outstanding figure modellers. Their skill may have influenced his decision to enter this field of porcelain making. These modellers were Joseph Hill and Isaac Farnsworth, both of whom were former apprentices at Derby where they spent their full working lives. To Joseph Hill, the more expert of the two, are attributed those figures marked with an incised triangle; Isaac Farnsworth is believed to have marked his work with an incised asterisk.

Pierre Stephan modelled at intervals between 1771 and 1795 a series of national heroes. He worked at Derby until 1774, earning two and a half guineas a week. He then transferred to Josiah Wedgwood but continued supplying the Duesburys with original models on a free-lance basis. Some biscuit figures made from his models have the name "Stephan" incised beneath the plinth.

The finest of Derby figures in biscuit porcelain date to the régimes of Duesbury II and Michael Kean. Early in this period there was intermittent employment of Jean-Jacques Spängler, usually known as John James, the greatest of Derby biscuit modellers. In 1790 he signed an agreement to work at Derby for three years. He left in November 1792 but returned for a year in 1795. Among the more outstanding of the Spängler figures, which were always modelled primarily for reproduction in the biscuit, were such four-figure groups as "Russian Shepherds and Companions" and three after paintings by Angelica Kauffmann: "Three Virgins Distressing Cupid", "Virgins Awakening Cupid", and "Virgins Adorning Pan". These titles are to be found, however, in the Derby sale catalogues of 1778 and 1782, probably referring to less elaborate versions. T. W. Coffee, later a porcelain manufacturer on his own account at Derby, modelled a number of figures between 1794 and about 1798.

Although the names and dates of the Derby modellers have been recorded by Llewellyn Jewitt, and price lists and names of figures have been preserved, there is little to associate one with the other, and no indications as to those figures made solely for production in biscuit, with, of course, flawed examples glazed and coloured.

George Cocker, a Derby modeller who had specialized in biscuit figures, began business on his own account in 1825, continuing until faced with the competition of parian ware in the early 1840s. His biscuit figures have the dry chalky appearance of Bloor biscuit, but may be distinguished by the name "Cocker" incised, or by a cross incised beneath the plinth.

During the Kean régime modelling generally deteriorated, colours became gaudy and were accompanied by vast quantities of bronzy-gilding. Bloor's enamels were lifeless, being inexpensive and applied over a hard glaze. Edward Keys, one of Bloor's chief modellers, was responsible for the long series of Dr. Syntax figures after Rowlandson's illustrations published from 1812.

At this time perforated porcelain lacework, used at Derby as early as 1771, might decorate figures, often being enriched with hand-modelled flowers. The Derby catalogue of February 1773 had recorded the sale of a "pair of sitting figures; a man sitting, lady playing on a guitar. Finished lace, in biscuit". This fragile decoration was made by soaking lace in porcelain slip of cream consistency filtered through fine lawn. Firing in the kiln destroyed the textile threads, leaving the filigree porcelain. Tiny blossoms in coloured porcelain were then attached, each petal being shaped by a girl on the palm of the hand, a process which impressed the paste with skin markings.

An extensive trade was done by the first two Duesburys in china trinkets such as seals, smelling bottles, tooth-pick cases and tiny plaques for mounting in such decorative trifles as brooches, cuff-links and breast-pins. Although considerable quantities were supplied to the Derby jewellery trade, the majority found their way to the jewellers of Birmingham and Clerkenwell. Some were sold in the white, others were coloured and gilded. The extent of this trade may be gauged from the 1795 list of models and moulds which included one hundred seal trinkets, fifty smelling bottles, and three hundred miscellaneous trinkets.

Derby porcelain of the eighteenth century is celebrated for its colours. Some collectors consider the beautiful apple green to be Derby's loveliest tint; others prefer the exquisite canary yellow, which several artists delighted to use as a background to their flowers and other decoration. Pale lavender was another Derby background, especially for trees and birds and figures etched in gold. Deep claret, brilliant orange, coral and faded old rose were also popular. The blue ground so typical of eighteenth-century Derby porcelain is of importance in dating a piece and also in identifying unmarked examples. Until 1782 an exclusive semi-matt overglaze enamel blue was used, described in catalogues as lapis lazuli, and known in the factory as Smith's blue in honour of its invention by an employee of that name. This was abandoned in 1782 and an underglaze cobalt-blue ground introduced: in the same year the crossed batons and dots were added to the crown and "D" mark. The presence of opaque chrome green indicates a date later than 1796: a translucent copper green was formerly used.

Decoration was symmetrical and simple until about 1784. Of Duesbury II's work W. Moore Binns says: "Blue or pink bands and festoons were largely used, the blue being, as far as useful wares are concerned . . . not an underglaze blue, but a rich enamel; in colour it is quite exceptional, brilliant and rich, and it may be felt slightly raised if the finger be pressed over it, showing that it was laid on as a thick coat."

Derby, like other contemporary porcelain factories, decorated in the conventional style. In about 1785 Derby decorators, such as Billingsley in the painting of flowers, and Brewer with landscapes, introduced naturalistic painting. This style continued fashionable until the Bloor period when Edwin Horatio Steele developed a hard formalistic ornament. Pattern completely covered the ware with bright colours and gilding, hiding defects in the cheaply produced china. Bloor set out to popularize decoration in the Japan taste, originated by Josiah Spode II before 1803. In 1817 Bloor advertised in the Staffordshire newspapers for "twenty good enamel painters who could paint different japan patterns". Derby Japan colours include a foxy red, deep orange, deep cobalt blue, green, sharp pink and gold, the latter often forming the outline of the pattern.

The most eminent of the Derby flower painters was William Billingsley, who joined Duesbury as an apprentice in 1774 and remained with the firm until 1795. Soon after 1780 he introduced to Duesbury examples of a new decorating technique in which sharp outlines were abandoned and the colour applied in soft washes. The London merchant houses received the samples with delighted approval. Instead of leaving a ground white for high lights, Billingsley swept the whole field with a single colour, producing light contrasts by removing surplus enamel with a cotton-wool stipple or a clean brush. The effect was more softly delicate than anything yet seen: Billingsley had initiated a new scheme of ceramic painting.

Concerning Billingsley's flower painting at Derby, William Bemrose writes that it "has a fatty, soft glaze, lovely when compared with that of his contemporaries: grouping is good and he often threw out from his bouquets long, delicately painted sprays. He also painted his flowers in true perspective by an effective treatment of shadows; his colouring is much more delicate than that of most other ceramic artists—he was fond of yellow and puce, and often introduced white flowers. Leaves are generally dark, but slightly veined and outlined: they are painted with greater freedom and want of detail when compared with his flowers."

Billingsley's mannerisms in floral groups are almost the equivalent of a signature. On good-quality porceiain the roses for which he is so famous are painted from countless angles. His favourite appears to have been the Maiden's Blush variety, and an outstanding feature of the work is the artist's obvious delight in the graceful play of the long reflex sepals. In many instances the calyx is turned right back from the corolla to emphasize the contrast between massy, rounded petals and feathery sepals. Invariably one rose in each piece is found bending over, leaving the calyx standing out from a deep cavity at the flower-base; foliage is often attached to the stem. When painting a small bouquet Billingsley placed one or more rose-buds bending over the main flower. Some of his Derby flowers were built up petal by petal and fired after each application of colour, frequently so costly a process that Dr. Johnson complained during a visit to the factory that "he could have vessels of silver, of the same size, as cheap as what were here made of porcelain".

Billingsley foliage is distinctively natural and irregular; thorns are very carefully painted. This understanding of foliage and habits of growth is seldom found elsewhere. His finest floral groups were painted between 1793 and 1795 when he gave an effect of great depth to his work by applying a pale-green or a delicate-brown undertint, painting the stronger, translucent colours over this. Most of Billingsley's Derby work is marked with a crown, crossed batons, and a script "D" in puce or blue. (See Chapter 16.)

John Stansby, one of Billingsley's imitative disciples at Derby, and the most rapid rose painter yet recorded, copied the technique of his master, but omitted the individual traits which gave life to Billingsley's portrayal of this most difficult flower. George Hancock, Moses Webster and Leonard Lead also painted in a manner resembling that of Billingsley. The Staffordshire potters were soon engaged in large-scale productions of imitations of Billingsley's style.

MARKS ON DERBY PORCELAIN

Porcelain of the Planché period 1749–55 have been found with a simple script "D" incised beneath the base and sometimes accompanied by the date 1750. Examples are also known incised with the name Derby.

Rarely, if ever, was porcelain marked by Duesbury until he acquired Chelsea in 1770. He added his own initial to the anchor already in use; the mark then used was a Chelsea anchor traversing the down-stroke of a script "D." From 1773 the mark, in gold, might be a jewelled crown above an anchor.

Duesbury's Derby productions 1770–84, if unmarked, are difficult to distinguish from earlier Chelsea examples, as the same models, moulds and paste might be used. Porcelain made at Derby 1773–82 might be marked with a jewelled crown above a script "D". The earliest were coloured blue, then purple or puce, occasionally in gold, light brown or black, all overglaze.

Until 1780 a cursive "N" might accompany the mark, sometimes incised, sometimes enamelled in red or blue. It is usually found on figures and its significance is unknown.

From 1782 and continuing until 1830, crossed batons with three dots on each side were placed beneath the jewelled crown and above the script "D". Until 1795 this mark was usually in cobalt blue or puce, afterwards in red. A pattern number might be incised below the "D" and a gilder's number might also be present.

For eight months in 1795–96 the script "D" was combined with a script "K" in monogram form.

After the death of Duesbury II in 1796 the crown, crossed batons and script "D" once more became the Derby trade mark, painted in vermilion, incised on vases and figures where it might be accompanied by the number of the model, the size of the piece, and the modeller's initial or a workman's mark. This mark was used by Bloor on fine quality porcelain until about 1830.

The Bloor mark from 1815 to 1820 and used as late as 1830, was a carelessly drawn crown, smaller than previously and without jewels on its bows, two brush strokes to represent crossed batons, and a pattern number below. This mark in vermilion enamel (rare examples have been found in grey) reflected the lowered artistic standards then operating at Derby.

From 1821 until the factory closed in 1848 marks painted in vermilion include a royal crown over a gothic "D" with the word DERBY below; two circles enclosing the words BLOOR DERBY and surrounding a royal crown; a royal crown superimposed BLOOR with DERBY below.

Adaptations of other factory marks were used largely on replacements or additions made to customers' requirements. Usually the Derby "D" or crown was incorporated into the design of the foreign mark.

PLATE 22

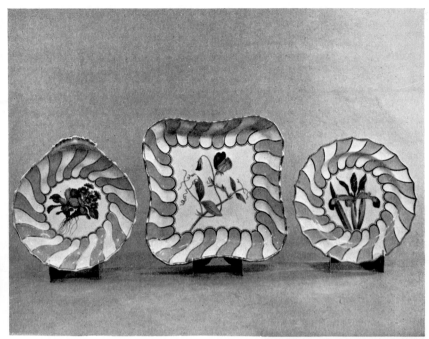

Worcester bone china made by Flight, Barr & Barr; part of a dessert service painted with botanical specimens in naturalistic colours, the borders composed of apple-green bands with gilded edges.

Two views of a Worcester porcelain mug painted with a silhouette of Dr. John Wall in black, set among flowers, fruit and insects in naturalistic colours. Dated 1759.

PLATE 23

A collection of early Worcester porcelain in the Victoria and Albert Museum. *Top row:* all moulded in relief and painted in underglaze blue: (*a*) tea-pot with barrel-shaped body and ribbon loop handle, *c.* 1760; (*b*) barrel-shaped cream-jug, *c.* 1760; (*c*) flower holder, *c.* 1755; (*d*) hexagonal cream jug, *c.* 1755; (*e*) tea-pot with scrolled feet, *c.* 1755. *Middle row:* (*a*) plate moulded in relief and enamelled in colours, *c.* 1755; (*b*) tray in the shape of a shell, enamelled inside, *c.* 1755; (*c*) oval spoon tray enamelled in colours, *c.* 1755; (*d*) plate pencilled in black, *c.* 1765. *Bottom row:* (*a* and *c*) sauce-boats moulded in low relief and printed in black, *c.* 1757; (*b*) basket with pierced sides, painted in under glaze blue in the Chinese style.

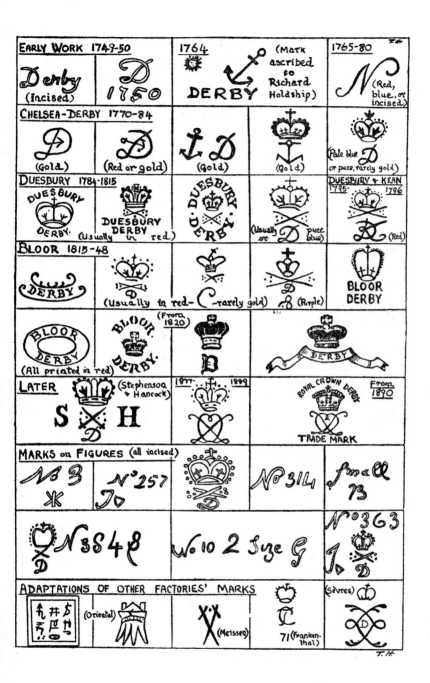

EARLY WORK 1749-50 | **1764** | (Mark ascribed to Richard Holdship) | **1765-80**

Derby (Incised) | *D 1750* | DERBY | N (Red, blue, or incised)

CHELSEA-DERBY 1770-84

D (Gold) | D (Red or gold) | D (Gold) | (Gold) | Pale blue D or puce, rarely gold)

DUESBURY 1784-1815

DUESBURY DERBY | DUESBURY DERBY (Usually in red) | DUESBURY DERBY | (Usually D or puce blue) | **DUESBURY & KEAN 1795- 1796** (Red)

BLOOR 1815-48

DERBY | D (Usually in red— rarely gold) | C | D B (Ripple) | BLOOR DERBY

BLOOR DERBY (All printed in red) | BLOOR DERBY (From 1820) | D | DERBY

LATER | S ⨯ H (Stephenson & Hancock) | 1877- 1889 | ROYAL CROWN DERBY From 1890 TRADE MARK

MARKS on FIGURES (all incised)

N° 3 K | N° 257 Jᴰ | (crown mark) D | N° 314 | small 73

N° 3848 D | N° 102 Size G | N° 363 Jᴰ D

ADAPTATIONS OF OTHER FACTORIES' MARKS

(Oriental) | (Meissen) | 71 (Frankenthal) | (Sèvres)

When Billingsley left Derby he was replaced by William Pegg, the Quaker, who stayed with the firm until 1823 with a period of absence from 1801 to 1810. His flowers are nearly life-size, much larger than those of any other Derby artist. They are seldom accompanied by arabesques or gilded borders, a band of gilding around the rim of domestic ware being his only concession to the period's delight in rich decoration. The name of the flower, unless very common, was painted in red. Although Pegg's drawing and finish were clever, his work usually displays a rather flat appearance. It has been observed that he painted the jewelled crown of the Derby mark wide and flat with crossed batons to match.

A prolific flower painter from early in the Duesbury régime to 1790 was Edward Withers, who painted leaves in two shades of translucent copper green over finely pencilled outlines in black or dark brown. One flower always sprays out from the group, a well-known Derby feature carried by their firm's artists to other factories.

Two celebrated landscape landscape painters worked at Derby: Zachariah Boreman and "Jockey" Hill. Boreman, who had been head painter at Chelsea, arrived at Derby in 1783 and returned to London eleven years later. According to Haslem he always washed in his subject with a neutral tint, over which he laid positive colours such as green, red or yellow, which, being transparent, allowed the neutral colour to be seen through them. The piece was then fired, shading and detail work being added afterwards in a darker colour with a pencil brush.

Boreman's trees were carefully delineated, and he introduced tiny, well-painted figures into his compositions. A subdued tone distinguishes his painting, an effect secured by the use of a light yellowish green. He was also an excellent portrayer of exotic birds usually painted over a transparent copper-green background.

"Jockey" Hill appears to have been a decorator at Derby throughout the Duesbury era and until 1800. He painted by the same method as Boreman, his work being recognized by his more vivid colouring, his ochre skies and his more delicate use of the pencil brush.

John Brewer, a former miniaturist, who worked at Derby from 1796 to 1810, painted landscapes in natural colours on backgrounds of chrome green and burnished gilding. He painted exotic birds equally well.

Outstanding among the early Derby subject painters was Richard Askew, who decorated from 1772 to 1795. His early work was chiefly in rose-pink camaieu, of cupids flying, sitting or lying on their backs among clouds. Outlines were filled in and shadows produced by broad washes of colour. Askew later specialized in figure subjects depicted without the use of hatching or stippling. (See Plate 38.)

Fruit was painted until 1795 by George Complin, whose work, though conventional, was always bright and gay. Complin was succeeded by Thomas Steele, who painted fruit more realistically in rich transparent colours. He obtained delicate effects by dabbing the wet colour with his fingers.

Derby was the first porcelain factory to decorate, from about 1817, with pictures in the style of the oil paintings already fashionable for a quarter of a century on japanned iron and papier-mâché tea-trays. Early examples were the works of William Corden.

Porcelain of the Planché period 1749–55 has been found with a simple script "D" incised beneath the base and sometimes accompanied by the date 1750. Examples are also known incised with the name Derby.

10

ALTHOUGH only the fourth soft-porcelain factory known to have been established in England, and one which was described in some detail in contemporary writing, Bristol remains aggravatingly elusive to the present-day collector of what was, in some instances, peculiarly attractive ware. As a precursor of the more famous Worcester in the manufacture of the soapstone ware, the firm is of some interest to the student, who may, with considerable justification, conjecture that its founders were none other than William Cookworthy of Plymouth hard-porcelain fame (see Chapter 18), and Benjamin Lund.

It must be stressed that Bristol, unlike its rivals at Chelsea and Bow, used steatite or soapstone as the plastic ingredient in the porcelain formula. The earliest written record noting the firm's existence lies in two letters by Dr. Richard Pococke, Bishop of Ossory, which comment on this fact.

Dr. Pococke's letters, with many others covering the period 1750–52, were published in 1888 by the Camden Society under the title *Travels Through England*. Writing from Tavistock under the date October 13, 1750, the bishop chronicled: "We went nine miles to the South near as far as Lizard Point to see the Soapy Rock, which was being sold at £5 a ton, for the manufacture of porcelane now carrying on at Bristol." On November 2 he wrote from Bristol: "I went to see a manufacture lately established here by one of the principal[s] of the manufacture at Limehouse, which failed. It is at a Glass house and is called Lowris' China House. They have two sorts of ware, one called stone china which has a yellow cast, both in the ware and the

PLATE 24

...amberlain's Worcester porcelain. *Top left:* ice-cream pail with cover and liner painted with a view ...Malvern Priory on an apple-green ground; pendant vine decoration, handles and knobs thickly ...ded; square foot veined on a yellowish-brown to resemble marble, the liner being similarly decor-...ed; marked in red script MALVERN, CHAMBERLAINS WORCESTER & 155 NEW BOND ...REET LONDON. *Top right:* cup and saucer in colours and gilt, *c.* 1802. *Below:* jardinière painted ...colours and gilded, the panel inscribed "Orpheus & Euridice". *c.* 1815.

PLATE 25

A collection of nineteenth-century Worcester porcelain and china in the Victoria and Alb
Museum: mugs and vases in top row, and tray in third row, *c.* 1810; pastille burner and cover
left of second row, *c.* 1820; ewer, centre of top row, 1859.

glazing, that I suppose is more of pipe clay and calcined flint. The other they call Old China; this is whiter and I suppose is made of calcined flint, and the soapy rock at Lizard Point, which 'tis known they use. This is painted blue, and some is white, like the old china of a yellowish cast; another kind is white with a bluish cast, and both are called fine ornamental white china. They make very beautiful white sauce boats, adorned with reliefs of festoons which sell for sixteen shillings a pair."

The name "Lowris'" was no doubt the transcriber's error for "Lowdin's". When collectors became aware of these letters in the early years of George V's reign it was at once assumed that the proprietor of the china works in Redcliff Backs, Bristol, had been William Lowdin whose family had been glass-makers in Bristol from about 1650. But this appears to have been too hasty a conclusion, for "a messuage in Redcliff Street, known on the sign of the Glass House, consisting of several tenements lately in the possession of William Lowdin, and extends from Redcliff Street to Recliff Backs" was advertised for auction in the *Bristol Oracle*, June 23, 1745, "for the remainder of a term of 40 years granted by the Dean and Chapter of Bristol, whereof 28 years are to come under the yearly chief rent of 30/–". This clearly indicated that Lowdin was no longer in business at Redcliff Backs: C. W. Dyson Perrins, F.S.A., and other writers have concluded that he died before June 1745. The term "Lowdin's China House" would be an obvious local name for the premises after their occupation for porcelain-making.

A more reasonable conjecture is that the proprietors were the two Quakers, William Cookworthy, a Plymouth druggist, and Benjamin Lund, a copper smalter and merchant of Bristol and London, with mining interests in the West Country, a third partner being William Miller.

Cookworthy had read Du Halde's *History of China* (1738) which contained Père d'Entrecolle's first-hand reports on the manufacture of porcelain in China. He was aware, therefore, that the Chinese on occasion substituted *hua shih* or soapstone for kaolin. He had also discovered soapstone or steatite (hydrated silicate of magnesia) deposits in Cornwall and acquired the sole mining rights (see page 148) knowing that finely pulverized and incorporated in porcelain instead of china clay it vitrified at a comparatively low temperature. Again, some of the marks on early Bristol soapstone ware resemble chemical signs, and Cookworthy marked his hard porcelain made at Plymouth with the chemical sign for tin.

Benjamin Lund in association with Francis Hawksbee in 1728 patented a method of copper refining which destroyed the volatile sulphur found in copper, resulting in a fine metal long known as "rose copper". Their copper-refining plant was in the Limehouse district of London. Thus it might be Benjamin Lund whom Dr. Pococke meant when he referred to a principal of the Limehouse factory which failed. Lund was granted a licence to mine soapstone at Lizard Point on March 7, 1748. Lund's name and his private address appear in various advertisements associated with the China House, and although authorities have considered him to be merely a selling agent, there is little doubt that he was the leading partner in this undertaking.

Shortly after Dr. Pococke's visit to Bristol the proprietors of the China House announced in a series of advertisements in the *Bristol Weekly Intelligencer* that they had for some time been in active production in a small way. From November 24 to December 22, 1750, and again in July of the following year, it was announced: "Whereas for some time past attempts have been made in this City to introduce a Manufactory in imitation of China Ware, the Proprietors having brought the said Undertaking to a Degree of Perfection, are determined to extend their Works and Sales of Ware, as soon as proper Hands can be either procured or instructed in the several Branches of the said Business; They therefore give this notice, That if Parents or Guardians of any Young Lads above the age of Fourteen are inclined that they shall learn the art of Pottery as practised in Staffordshire and will find them Lodging and all necessaries, during the term of that Apprenticeship, No Money will be required for learning them in the best Manner; and in particular children of either sex not under the above Age may be learned to draw and paint by Persons appointed for that Purpose, that they may be Qualified to Paint the sd Ware either in India or Roman Taste whereby they may acquire a genteel Subsistance. The Consideration expected for such Instruction, being the Perquisite of the Painters, is left to them and the Persons to agree. Any person that is inclined to purchase a six or four leaved Screne, or to have one or more made to any particular Hight or Dimensions may be directed where to apply by Mr. Lund on St. Philip's Plain, who will also inform them concerning the above Particulars." Lund's address was the one given in connection with his copper-refining enterprise nearly a quarter of a century earlier.

Porcelain production was already large enough to warrant storage in a warehouse at Castle Green, Bristol, for a further advertisement in the same issue of the *Bristol Weekly Intelligencer* gave notice "That the Ware made in this City for some Time past, in Imitation of Foreign China is now sold at the Proprietors' Warehouse in Castle Green. . . . For the future no Ware will be sold at the Place where it is Manufactured; nor will any Person be admitted to enter there without Leave from the Proprietors." An advertisement in the following January refers also to "the Warehouse next the Bell Inn in Temple Street".

The story of Bristol's first venture into porcelain-making is carried further in another advertisement dated July 24, 1752, announcing that "the Proprietors of the Manufactory for making Ware in this City in Imitation of Foreign China are now united with the Worcester Porcelain Company, where for the future the whole Business will be carried on; therefore the said Proprietors are determin'd to Sell their Remaining Stock of Ware very cheap at their Warehouse in Castle Green till the whole is disposed of".

Formulæ, processes, plant, moulds, workers and decorators all appear to have been transferred from Bristol to Worcester, further up the Severn, to the porcelain works established there a year earlier by Dr. Wall and his associates. Whether the Bristol firm had been a financial success is unknown: nor is there any record of the Worcester firm making any payment in connection with the transfer.

There would, obviously, be little change in the soapstone

ware made at Worcester until the influence of the new firm became manifest. Examples are known in which the mark BRISTOL in relief has been overpainted, suggesting such pieces to be of early Worcester origin. No difficulty would have been experienced, however, in removing the name from the moulds.

Considering the short life of the Bristol factory, extending from the summer of 1748 to mid-1752, attributions are now astonishingly large. William Pountney and Hugh Owen believed other porcelain-making firms to have been established at Bristol during the following decade. It is unlikely, however, that the soapstone formula was used elsewhere, apart from Worcester, where the mixing was carried out behind double-locked doors. Pountney noted that the warehouse in Castle Green was in use as a Worcester agency until 1757.

In Bristol soft-paste porcelain the soapstone or steatite added to the glassy paste instead of china clay is a silicate of alumina and magnesia. A sauce-boat moulded with relief panelling was analysed by Herbert Eccles and the result reported in *Analysed Specimens of English Porcelain*.[1] The soapstone content was about 40 per cent and the presence of lead oxide to the extent of 8 per cent suggests that alkalis were introduced by adding about 25 per cent of cullet or broken flint-glass to the batch. Such glass was easily available from the flint-glass houses of Bristol but not at all in Worcester. Lead oxide is not present in early Worcester porcelain.

Bristol soft-paste porcelain has a hard compact texture and is found in two distinct types: (*a*) with a creamy-white tinge, of high translucency and showing ivory by transmitted light; (*b*) with a greyish tinge, less translucent, and showing a greenish tinge by transmitted light. The second is the more frequent and it has been suggested that this was caused by the addition of smalt in an effort to whiten the creamy tinge.

The thin glaze, imperfectly opacified, at first displayed tiny bubbles, quickly improved but always flawed with a multiplicity of microscopic pittings. A starchy blue tinge

[1] H.M. Stationery Office, 1922.

is characteristic of the glaze in association with blue underglaze decoration. Authorities usually suggest that this was due to the addition of cobalt to impart to the ware a cold bluish tone reminiscent of Chinese porcelain at that period. Actually smalt was used, a finely pulverized rich-blue glass prepared from cobalt. The most reasonable explanation is that the smalt used in the underglaze decoration "flew" in the kiln and the bluish tinge was unintentional. In enamel-painted ware the glaze has a warm ivory tint. The glaze is of a quality which recedes a little from the foot ring when fired.

Blue underglaze decoration is usually badly blurred, and most frequently in poorly executed *chinoiserie* designs. Enamel-painted decoration is in the *famille verte* and *famille rose* styles. W. B. Honey[1] mentions that "one painter in particular used a very fine brush with remarkable skill, and his Chinese figures amid furniture and trellises, and very distinctive birds and flowers, include some of the most delightful brushwork seen on English porcelain".

Figures of Lu Tung-pin, one of the eight Taoist Immortals, were made in white porcelain with the name "BRISTOL 1750" in raised characters on the back of the plinth—not beneath. A few examples are known in which the plinth is enlivened with touches of manganese purple. No other figures have yet been attributed to Bristol.

Sauce-boats were seen in production by Dr. Pococke in 1750 and at a factory price of 16s. a pair the retail price, via a merchanting house, would have been in the region of 30s. a pair. Sauce-boats in porcelain were therefore luxury pieces, yet they appear to have been issued in considerable numbers if the quantity of existing examples is any indication. Butter-boats, it appears, were rather less frequently made. Like sauce-boats from contemporary factories, the patterns were based on designs in silver plate. Bodies were moulded, but with the joints poorly trimmed; feet and handles were attached with liquid slip.

Characteristic features of Bristol sauce-boats are: rosettes at the points where body and handle join; always a thumb-rest on the handle; an expanded lip usually painted with

1 W. B. Honey, *Old English Porcelain*.

flowers or oriental emblems; decoration with running scrolls inside the rim; and a small shell painted inside the lip. Exteriors are ornamented with relief work, usually scrolls and festoons, often forming a shallow cartouche on

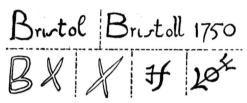

Soft-paste Bristol:
  Top, left and right, impressed in relief.
  Bottom, left and left centre, incised; *right centre and right,* probably workmen's marks also, rarely, found on Bow and Worcester porcelain.

each side of the bowl enclosing decoration in blue or enamels. Examples in the British Museum bear in relief the name BRISTOLL.

Soft-paste Bristol porcelain also includes leaf dishes, dishes in the form of scallop shells, cream-jugs, cups and saucers, mugs—notably a series with outspreading bases—tea-pots, small bottles and vases in shapes adapted from Chinese porcelain of the K'ang-hsi period.

Marks, in addition to the name BRISTOLL in relief, and occasionally the date 1750, include a single short stroke or two; such strokes either detached or crossed in saltire, incised in the base before firing. Sometimes there is a painted mark in blue under the glaze or in black or red over the glaze. A frequent mark is an arrow with a circle on the shaft: this mark is also found on early Worcester. A peculiarity of this ware is a short incision made with a sharp-bladed tool on the inner side of the foot ring.

Several authorities have associated transfer-printing with Bristol soft-paste porcelain. Not until the year following removal to Worcester, however, is transfer-printing known to have been developed through the combined efforts of Stephen-Theodore Janssen the paper merchant, John Brooks the engraver and Henry Delamain the potter. Transfer decoration on ware made from Bristol moulds may with some certainty be given a Worcester origin and be dated from 1756. (See Chapter 5.)

11

EARLY Georgian potters were inevitably influenced by the beauty and grace of oriental porcelain. The richness of colour and design in the eastern work attracted the eye and suited the cultivated taste of the period. It was to cater for this discriminating section of the public that the Worcester china works was established in 1751 by a group of local businessmen who realized that the growing demand for porcelain domestic ware offered opportunities for an extensive and profitable industry. The term "old Worcester" refers to the soft porcelain sponsored and developed by them at the famous Warmstry House works between 1751 and 1783.

The crescent adopted as the Worcester trade mark was taken from the Warmstry coat of arms, to be joined five years later by the script "W", representing Worcester rather than, as is so often stated, Dr. John Wall. Nevertheless, it was Wall, as one of the fifteen founder shareholders of the company, who took the initiative in establishing the factory, and continued as the chief driving force until his death in 1776.

Dr. Wall, born at Powick, near Worcester, was a Fellow of Merton, a medical practitioner with a considerable local practice and author of several medical papers, a portrait artist of some ability, and a designer of stained glass.

In 1750 he found himself possessed of the formulæ for making a soft-paste porcelain in which soapstone was a basic ingredient. In all probability he acquired these recipes and other essential information from two potters named Podmore and Lyes, former employees at the China

119

House, Bristol, where a small porcelain factory was already operating. Herbert Eccles' analyses of Bristol soft porcelain and of examples of early Worcester have revealed in each the presence of steatite or soapstone, an ingredient not known to have been incorporated in any other porcelain of that period.

As explained in Chapter 1, soapstone porcelain is a soft frit body with finely pulverized steatite added to the glassy paste instead of china clay. Examples made in about 1760 are specified in *Analysed Specimens of English Porcelain* as containing from 35 to 45 per cent of soapstone.

Dr. Wall organized the early experiments in the "secret art, mystery, and process of porcelain making" in association with William Davis, a Worcester apothecary who became a shareholder, technical director and works manager in the new venture, which was launched with a share capital of £4,500. The company, which operated profitably from the beginning, was named the Worcester Tonquin Manufactory for the same reason that the new factory at Bow was calling itself New Canton, the ambition of both being to produce domestic table-ware capable of competing with the true oriental porcelain then being imported from Nankin.

Worcester proved a stronger organization than Bristol, and in July 1752 the *Bristol Intelligencer* was able to announce that "the Proprietors of the Manufactory for making Ware in this City in Imitation of Foreign China are now united with the Worcester Porcelain Company, where for the future the whole business will be carried on". Early Worcester duplicated the Bristol style and was decorated with ornament in low relief, underglaze blue painting, sparse gilding and enamelling over the glaze, the ornament representing a western interpretation of the popular Chinese motifs.

Throughout what is known as the Dr. Wall period (1751–83) a soft or artificial porcelain was made possessing the densest texture then known, harder, thinner, and with a less undulating surface than either Bow or Chelsea wares. Although it must be classed as a soft-paste porcelain, the body is so hard that it will resist the file. Unique among eighteenth-century English soft-paste porcelains, soapstone domestic ware could withstand boiling water. If held to the light the creamy-white paste displays a faint bluish-green tinge. Moreover, paste and glaze were so closely considered in relation to each other that Worcester largely overcame the common fault known as crazing. The expansion and contraction of the glaze and the paste were so well matched that it is rare to find a piece of Worcester bearing this disfigurement of fine cracks.

The collector of old Worcester lays considerable stress upon the quality of this heat-resistant glaze, which was harder than that of Derby. It should be softly white with a suspicion of green, of even smoothness, glossy rather than brilliant. The glaze was thinly applied with a brush, so that the base was left uncovered and, even around the base rim, shrinkage in the glaze tended to result in a lack of glaze at the junction of base and rim. The glaze was free from blotchiness, a well-known defect of early Bow and Chelsea porcelain, but owing to the presence of lead there has been a slight tendency for it to discolour during the two centuries since its manufacture. Late in the period a glaze containing finely ground wasters and oxide of tin might be used. This had a faintly opalescent appearance and was evenly distributed, none being applied within the base rim.

Worcester domestic ware painted in enamel colours and underglaze blue on white grounds continued in manufacture until about 1776, the amount remaining to this day proving its toughness to be no fanciful legend. The white varies from a creamy tone to a faintly bluish-grey caused by the addition of cobalt in an effort to disguise the unpleasant greenish hue produced by impurities in the basic ingredients. The blue itself varies in tint from a clear bright sapphire to a dark indigo which with the passing of years has become blue-black. Moulding and finish are excellent, finer than any produced at other contemporary factories.

The period associated entirely with the production of domestic ware at Worcester lasted until 1763. Even then the *Annual Register* was complaining that Worcester had not managed to furnish a complete dinner table. In 1763, however, a notable change of policy was to be observed and

Worcester began to cater for a richer clientele. Some of the finest Worcester porcelain was made between about 1764 and 1783, a period famous for the elaborate beauty of its ware, the perfection of its potting, the supreme richness of its decoration. By 1769 the firm was advertising porcelain decorated with "beautiful Colours of Mazarine blue and gold, Sky-blue, Pea-green, French-green, Sea-green, Purple, Scarlet and other varieties of Colour", on dinner, dessert, tea and coffee services.

Turning from the comparative simplicity of the early patterns in the Chinese style dominated by blue underglaze painting, the Worcester designers now sought the vivid complexities of colour and pattern which characterized the porcelain of neighbouring Japan. Such designs, however, were modified and mingled with the patterns and colours of Meissen and Sèvres, and out of the medley emerged the typical oriental Worcester.

The famous Kakiemon-style decorations were among the most popular Japanese designs. The work of that brilliant porcelain painter was imitated over the whole of Europe, his pheasant pattern being the most widely known. The early Worcester version cleverly follows the original in the Japanese colour scheme of soft red, yellow, blue and green. This "fine old pheasant pattern", as it was called in the sale catalogue of 1769, returned to fashion a century later, but as a poor and lifeless creature. The same catalogue refers to "fine old scarlet Japan pattern", "old rich dragon pattern", "old scroll Japan" and several other exotic designs derived from the Japanese. By 1770 the Worcester decorators had firmly established the types now known as Worcester-Japan. The intricate Imari patterns were also followed at Worcester—a more massive and less charming style of decoration in a dark, indistinct blue, gold and Indian red.

This twenty-year period of Worcester's finest output coincided with the engagement of artists who had become experienced in colour work at Chelsea. In 1768 the proprietors advertised that they had "engaged the best Painters from Chelsea". The influence of contemporary flower painters at Sèvres led to the establishment of a Worcester

School of painters with an individual style typified by meticulously painted, tightly grouped flowers. These decorators introduced, too, the handsome richness of the Sèvres style, the most successful colours being apple green, pea green, copper green (sometimes over black scale outlines), turquoise, deep claret, manganese violet, and a beautiful pale canary yellow. This last was used over a ground of relief basketwork to represent woven straw. From about 1769 a plum-colour was often associated with exotic bird panels rivalling the famous Chelsea claret colour.

Every fashionable design of the day was appropriated by Worcester. Binns refers to "lovely exotic birds, those gorgeous ornithological fantasies of the imaginative painter, impossible but quite beautiful; these vary in style and were evidently the work of more than one artist. Quaint posies of old-fashioned flowers—chrysanthemums, roses, carnations (generally striped) and picotees, the sweet blue nemophila and the dainty auricula in colours soft and harmonious, always pleasing and without a jarring note; curious old landscapes in more than doubtful perspective, generally framed in turquoise husk borders shaded with black and gilt; rich and luscious-looking fruit; butterflies and insects, occasionally animals, and, apart from the Chinese style, rare figures." During the Wall period figure subjects were unusual among Worcester decorations.

The Meissen style is expressed in many Worcester designs, particularly in colourful birds, pink scale patterns, scattered posies and flower sprays, and bunches of fruit thought by Hobson to have been painted by artists from the Saxon factory—probably those who left Bow in 1763. Even the Meissen mark was copied.

These colourful birds, painted by all porcelain-ornamenters at this period and conveniently termed exotic, offered Worcester decorators particularly happy opportunities to express individual tastes. Each painter introduced his own types, such as the distinctively large-eyed bird with a close in-curving tail, now sometimes described as a partridge. The birds were usually painted against perfunctory landscapes and, like the other decorative motifs then employed—rural scenes, flowers and so on—they appeared on panels "in reserve". This term implies that, while a ground colour was applied to the piece of porcelain, panels were left white and it was upon these that the artists applied their ornament.

Even the ground colour was seldom left entirely plain, however. The blue grounds of old Worcester are famous, the best known being salmon-scale blue, powder blue, mazarine or dark blue, and overglaze enamel blue, all derived from cobalt oxide which could be fired at a high temperature without altering in colour. The device of breaking up a blue ground by diapering it with a close scale pattern known to some collectors as salmon-scale, is thought to have been used at Worcester as early as 1760. On early examples large scales were laboriously outlined and washed in. The later smaller scales were more speedily produced by wiping out the high lights of the pattern from a blue-ground.

The general impression is that the scale pattern is of eighteenth-century origin, but actually its use on ceramics dates to the fifteenth century, being found on Ming vases. Even then it was an adaptation of a design from tapestries and embroideries of a previous dynasty.

The Chinese indicated the scale design only by outline, but from direct copying the Worcester decorators soon developed their own interpretations of the pattern. This design has been successfully reproduced by those clever French artists who have been responsible for so much fake porcelain.

The term powder blue is given to the familiar stippled effect copied from Chinese porcelain and caused by blowing the colour on to the ware through a piece of silk gauze. The method may be recognized by the resultant granular effect, the bright blue being mingled with pin-points of a steely grey-blue shade.

Worcester's powder blue is more vivid than its mazarine blue. This deep blue ground, less brilliant than the *gros bleu* of Chelsea, and with a hint of indigo in its composition, was applied direct to the biscuit in wet washes. The brush-work resulted in subtle gradations of tone which saved such ware from monotony, particularly when the colour was laid on thickly.

Powder blue, scale blue and deep mazarine blue—all underglaze—were the ground colours of pieces on which the white reserves were filled with elaborately painted flowers, fruits, birds, insects or figures. Fan-shaped reserves are usually found with powder-blue backgrounds. Worcester's overglaze enamel blue, full and brilliant, with a shining lustre, might justly be called royal blue because of its close resemblance to the *bleu de roi* of Sèvres. Overpowering as a ground colour enclosing reserves, it was chiefly introduced in border designs, being applied over the glaze by the process known as ground laying.

Gilding now became an important medium of decoration associated with coloured grounds. A fine glaze was developed upon which gold leaf ground with honey could adhere in the form of delicate tracery, rococo scroll designs, lacework, and honeysuckle patterns. By this improved method of gilding, the gold was painted on the ware and fired until attached firmly to the soft glaze.

In 1768 London enamellers began to buy Worcester porcelain in the white, or partly decorated in underglaze blue, and painted it to suit the personal tastes of their customers. Among artists employed by Worcester at this period were two London miniaturists whose work dates from 1770. These were John Donaldson and Jefferyes Hamett O'Neale. Both decorated flamboyant vases and hexagonal jars, and both signed examples of their work. Donaldson was responsible for some crude peasant scenes and clumsy exotic birds. O'Neale's panels often contain hunting scenes in the style of Wouverman, classical subjects and animal paintings. His signature has also been found on landscapes with stiff-looking waterfalls and peculiar trees.

Meanwhile, from 1757, a notable innovation for the inexpensive decoration of domestic ware made its first appearance on Worcester porcelain. This was transfer-printing, widely used until the factory was reorganized in 1774. The process had been introduced on enamelled copper as a triumph of industrial art as early as 1753 at

Janssen's Battersea enamel works. Robert Hancock appears to have done a considerable amount of engraving for these transfers and it is presumed that it was he who introduced the process of transfer-printing to Worcester after the closing of Battersea early in 1756, although it appears probable that he had already acquainted Bow with the technique. (See Chapter 5.)

Hancock's copper plates were beautifully engraved. His work cannot be too highly prized. On a few pieces a monogram "R H" and the word "Worcester" are found mingled with the design, but more often with this the piece also shows an anchor, indicating the engraving to be the work of Richard Holdship, a partner in the firm.

Among the earliest of transfer-printed designs was the well-known portrait of Frederick the Great, King of Prussia, which decorated many mugs during 1757, following Frederick's victory at Rossbach. Although the printed portrait is signed "R.H. Worcester" accompanied by an anchor, it is certain that Hancock was associated with the decoration of this commemorative mug, for in the same year the *Worcester Journal*, in reply to some verses addressed to Richard Holdship in the *Gentleman's Magazine*, edited by Edward Cave a partner in Worcester, declared:

"Hancock, my friend, don't grieve tho' Holdship has the praise,
'Tis yours to execute, 'tis his to wear the bays."

Other transfer-printed portraits of this period included those of George II from a copper-plate by Hancock adapted from the painting by Thomas Worlidge in 1753; Admiral Boscawen, from the engraving by John Faber the younger, published in 1747 after the painting by Allan Ramsay; General Wolfe, after an engraving by Richard Houston; General John Manners, Marquess of Granby, from Houston's engraving of 1760, after the painting by Sir Joshua Reynolds; William Pitt, Earl of Chatham, after the painting by William Hoare, now in the National Portrait Gallery; Shakespeare leaning on a pedestal, after the monument in Westminster Abbey by Peter Scheemakers from William Kent's design; George III after an engraving by James McArdell, 1761, from the painting by Jeremiah

Meyer; Queen Charlotte after the portrait drawn and engraved in 1762 by James McArdell. Examples of these, together with a proof of the portrait of George III pulled from the original plate, are all to be seen in the Schreiber Collection at the Victoria and Albert Museum.

The usual colours for the transfer-prints—which were of course in monochrome—were jet black, deep red, lilac and pale purple over the glaze until 1770, when underglaze printing was introduced. Thereafter, the transferred designs might be treated with bright-coloured washes of enamel, enlivened with touches of gilt—a questionable improvement. Jet black and deep red gave the clearest impressions, black being the favourite. Little transfer work was marked, but rare examples have been found painted with the crossed swords of Dresden.

After the reorganization of the company in 1774 transfer-printing appears to have been abandoned until early in the Flight period (1783–93) when the bat process of engraving was introduced. Pictures in meticulous detail became possible by this method (see pages 55–56).

As might be expected from a newly established factory, Worcester's early domestic ware showed a marked lack of originality in form and shape. The first cups and saucers were exact reproductions of small plain oriental prototypes without handles. These were thrown on the wheel and are of comparatively thick section. Quickly, however, the tea-ware was developed and made from porcelain of eggshell fineness and delicacy. Decoration included somewhat stiffly arranged floral patterns, delicately traced or slightly embossed. The design of the cups was modified, their size increased and their rims given a slight flare to fit the lips. Handles were soon supplied, at first consisting of thin rolls of clay, then moulded. At first tea-pots, jugs and sugar-bowls also were given rolled handles; later came rather thin designs, with only the inner surface rounded and the outer one plainly flat. Some handles were grooved at the top, near the outer edge, and towards the end of the period scroll handles might be used. Handles were always given a good outward projection and were gracefully curved.

Each tea-pot had its stand, and each sugar-bowl its cover. Sauce-boats were made in the form of two conjoined leaves, the stems forming a loop handle. A cabbage leaf was a favourite mould for jugs, pickle-trays, asparagus-bowls and other table-ware. Tea-jars were made with spoons and oblong trays. Rock-work and shell sweetmeat stands were also made.

Cylindrical mugs were a feature of early Worcester ware. These were designed with foot rims lifting their flat bases from the table. These rims flared outward, and the deeper the foot-ring, the earlier the mug. Foot-rings on early Worcester domestic pieces were triangular in section.

Some of the early domestic ware known to have been made at Worcester is copied from silver models, with rococo relief designs painted in vignette style with reserve panels in underglaze blue or polychrome enamels. These resemble porcelain issued by St. Cloud. One of the partners in the concern, Samuel Bradley, was a goldsmith of Worcester and it was possibly at his wish that such designs were issued in competition with Chelsea.

Soft porcelain containing soapstone possessed little plasticity and so was unsuited to the modelling of figures. Until about 1920 it had been thought that no figures were ever manufactured at Worcester. It was then noticed that the diary of Mrs. Philip Lybbe Powys, under the date of August 1771, contained accurate details of a visit to the figure building department in "the sixth room" of the Worcester porcelain works. Several specimens containing magnesia, proving the use of about 30 per cent of soapstone in the paste, have been recognized by analysis. These are unmarked, and the base of each is fire-cracked.

Among the rare relics of the early history of Worcester are the porcelain tokens issued in 1765. On one side of such a token is printed "Promise to pay bearer", to which the amount of 1s. or 2s. 6d. was added. On the reverse are the letters "W P C". No examples of larger amounts are known. Tokens in place of cash in the payment of wages were used to a considerable extent by eighteenth-century manufacturers.

The Hon. John Byng visited Worcester late in the Wall

PLATE 26

amberlain's Worcester bone china. *Top:* a pair of dishes painted with colours and gilded; shaped
1els outlined with gilt scrollwork, the larger panels painted with exotic birds and the smaller
th butterflies and insects, *c.* 1815. *Below:* dish with border modelled and gilded with shells and
olls in high relief, decorated in natural colours, the centre painted with a view of Buckingham
ace from the garden front; marked "Chamberlains" in red.

PLATE 27

Caughley porcelain: (*a*) jug, *c.* 1795, printed in underglaze blue with the royal arms of George III as borne before 1802, and with figures of volunteers. Inside the rim is the inscription "Brimstree Loyal Legion", Brimstree being the name of a hundred in Shropshire in the neighbourhood of Caughley; (*b*) mug painted in underglaze blue and gilded, with a grooved loop handle; (*c*) tea-cup and saucer decorated in underglaze blue and gilded, marked "S" in underglaze blue, *c.* 1790.

Mansfield porcelain: two sides of a large jug with monochrome views of Sherwood Forest and Nottingham Castle. Signed "Billingsley Mansfield".

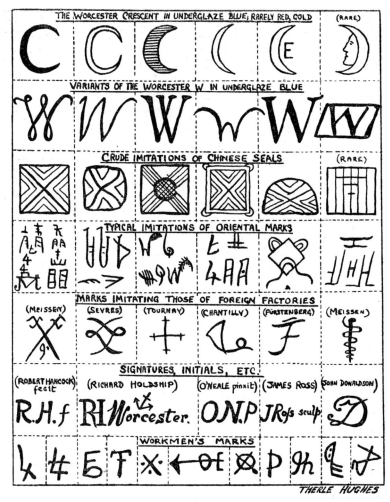

Worcester marks, 1751–1783. (See page 130.)

period. In *The Torrington Diaries* under the date July 2nd,
1781, he wrote: "We went to the china manufactory [at
Worcester] of which we took an accurate survey, from the
first handling to the last removal from the furnace: the
trade is now very flourishing, owing to the great demand
from Holland; the china is very clumsy and probably suits
their taste."

Three years later he made a second visit and "surveyed

the china manufactory from the first clay to the last gilding; and were then introduc'd into the ware house, to tempt our money out of our pockets. The colours of this china are very fine, and their imitation of old Japan are excellent; but, I think, there is a want of taste, and of good painters: the people about it seem properly secret and to envelope their art in as much mystery as possible."

The study of the early emblems used to mark Worcester porcelain during the Wall period calls for great care, for the marks used were many and varied. Only two can be regarded as true trade marks, the crescent and the cursive capital or script "W". The block capital is also found, but only on blue-printed wares.

The well-known "Chinese seal" in underglaze blue, a fretted square, appears in five different designs on porcelain printed in underglaze blue. Other varieties of the seal—square, round or semicircular—are found on all classes of porcelain throughout the period. Some of these marks bear very slight resemblance to oriental date seals.

The crescent is found in outline, outline with shading lines, and blocked in, the small open crescent in blue underglaze being most frequent. A red open crescent marked some enamelled porcelain from 1770. In varying forms the crescent seems to have remained in use until about 1793. Its size varies and a printed letter is sometimes added on blue-printed wares.

The script "W" in blue and in several forms was used on all classes of ware from 1755, sometimes in association with the crescent also in blue.

Several types of Meissen crossed swords in blue were common on many classes of Worcester porcelain. Numerals, generally 6, 9 or 91, were often placed between the blades of the crossed swords and there may be a dot between the hilts. This is the only mark to be found on black-printed wares, usually unmarked. Worcester also copied the anchor of Chelsea, the crossed L's of Sèvres, the F of Fürstenberg, the cross of Tournay and the horn of Chantilly.

Sometimes as many as four different marks will be found on various pieces in the same service, but a considerable amount of table-ware made during the Wall period was not marked.

12

THE prestige of the Worcester Tonquin Manufactory tended to decline after the death of Dr. Wall in 1776, when the factory came under the control of William Davis, an original shareholder who had been works manager from the time of the company's establishment. Upon his death in 1783 the business was sold for £3,000 to Thomas Flight, jeweller to the royal family and London agent for the company. Flight controlled the factory from London, placing his sons John and Joseph in charge of the works.

The soapstone paste produced during the Flight period has the appearance of being a compromise between vitreous stoneware and hard porcelain. It never had the clearness and translucency of earlier productions or of the later bone china. If held to the light a faintly yellow tint is seen. This body was extremely successful commercially, but it was not an improvement in the eyes of the present-day collector. The harmonious blending of paste with glaze and decoration which so distinguished Dr. Wall's porcelain is missing.

Costly table services were ordered from Thomas Flight by various members of the royal family to whom he had already sold jewels. In 1788 George III with Queen Charlotte and three of the princesses visited the factory at Worcester. As a token of appreciation His Majesty honoured Thomas Flight with permission to prefix the word "Royal" to the works' title. Under the influence of such patronage the Flights inaugurated an era of sumptuous decoration which lasted until the end of the century, specializing in dinner, dessert and breakfast services painted with armorial devices in full colours.

Styles and designs were in the fashionable classical mood. Decorators of pictorial panels developed a technique which became characteristic of Worcester. If these miniature paintings are examined beneath a magnifying glass it will be seen that outlines are perfect and that the colours are applied with careful precision. Such pictorial panels comprised landscapes, figure subjects, copies of paintings by eighteenth-century artists, allegorical pictures, scenes from Shakespeare's plays, and illustrations to poems. Groups of flowers and finely painted shell patterns were in great demand. Flight's early patterns for less expensive tableware were simple, many of them consisting of blue painted or printed flowers and blue bands, with or without gold decorated sprigs. One popular pattern known as the blue lily was selected by the king for a breakfast set and afterwards called "royal lily", immense quantities being sold.

Thomas Flight died in 1793, whereupon Joseph became owner of the Royal Porcelain Works, into which he took Martin Barr as partner. The latter's son, Martin Barr II, joined the firm in 1807 when it became styled "Barr, Flight and Barr". In 1813 George Barr went into the business and the name was changed to "Flight, Barr and Barr" until 1840 when the concern was acquired by the firm of Chamberlain (see pages 135, 136).

Shortly before 1800, following the lead of other eminent potters, Flight and Barr began to manufacture bone china. For this they used the Cornish clay and china-stone then released for general use by the expiry of the Cookworthy patent, which had monopolized the use of these materials for porcelain from 1768 to 1796. The first Worcester bone china was hard-looking, faintly grey, and less attractive than that made elsewhere. Pure whiteness and high translucency were reached by about 1820.

During this period a steatitic body made from Thomas Flight's soapstone formula also continued in use. This was improved by William Billingsley and his son-in-law Samuel Walker who joined Barr, Flight and Barr in October 1808 and for whom experimental facilities were provided for developing a fine soft-paste porcelain. During the early months Billingsley gave some of his attention to decorative

PLATE 28

op: Liverpool porcelain jugs decorated with transfers in black, *c.* 1780 (left) Masonic emblems, ansfers signed "Kennedy"; (right) one side "The Death of Gen. Wolfe", and reverse Britannia. *ower left:* Lowestoft porcelain jug painted with cricket scenes in colours, *c.* 1765. *Lower right:* iverpool porcelain mug with barrel-shaped body painted in colours, *c.* 1765.

PLATE 29

Lowestoft porcelain. *Top row:* cup, saucer and cream-jug painted in colours, *c.* 1780. *Middle row:* mug painted in underglaze blue, marked "8" in underglaze blue on base, 1790s; and sauce-boat painted in underglaze blue, with long spout, shaped rim, loop handle, and sides moulded in relief with shaped panels, 1770s. *Bottom row:* tea-pot and cup painted with Chinese scenes and figures in underglaze blue, *c.* 1780.

work, painting floral groups and borders. Few of these have been identified. In 1810 Martin Barr I reported that there was very "great improvement in the texture, whiteness, and beauty of our porcelain". In November 1812 Billingsley sold to his employers "a certain secret relating to a new method of composing a finer and more translucent porcelain" for £200. This was never made commercially, although the trial pieces, bearing the script "B", are remarkably translucent.

Until about this period old-fashioned, square, iron-box kilns were used at Worcester for enamelling. Samuel Walker then developed a new muffle kiln of the reflecting or reverberatory type which made firing less hazardous and results finer. This was first used by Barr, Flight and Barr.

During the Flight and Barr régime the vogue for magnificent armorial services and table equipages reached its height. Early in the nineteenth century began a return to simpler decoration, chiefly on dull classical forms in which enamel colours, cruder and harder than formerly, were used for naturalistic and meticulous but mechanical flower painting in the mood of the period. There was a decline in artistry and designs coarsened to cater for a wider, less-moneyed market.

Under the Barr, Flight and Barr proprietorship the Royal Worcester Porcelain Company produced considerable quantities of flat-ware, the borders and rims decorated with raised rococo moulding. These might be enamelled with sprays of garden flowers in full colours or in blue and gold. After Walker's muffle had been brought into use Worcester became famous for its colouring. Particularly successful was the firm's rich cobalt blue and a softer, lighter tint of sky blue, a dull opaque green, and an excellent shade of ruby. Fine work was made radiant with heavy gilding which became rather brassy after about 1820.

From about 1820 until 1840 Flight, Barr and Barr concentrated chiefly on table-ware and vases, style and flamboyance of decoration resembling that on competitive ware, but with considerably more attention given to details. Colouring too was more subdued and gilding less lavish. Pairs of vases at a casual glance would appear to be identical, but there were variations in the shapes of the panels and their decoration.

Trays intended to hold writing quills were a feature and it is doubtful if any other firm produced such exquisitely painted examples. As a rule such a tray was a narrow oblong about 9 inches long, often with shaped edges. Thomas Baxter (see frontispiece) and Solomon Cole decorated them with rustic scenes and figures. Scenes from Scott's novels were by Baxter, often in small ovals set in deep rich-blue grounds with gilt gadroon edges. The firm catered also for the amateur painting craze, producing china slabs, vases and table-ware in the white which were afterwards fired and finished for the decorator's personal use. This explains the existence of marked bone china covered with some very remarkable decorations. Solomon Cole, an artist-pupil of Baxter, wrote his reminiscences detailing the processes used, names of artists and their types of work, and much other information of great interest to collectors of early nineteenth-century Worcester china. Views of country seats in full colour were fashionable decorations for cabinet plates and cups. Some exceptionally fine examples, and some flower subjects, were signed and dated C. Hayton.

Bat printing, which originated at Worcester, was a type of decoration extensively used on cheaper tea-wares by Flight and Barr. By this process stipple engravings after works by Bartolozzi, Kaufmann, Cosway and other popular artists and engravers were reproduced in profusion, continuing to a lesser extent during the reign of George IV. (See Chapter 5.)

The earliest of Thomas Flight's marks was the name "Flight" in script either alone or accompanied, above or below, by an open crescent in blue, red or gold. The name FLIGHTS might be impressed in the paste. A crown was added to the mark in 1789 after the firm received the royal patent.

During the Flight and Barr partnership (1793–1807) porcelain and bone china were marked with the name of the firm below a crown. An incised letter "B" belongs to this period, indicating the piece to be made from one of the various experimental pastes initiated by Martin Barr I.

In 1807 when Martin Barr II joined the firm the mark was

Marks used by Worcester:

1-4. Marks of Flight, Barr and Barr, 1813-40: (1) in red or black; (2) impressed; (3 and 4) printed in red or black.

5-6. Chamberlain's marks, printed in red, 1820-40.

7-11. Some of the marks used after the amalgamation of Chamberlain and Barr: (7) 1850-51; (8) 1840-45, printed in red, until the Coventry Street address was given up; (9) printed; (10) printed or impressed; (11) incised.

12. One of the marks of Grainger, Lee and Company after Lee joined Grainger in 1812.

13-14. Marks of Kerr and Binns, 1852-62: (13) on best-quality work, printed; (14) printed or impressed.

15. Mark of the Worcester Royal Porcelain Company Ltd. founded in 1862.

changed to BARR FLIGHT AND BARR printed in red or blue underglaze and accompanied by the Worcester and London addresses. The impressed initials "BFB" surmounted by a crown belong to this period.

From 1813 to 1840 the mark, printed in blue, was FLIGHT BARR & BARR in script or "FBB" impressed.

Robert Chamberlain who had been Dr. Wall's first apprentice and rose to become chief decorator, left early in the Flight régime, to establish enamelling workshops of his own in King Street, Worcester, buying in the white from

Caughley, New Hall, Lowestoft, Derby and possibly Liverpool. His two sons, Humphrey and Robert, were employed as decorators. Humphrey is associated with meticulous renderings of sporting subjects while Robert junior specialized in flower painting. In 1788, financed by Richard Nash, Robert Chamberlain built more extensive premises at Diglis, the same factory as that occupied by the Worcester Royal Porcelain Company of to-day.

Upon the death of their father in 1798, or perhaps a year or so earlier, the two young Chamberlains launched into the manufacture of bone china and early in the nineteenth century were making some fine table-ware. Orders were too heavy for their limited resources, and from 1804 until 1811 they were financed by G. E. Boulton. In 1828 the firm came under the control of Walter Chamberlain and John Lilly, and by 1840 these men acquired the Royal Worcester Porcelain Company, abandoning the old premises and moving plant, moulds and stocks to Diglis. The united firms traded as Chamberlain and Company until 1852 when W. H. Kerr and R. W. Binns became proprietors and ten years later converted the business into a limited company known as the Worcester Royal Porcelain Company Ltd.

The Chamberlains' early bone china resembles that of the contemporary Flight and Barr product with a faintly grey paste and glaze. By 1815 its translucency equalled that of Spode's, but the paste was hardly so white. In 1811 a special soft-paste porcelain was introduced under the name of "Regent china". This was very translucent with a fine clear surface. It was used first in the manufacture of matching dinner, dessert and breakfast services commissioned by the Prince Regent at a cost of £4,047 19s. od. So successful was this that many orders from the nobility followed. In 1818 the East India Company ordered a "dress" or armorial service for use on state occasions, the 1,400 pieces costing £2,170. This included 1,450 coats of arms emblazoned in proper colours at 15s. each. The ground colour was of delicate salmon-pink with enrichments of burnished gold. A second service ordered at the same time consisted of 4,973 pieces and cost £2,019, with coats of arms painted in one colour at 2s. each.

Although at this time executing orders of lavish dimensions in Regent china, the Chamberlains built up a thriving trade in bone china—in spite of the fact that by 1818 two dozen makers of bone china were operating in Staffordshire alone. A Chamberlain characteristic in table-ware consisted of borders of a chain or net-like design giving to the ware a hard appearance. Decorations of carefully painted bouquets of garden flowers saved this ware from banality.

During the reign of George IV the Chamberlain firm decorated many services of bone china with a series of old castles, each piece showing a different scene, with its name impressed or printed on the back. Mythological legends were favourite subjects for illustrative decoration during this period, as were copies of the works of eighteenth-century French artists. Japan patterns in red, blue and gold in a style resembling those of Spode and Derby date from about 1825. During the 1830s the Chamberlains were successful with a long series of vases lavishly gilded and decorated with views of eastern towns. Following the Queen's acceptance of a set they became known as Adelaide vases.

The apple-green ground of the Chamberlain Worcester porcelain is celebrated for the beauty of its tint. This is slightly darker than the apple green of Derby. In place of coloured grounds the meandering vermicular pattern in gilding might be used.

The impetus given to production by uniting the old works with that of the Chamberlain firm was responsible for the appearance of many new lines and decorations in the pattern books. Within ten years the factory had considerably expanded. In addition to the wide range of cabinet and table-ware, the united firm made many novelties including bracelets, brooches, buttons and gold and white pseudo-Dresden baskets decorated with paintings in the naturalistic style. Snake-handled vases were a feature of this period, decorated with views of the districts in which they were sold. Eggshell china dates from about 1850. Enamelled and gilded porcelain trays for dessert and for decanter tables were a feature. During the decade 1840–50 Worcester appears to have been responsible for the major part of the fine china produced in England.

The marks used by the Chamberlains always bore their name and few pieces were issued unmarked. The early mark until about 1808 was CHAMBERLAINS or CHAMBERLAIN'S WORCESTER painted in red script and often accompanied by a pattern number. The same marks in purple were used from 1808 to about 1820 and rarely in gold during the same period.

The first of the printed marks was CHAMBERLAIN'S WORCESTER & 63, PICCADILLY LONDON in red script. This was used 1814–16. On Regent china from 1811 to 1820 the mark in red was a crown above CHAMBERLAIN'S REGENT CHINA WORCESTER & 155 NEW BOND STREET LONDON. The name CHAMBERLAINS in script belongs to the period 1844–50 and is found on a very hard body decorated with thick raised gilding. The usual Chamberlain mark printed in red from 1820 to 1840 read CHAMBERLAIN'S WORCESTER & 155 NEW BOND STREET LONDON. ROYAL PORCELAIN MANU-FACTURERS with a royal coat of arms or crown above. The same wording in roman characters without crown or coat of arms but with the addition of NO 1 COVENTRY ST. LONDON indicates the period 1840–45. The name CHAMBERLAIN & CO WORCESTER enclosed in the border of an oval containing a crown belongs to the years 1850 and 1851.

The firm of W. T. Grainger was absorbed by the Worcester Royal Porcelain Company Limited in 1889. This factory had been established at St. Martin's Street, Worcester in 1801 by Thomas Grainger, a nephew of Humphrey Chamberlain and a former decorator with the Chamberlain firm. At first he decorated bone-china table-ware bought chiefly from Coalport in a style similar to that used by Chamberlains. In 1812 he was joined by a Mr. Lee, the firm then being styled "Grainger, Lee and Company", their address being the Royal China Works, Worcester. By 1815 they were manufacturing a fine soft-paste porcelain, but abandoned this by 1820 in favour of bone china. During George IV's reign their table-ware was embossed with sprays of wild roses and leaves, birds and other flowers enriched with polychrome enamelling. An intensely deep opaque *gros bleu* was also used in sprays and stripes.

13

THE last quarter of the eighteenth century was a period of significant changes in English porcelain manufacture. By 1770 the splendid triumphs of Bow and Chelsea were at an end; Bristol was launching on a brilliant but brief and troubled career with hard porcelain; at Worcester continual bickerings made the future of the factory appear precarious.

Obviously the time was ripe for new developments. An extensive market for porcelain was wide open to the potter capable of gauging and meeting the public's demands, and yet organizing the venture so that it would be economically sound.

One result of the unrest at Worcester in 1774 was the resignation of Thomas Turner (1749–1809) who severed his connection with the firm and went to Caughley—pronounced "Calf-ley"—near Broseley in Shropshire. Here he succeeded the part-proprietor Mr. Gallimore in the management of an earthenware factory founded some thirty years earlier. Though his coming was ostensibly to put new life into Gallimore's pottery, there can be little doubt that Turner's real mission was to manufacture porcelain, using the soapstone formula so successfully employed at Worcester. At Caughley clay and coal were plentiful and near the surface, and the Severn provided a cheap means of transport for the Cornish soapstone and was suitable for the despatch of fragile goods.

Thomas Turner, son of Dr. Richard Turner, rector of Cumberton in Worcestershire, had been brought up in comfortable surroundings with every educational advantage the period could offer. Jewitt[1] says that he was "an excellent chemist, had thoroughly studied the various processes relating to porcelain manufacture, was a skilful draughtsman, designer and engraver, and was also a clever musician". While associated with the porcelain factory at Worcester he worked for a time as assistant to Robert Hancock the engraver during the period of his partnership from March 1772. They appear both to have resigned in October 1774 following a dispute with Dr. Wall.

Upon arrival at Caughley, Turner at once began building a porcelain factory quite independent of the old earthenware works. This was known as the Salopian China Works. Production started in the middle of 1775, and on July 3 an advertisement in *Aris's Birmingham Gazette* indicated that Hancock was associated with the project as an engraver. A Shropshire newspaper on November 1, 1775, reported that "the porcelain manufactory erected near Bridgnorth is now quite completed, and the proprietors have received and completed orders to a very large amount. Lately we saw some of their productions, which in colour and fineness are truly elegant and beautiful, and have the bright and lively white of the so much extolled Oriental." Instead of letting artistic enthusiasm plunge him into elaborate work before he was firmly established, Turner's business instincts urged him to concentrate on domestic products, for which there was an overwhelming demand.

Turner married Dorothy Gallimore in 1783 and eventually became proprietor of the works at Caughley. He was thus enabled to direct the factory without the interference of exacting shareholders, a trouble that had almost ruined the Worcester works. Turner always remained closely linked with Worcester socially and commercially. Shortly after his marriage he was made a county magistrate for Shropshire and a freeman of Worcester, Bridgnorth and Wenlock, from each of which he received certain financial advantages.

Turner controlled the works until 1799, when the competition of bone china removed almost overnight all demand for his steatitic porcelain. He sold to John Rose of Coalport

1 Llewellyn Jewitt, *Ceramic Art of Great Britain.*

PLATE 30

oft-paste porcelain. *Top left:* Lowestoft punch-bowl, interior painted with the sailing ship *Frances*, 1765. *Top right:* Lowestoft sugar-bowl painted in colours and gilded, *c.* 1765. *Lower left:* Liverpool ιg painted with a hare-hunting scene in colours and gilded, lip moulded with a mask: the top border in underglaze blue veined with gold in imitation of marble, *c.* 1760. *Lower right:* Lowestoft ɔffee-pot painted with a coastal scene in underglaze blue, *c.* 1765.

PLATE 31

A collection of Plymouth hard-paste porcelain, about 1770, in the Victoria and Albert Museum
Top row: plain white glazed: (*a* and *c*) pair of *bocage* candlesticks with figures of gardener and his
wife on high pedestals, the glaze much discoloured; (*b*) pheasant perched on tree trunk. *Middle row:*
lion couchant on oval plinth, painted in colours; (*b*) salt-cellar in form of large shell resting on
heap of smaller shells and coral; (*c*) cow lying among flowers on shaped base. *Bottom row:* (*a*) vase-
shaped mug with grooved loop handle, painted in underglaze blue and inscribed " Josiah & Catherine
Greethead March 13 1769"; (*b* and *d*) pair of musicians in plain white on tall pedestals; (*c*) continental figure; (*e*) mug painted in overglaze blue in Chinese style.

who continued operating the works for the manufacture of table-ware in bone china, sending the biscuit to Caughley for decoration. Caughley was closed in 1814, the plant transferred to Coalport and the premises demolished.

The paste of Caughley porcelain, steatitic like Worcester, and capable of withstanding boiling water, was at first almost pure white with a cloudy orange or straw-coloured tinge when held to the light. It is whiter and more translucent than the creamy-white Worcester paste, which displays a faint bluish-green tint when held to the light. A change was made in the paste during the early 1780s resulting in a grey, hard-looking porcelain with an "orange-skin" surface but retaining the straw-coloured tint when held to the light.

Clear, brilliant, Caughley glaze has a distinct bluish tint entirely unlike the clear glaze of Worcester. Like Worcester, however, paste and glaze were so closely matched that the defect of crazing was largely overcome. There was some difference in the method of applying the glaze. Caughley used glaze more lavishly than Worcester, the result being an uneven surface, with small pools of glaze collecting in crevices and sometimes on the bottoms of hollow-ware. Worcester glaze was thinly applied with a brush.

When Turner established Caughley in 1775 there was a huge potential demand for English porcelain inspired by the Nankin blue-and-white table services being imported by the East India Company. Both Bow and Worcester had successfully copied these. The English potters had at first been asked to fill gaps in the extensive oriental services when breakages occurred or when the original sets had been incomplete. This explains the often recurring advertisements of the old porcelain makers that they could "produce services as good as the Nankeen".

Thomas Turner early realized the commercial value of decorating porcelain with transfer-printing under the glaze. There is no doubt that the Salopian Works was established at Caughley with the fixed intention of developing the manufacture of table-ware decorated by this process. Robert Hancock was one of England's pioneer engravers of copper plates cut for transfer-printing, with the advantage of twenty years' practical experience. It is more than probable that with the scientific Turner as his assistant at Worcester they developed technical improvements in the process of blue printing underglaze which for some years had been operating at Worcester. This secret they apparently carried to Caughley. Soon after their departure Worcester abandoned decoration in blue printing.

At first Caughley issued porcelain printed overglaze in black, sepia and blue. Then came blue printing underglaze in what were then considered mass-production quantities. Little more than blue-printed ware was issued from Caughley until about 1781. At a later period four printing presses each operating a seventy-hour week were required to produce the necessary transfers.

The production of the willow and other all-over patterns seems to have set the seal of success on the Caughley factory, although the earlier porcelain had met with a very favourable reception. In about 1780 Turner opened a London sales branch naming it, after its Shropshire origin, the "Salopian China Warehouse", at No. 5 Portugal Street, Lincoln's Inn Fields. At this time, too, Turner visited the principal porcelain factories of France and returned with several experienced potters and artists.

Whether its introduction was due to these imported decorators or not, rich, elaborate gilding now became a Caughley characteristic, and polychrome enamelling was introduced. Turner's designs in blue and gold were in the form of vertical bands or stripes of blue, edged with gold and separated by white bands of equal width; the blue bands were closely covered with a fine gold network of geometrical hatchings, while the intervening white stripes were frequently filled with scrolls or arabesques traced in gold. Alternatively, intricate floral or foliated scrolls in gold might be set off by enclosed areas of deep mazarine blue, either in the form of bands or introduced in some of the larger flowers. A variant of these striped and scrolled schemes consisted of continuous vertical lines of blue S-scrolls, edged with gold, separating bands of multi-coloured flowers painted on the intervening white spaces. Still another use of gilding occurred as accenting lines and edgebandings for some of the ware decorated in blue with Chinese patterns.

Queen Charlotte's pattern, made by both Caughley and Worcester, was an elaborate form of the Strohblumen Muster design made at Meissen from about 1740. In the case of Caughley the plate was divided into ten radiating panels instead of the eight of Worcester and the six of Meissen. The flowers were large, scrolls and foliage filling the whole ground, but each panel was exactly symmetrical. Sprays and foliage in blue and in gold, the cornflower, and many other motifs were copied from Chantilly porcelain. The dragon was another popular pattern, painted in either cobalt or lavender blue touched with gold.

Raised decoration in the form of small flowers in white or blue superimposed is found on baskets and other pieces, characteristic being a flower in white forming the knob of a teapot or butter-dish. Dishes in the shapes of leaves, shells and hearts were made in large numbers. Many of the cups and other pieces are fluted in the style of Worcester. The celebrated "Fisherman" pattern (see page 51) was marked with various forms of arabic numerals. This pattern usually decorated the miniature tea and coffee services and dinner services made at this time as toys.

Caughley polychrome painting, although trying to emulate the work of finer artists at other factories, is laboriously executed and for this reason is not difficult to distinguish if unmarked. The crowding of flowers into a tight mass is another Caughley characteristic. Sparse flower ornament and Chinese figures often display a sharp, distinctive pink not found elsewhere, and there is a hard shading of the petals. Thomas Fennell and Edward Jones are both recorded as flower painters from about 1775 until 1799, suggesting that more polychrome decoration was issued than collectors have generally believed.

The blues used for transfer work at Caughley varied from a greyish blue, through a dull purple to a fairly bright violet blue used in the late period: sometimes a pale misty blue is found. Colour was strong and clear when it did not run. In later productions the peculiar vivid blue, almost violet, is noteworthy as this colour, prepared by Turner, does not appear on any other English porcelain. A dark underglaze blue was used in combination with thin gilding from about 1790.

Painting in blue underglaze decorated Caughley porcelain in limited quantities throughout the period, birds and flowers being the usual motifs. The Chinese designs of Worcester were extensively copied in this medium. A characteristic blue-and-white design was carried out in powder blue. This had a central reserve decorated with roses and flowers from which radiated six rectangular reserves filled with oriental diaper, flowers and symbols. Later designs might be partly printed and partly painted.

Resemblances between early Caughley blue and white and that of contemporary Worcester are very marked, for the paste is similar and designs are frequently identical. Similarity is still further explained by the fact that when Robert Chamberlain parted from the old works at Worcester in 1783 and established a rival business he bought porcelain from Caughley, hand-decorated it and added his own mark. This porcelain was usually of poor quality with a yellowish or brownish tint if held to the light. When the Chamberlains were producing their own porcelain they sent large consignments to Caughley for blue-printing: in 1789 £2,000 was paid to Turner for such decoration. When Thomas Grainger established a third porcelain factory at Worcester he merely painted and finished bone china supplied at Caughley, then controlled by John Rose. (See Chapter 22.)

The majority of designs in polychrome enamel appear to have been freely adapted from the designs of other contemporary factories, but a sharp pink distinguishes Caughley as well as the steatitic paste. A Caughley feature in this medium was to crowd colourful flowers into a tight mass. Finely pencilled floral motifs in black and brown with gilding constituted another style peculiar to Caughley.

A special form of jug made at Caughley had a design of cabbage leaves moulded in relief on the body. Many jugs had mask spouts, and the bodies of mugs might be decorated with low-relief panels in the white enclosing blue-printed designs. Foot rims were usually rectangular in

PLATE 32

collection of Plymouth hard-paste porcelain painted in enamel colours, about 1770, in the Victoria
d Albert Museum. *Top row:* (*a* and *c*) boy and girl with vases of flowers; (*b*) group of two boys
eding a goat on a pedestal with symmetrical rococo-scrolled feet. *Middle row:* (*a* and *d*), together with
'o figures in bottom row: set of figures emblematic of the four Seasons; (*b*) tea-pot painted in
e Japanese style, marked with the sign for tin in red; (*c*) tea-pot with body and cover vertically
)bed, marked with the sign for tin in gold. *Bottom row:* (*a*, *c*, and *e*): part of a garniture of five
ses and beakers. Mark, on vases and one beaker, the sign for tin in red; on the other beaker, a
oss incised through the glaze.

PLATE 33

A collection of Bristol hard-paste porcelain in the Victoria and Albert Museum. *Top row:* (*a* and *c*) pair of figures with dogs, one impressed beneath with the mark "T°", *c.* 1775; (*b*) jug with bearde mask in relief on the lip, marked with the sign for tin in gold and "T" impressed, *c.* 1772. *Secom row:* painted in colours and gilded in Champion's cottage style; tea-pot on right marked with a cro in dull overglaze blue enamel and with "6" in yellow, 1776. *Third row:* (*a* and *e*) figures of girl and bo playing triangle and hurdy-gurdy, the former marked "T°"; (*b* and *d*) sauce-boats moulded i relief, *c.* 1770; (*c*) plaque with bas-relief in unglazed white porcelain, *c.* 1775. *Bottom row:* (*a*) pla with strengthening ring in addition to foot-ring, marked "6" in gold, *c.* 1780; (*b*) figure of goa herd, *c.* 1775; (*c*) plate marked with a cross and "1" in overglaze blue enamel, *c.* 1775.

section, but others were bluntly triangular like those of Worcester.

Caughley marks are simple, easily recognized, not unduly numerous, and as yet have not been greatly counterfeited. Turner never applied his name to Caughley porcelain.

Caughley:
Top, impressed; *middle line*, blue (*second from left* rarely in gold). *Bottom, left*, mark often mistakenly assigned to Caughley; *bottom, centre and right*, typical disguised numerals.

An early mark, continued throughout the Caughley period, was the letter "S" standing for the word "Salopian". Painted, or printed in underglaze blue, it is found in numerous sizes and shapes, sometimes plain, occasionally florid. Although usually found alone it might be followed or preceded by a star, or be accompanied by the word SALOPIAN impressed, or the letter "C". This mark appears on all kinds of blue-printed ware with the exception of the vivid blue characteristic of the finest Caughley porcelain. From 1782 porcelain painted or printed in the French manner was marked with the "S".

The name "Salopian" might be impressed in capitals of various sizes differing by as much as ¾ inch on a single service. It was chiefly used on dessert and dinner services decorated with the mazarine blue and gold made from 1782.

The crescent, borrowed from Worcester, appears on all classes of Caughley ware except those on which the influence of the French school is apparent. It might be fully filled in or horizontally barred. Neither the open crescent nor the small truncated crescent is found on Caughley porcelain.

The capital "C" is always printed in underglaze, never painted. It is found in association with the word SALOPIAN impressed, the letter "S", and the small star impressed. Erased numerals were often used as marks, the figure 5 being a favourite. These consisted of arabic numerals up to

10   145

8, disguised with small flourishes and crescent marks to resemble Chinese characters. The basic numeral is generally printed in underglaze blue, the erasures being painted.

Salopian porcelain has been faked for at least half a century. Early forgeries are in a paste far too white and with a glaze too glassy; they bear a Worcester design of flowers and fruits and are marked with a C. The painting is in a very vivid, brilliant blue never found on genuine Caughley. Several authorities assign to Caughley a mark of crossed swords used in conjunction with a letter S between the hafts. This mark is found on ware described by Chaffers as "in imitation of Oriental with blue stripes and red flowers". The paste, however, is not steatitic and is pure white, and the glaze hard and glassy, and the form of S is not such as is found on genuine Caughley ware. This appears to be a Victorian hard-paste porcelain imported in considerable quantity. Other marks attributed to Caughley are an arrow head, a trident head, an open crescent, and a truncated crescent: none of these seems to be authenticated.

14

"EARTH potters" were active in Liverpool early in the reign of Charles II, chiefly as specialists in mugs and jugs for export. This trade progressively expanded: by 1710 blue-painted delft ware was being made, and half a century later at least three establishments were producing domestic porcelain. As was to be expected the main output still consisted not of the many-piece services chosen by the wealthy, but of the most basic home requirements, mugs and jugs. The majority were designed for north-country and foreign markets, particularly the American colonies where strength of material and low price were overriding considerations. During the second half of the eighteenth century more than eighty potters were recorded as operating in Liverpool, six of them specialists in porcelain.

Several of these firms are well known to collectors: Richard Chaffers, who in 1756 advertised that his porcelain was "proved with boiling water before being exposed for sale"; John Sadler and Guy Green, the first to realize the significance of transfer-printing on ceramics as a separate industry; Zachariah Barnes who issued blue-printed underglaze in advance of the Potteries; and the Herculaneum Pottery, which may be numbered among the first half-dozen factories in England to make non-frit bone china.

The characteristics of the soft-paste porcelains made in Liverpool are so varied that no hard and fast rules regarding identification are possible, and rarely indeed is a marked example to be found. Taken as a group, however, the Liverpool porcelains display a distinctly greyish hue when compared with porcelain made elsewhere. The basic clay appears to have contained impurities which cleansing methods of the period failed to remove. Pure white porcelain does not appear to have been possible until supplies of Cornish stone became available after 1796.

Richard Chaffers (1731–65) is credited with having founded the Liverpool porcelain industry early in 1756. This was a frit porcelain containing soapstone, in that way resembling ware already being made at Worcester. The introduction of soapstone or steatite into soft-paste porcelain lessens the risk of fracture from sudden changes of temperature, such as would be caused by pouring boiling water into a tea-pot or hot tea into a cup.

Chaffers was already operating a pottery specializing in blue-and-white delftware for export to the American colonies. Apprehensively aware that the improvements then taking place in Staffordshire earthenware would quickly outmode delftware, he was experimenting with soft-paste porcelain when he made the acquaintance of Robert Podmore, passing through Liverpool on his way to establish himself as a master potter in America. Podmore had just left Worcester where soapstone porcelain was in profitable production. Formerly he had been employed as a delftware potter at Bristol, and later in the soapstone-porcelain factory there. He had accompanied its removal to Worcester, receiving a substantial bonus with a three-year contract. At Worcester he had been highly paid and worked in a private room "the better to engage his fidelity to keep such part of the secret as may be entrusted to him".

Chaffers persuaded Podmore to abandon his American project and join him in the manufacture of soapstone porcelain. A seven-year contract was drawn up in 1755 in which Podmore agreed to act as works manager in the production of such ware at Liverpool. In this document he is described as "very knowing and expert in the making, painting and burning of earthenware in imitation of and to resemble china ware".

The only difficulty now facing Chaffers was to obtain supplies of soapstone. Joseph Mayer[1] has recorded that it was Cookworthy who discovered soapstone deposits in

1 *The History of the Art of Pottery in Liverpool, 1854.*

Cornwall and acquired the mining rights. When, as has been justifiably conjectured, Cookworthy established a pottery at Bristol to make soapstone porcelain, the firm had sole rights in supplies of soapstone. When this firm was taken over by Worcester the soapstone mining rights were also acquired.

Chaffers therefore set out to prospect for soapstone in Cornwall, carrying letters of introduction from the Earl of Derby to leading landowners. Podmore was left in charge of delftware production. The thousand guineas allocated by Chaffers to this project was almost spent when a large deposit of soapstone was revealed near Mullion. Consignments were despatched to Liverpool by sea, Jewitt recording that the first soapstone-laden ship sailed into "the Old Dock dressed in colours, amidst the cheers of assembled spectators".

The heat-resisting soft-paste porcelain made under the Chaffers-Podmore régime closely resembled that of Worcester, but was a trifle coarser and slightly less translucent. Production was obviously active by December 1756 when an advertisement in *Williamson's Liverpool Advertiser and Mercantile Register* announced: "Chaffers and Co., China Manufactory. The Porcelain or China Ware made by Messrs. Richard Chaffers and Co. is sold no-where in the town but at their Manufactory on Shaw's Brow. Considerable abatement for exportation and to all wholesale dealers. N.B. All ware is proved with boiling water before it is exposed for sale."

Chaffers concentrated on domestic table-ware, quickly building for himself an enviable reputation. When in 1760 he presented a porcelain tea-set to Josiah Wedgwood that great potter exclaimed, "Mr. Chaffers beats us all in his colours, and with his knowledge; he can make tea-sets for two guineas which I cannot produce so good for five."

Chaffer's soapstone porcelain has a clean, hard-looking faintly grey body with a faintly bluish milky glaze. When held to the light a greenish translucency is seen, varying in intensity according to the thickness of the ware. Herbert Eccles analysed a transfer-printed jug of about 1760 and the paste was found to contain $8\frac{1}{2}$ per cent of lead oxide. This suggests that about 25 per cent of flint-glass was incorporated in the formula. The glaze, often marred with tiny bubbles, was brush-applied, leaving bare patches on foot-rims. Where it has collected thickly, as in crevices, a bluish-grey tint is displayed, known to collectors as "thunder-cloud".

Chaffers' jugs are believed to have been the first in which the lip was raised slightly above the level of the rim, a style continued by his successors. He was responsible for the vogue for flat-based barrel-shaped mugs with everted rims and concave rings encircling their bases. Foot rims were triangular in section and might be either vertical or slightly undercut. Handles were shaped in the Worcester style, but were of thinner section.

Some of Chaffers' porcelain was decorated with moulding in low relief forming reserves for painted decoration in cobalt-blue or coloured enamels. Blue-and-white work was cleanly painted, obviously by decorators already skilled in the use of the brush, designs being copied or adapted from the Chinese. The blue itself inclines towards a slaty tinge.

The colours most frequently used were pale yellow, brick red, emerald green and blue, applied over the glaze in the Chinese style, motifs including rocks, flowering plants, birds and robed figures. High lights on relief work might be accentuated with colour. A red border encircling the rim was characteristic of this hollow-ware. Simple diaper borders were also used, the most common being a trellis of repeated X's in various forms. A more elaborate border had a thick outer line, a thin inner and a series of lunettes joining at their points and with a dot below each point. Another characteristic border was composed of a thick outer line broken at intervals by groups of five irregular ovals.

Chaffers designed a bird vaguely resembling the partridge type already decorating Chelsea and Worcester porcelain, but, catering for a less-moneyed market, his bird had to be more speedily painted. Known to collectors as the Liverpool bird and usually perched on a leafy branch, it has a red head and neck, a breast speckled with red dots, the upper wing blue and the flight feathers outlined in black. The yellow body is speckled with reddish dots and there is a patch of red before a purplish tail. This bird was copied by succeeding Liverpool potters.

Some of Chaffers' porcelain was decorated with transfer prints in black or red. The majority of transfer lines are coarse and blurred owing to some defect in the glaze. The transfers were engraved and applied by the firm of Sadler and Green, some being signed "J. Sadler", others "Sadler, Liverpool".

Chaffers and Podmore, both still young men, died within a few days of each other in 1765. Simultaneous loss of both chemist and works manager was a severe blow. The business appears to have been operated on behalf of Chaffers' widow and two sons by his friend and executor Philip Christian, a maker of tortoiseshell earthenware. Within a short time Christian had become owner, probably in 1767. Gore's *Liverpool Directory* for 1766 gives Christian's address as Lord Street: in the 1769 issue he is entered as "Philip Christian and Co., potters, Shaw's Brow".

An entry in John Sadler's notebook under the date January 1769 includes the following formula: "Christian's China Body—To 100 parts [soap] rock; flint, 24 parts; best flint glass 6 parts; small glass 6 parts; crown glass, 6 parts. To every 20 lb. of the above put 1 lb. salts. Glaze—4 china body (foreign); 16 flint glass; 3 white lead; 12 oz. pearl ashes." This paste differed from that made by Chaffers in being non-frit, and contained a substantially smaller proportion of flint-glass. The resulting porcelain had a faintly brown tinge and translucency was poor.

It is possible that the original formula died with Chaffers and Podmore, and that Christian was compelled to originate a paste from the materials known to have been used. At any rate results were unsatisfactory, and in the early 1770s Christian abandoned the soapstone paste in favour of one containing bone ash. In 1774 the lease of the Mullion soapstone quarries was sold to Thomas Turner of Caughley. Joseph Mayer records that Christian's new paste was very compact and highly translucent, and that finished examples placed beside costly oriental porcelain rivalled them in brilliancy of colour and glaze.

Christian now took his place as the leading Liverpool potter, the quality of his painted porcelain often surpassing that of Derby and Worcester. He issued some excellent table services as well, described by Mayer as "elegantly formed ornaments for the chimney piece and the corner cupboard, the tops of which it was then the fashion to decorate with choice bits of china". Large quantities of jugs and mugs were transfer-printed for the American market.

While Richard Chaffers was organizing the production of colourful domestic ware in soapstone porcelain the firm of Reid and Co., proprietors of the Liverpool China Manufactory, Brownlow Hill, planned to make a soft-paste porcelain, announced in the *Liverpool Advertiser*, November 1756, as "blue and white china ware, not inferior to any made in England". In the previous September they had advertised for several apprentices: "young persons with capacity for drawing and painting". The same advertisement stated that large quantities of cordwood were required, indication that coal was not yet being used for firing the porcelain kilns. The first coal-burning kiln had been built only four years earlier by Henry Delamain at his pottery in Dublin. Reid & Co. advertised for more apprentices in 1760, after which nothing further is heard of the firm. No porcelain from this factory has been identified, but it is known that considerable quantities were exported to the American colonies.

Three brothers Pennington were well-known potters in Liverpool, James and Seth making soft-paste porcelain. James Pennington was established as a manufacturer of porcelain in Park Lane by 1768. Sadler's notebook for March of the following year contains the formula for the paste used by James Pennington: "bone ashes 60 lb; Lyme [Lynn] sand 40 lb; flint 35 lb; fritted together. To every 60 lb of the frit add 20 lb clay". So successful was Pennington that in 1774 he moved to larger premises at Copperas Hill, naming the premises "Chelsea", and advertising "elegant, cheap and serviceable chinaware which for brilliancy of colour is equal to any made in Great Britain". Seth Pennington is celebrated among the later Liverpool potters for the quality of his porcelain. It is thought that his firm was taken over by Philip Christian's establishment in the early 1780s. Bone ash was an ingredient of his ware, which displays a duck-egg-green tinge in the glaze. Many vases and punch bowls were decorated with panels of flowering plants in blue underglaze, enriched with coloured overglaze enamels. His table-ware was exceptionally heavy and thick, particularly at the base, and might be decorated with relief ornament beneath the rim. These borders were usually composed of flowers and foliage or designs of a mythological or symbolical character, which might be touched with blue. His blue enamel is exceptionally light in tone and was probably the most attractive used on Liverpool porcelain. Because of its wet appearance collectors have termed it "sticky".

Three characteristic borders have been credited to Seth Pennington. The one most frequently seen is composed of a thick line and a thin line enclosing a row of wheel-like circles each containing numerous radiating spokes. Another border consists of a series of lunettes, each containing an inverted "Y" with zig-zag lines linking the motifs. A shamrock leaf is painted beneath each semicircle. A third Pennington border consists of a single line of diamond trelliswork with a cross at each intersection: below is a thin scallop line with three dots at each arc junction.

Zachariah Barnes (1745–1820) was a well-known maker of delftware tiles until the early 1780s, when the trade declined. He then began to make underglaze blue-printed porcelain. The paste shows considerable variation. Much of his porcelain table-ware was so thick as to suggest earthenware: thin pieces display a faintly brown or blue translucency. The glassy glaze is tinged with blue, and faulty firing has flawed the surface with specks in black and blue.

The thick, blurred lines of the underglaze transfer-printing in dark cobalt blue suggest that Barnes had not thoroughly mastered the process. As blue-printing underglaze was not perfected by Spode until 1785 it must be assumed that Barnes was a pioneer in this medium. Gold was sometimes sparingly applied. H. Boswell Lancaster discovered one of the few Liverpool marks on blue-printed underglaze porcelain formerly in the possession of the Barnes family. The mark is a lion rampant surmounted by a crown.

Transfer-printed designs decorated Liverpool porcelain from the very first, the firm of Sadler and Green being established for this purpose. Most authorities give John Sadler and Guy Green the credit for the invention of transfer-printing and many are the apocryphal stories associated with them. It has not been observed previously, however, that the *Journal of the House of Commons*, November 1, 1753, records a petition by Henry Delamain, a delftware potter of Dublin, in which Delamain stated that he had "purchased the Art of Printing Earthen Ware with as much Beauty, Strong Impression, and Dispatch as it can be done on paper". Delamain was at that time also a partner in the Battersea enamel works established earlier in that year and the first firm to develop and make successful use of the transfer-printing process. It seems reasonable to conjecture that transfer-printed tiles were made at Delamain's pottery in Dublin, particularly as he withdrew from the Battersea enterprise in 1754.

Sadler and Green had meanwhile been developing a process on precisely similar lines, and established a "Printed Ware Manufactory" at 14 Harrington Street in 1756. Earthenware and porcelain makers sent ware to Sadler and Green for decoration. Wedgwood was for many years one of their most valued customers, sending large loads of earthenware by canal. Until Sadler retired as a wealthy man in about 1770 black and red were the only colours used. Green, then styling himself "china printer", produced finer transfers than formerly and used subjects of greater popular appeal. He introduced outline work in 1776, the transferred designs being filled in with enamel colours. Joseph Mayer possessed invoices showing that as late as 1794 Wedgwood was sending earthenware to Guy Green for transfer-printing. In 1783 Green charged Wedgwood £8 6s. 1½d. for "printing a table and tea-service of 250 pieces for David Garrick".

Richard Abbey, an engraver formerly employed by Sadler and Green, and designer and engraver of the famous series of quasi-heraldic jugs, established a factory in 1793, specializing in the manufacture of finely printed pottery jugs In 1796 the premises and plant were acquired by the firm of Worthington, Humble and Holland, who reorganized the factory and introduced more up-to-date methods from Staffordshire, including new kilns invented by John Pepper. As Wedgwood had called his settlement "Etruria", the Liverpool venture was named "Herculaneum". About forty workers experienced in the various branches of the Staffordshire pottery industry were carried by barge on the Grand Canal from Burslem to Toxteth. Thus at the very outset the Herculaneum factory abandoned the traditional potting methods of Liverpool.

This was the period marked by the startling success of Josiah Spode's bone china, white and of even translucency, which had created apprehension among the old-established porcelain potters. Herculaneum decided to make the non-frit bone china, the first oven for this purpose being fired in 1800 by Thomas Walls, the paste mixer being the factory manager Ralph Cordon.

So prosperous became the Herculaneum Pottery that further expansion was necessary by 1806. The firm continued under Cordon's management until 1833, when it was sold to Case, Mort and Company for £25,000. Thomas Case, the financier, withdrew his support three years later. The factory traded as Mort and Simpson until 1841 when it was closed, bringing to an end the manufacture of porcelain in Liverpool.

All kinds of table-ware were made in the new dead-white bone china, and transfer decoration was used extensively. Bat-printed tea and coffee services were a feature, decoration in various colours showing views of celebrated country seats and spas, or stippled figures of men and women adapted from Bartolozzi prints. These were sometimes finished in coloured enamels. Table services might be decorated with local scenes painted in sepia. Landscapes in colours were also issued. Views, whether local or famous, were often identified by printed titles underneath. Heraldic services were made from 1805.

Urn-shaped vases in sets of three were decorated in brilliant colours, the body usually being of a solid tone—

HERCULANEUM.

REID & Co. | CHRISTIAN.

Richard ♥ Chaffers.
1769

Liverpool:
> *Top line, from left,* Herculaneum 1790–1822 impressed or blue prints; Herculaneum 1822–33 impressed; Herculaneum 1822–41 generally impressed.
>
> *Middle line, from left,* Reid and Company 1756–60; Philip Christian of Shaw's Brow 1760–75; impressed mark found occasionally.
>
> *Bottom line, left and centre,* Case, Mort and Company, 1822–41 (from Liverpool crest); *right,* Richard Chaffers.

red, blue or orange—with a reserve on either side containing a well-known landscape, flowers or figures. Handles were in the form of conventionalized birds, dolphins, winged heads and so on. Porcelain busts were made from the same moulds as pottery, but because of greater shrinkage during firing they are noticeably smaller. During the final period cheaper, more commercial wares were made. The paste was heavy and opaque although glaze and potting were excellent. Decoration has little to recommend it to the collector.

Marks on Liverpool porcelain of the eighteenth century are extremely rare. These include the signatures of the engravers John Sadler, Guy Green, Richard Abbey and Joseph Johnson, and the lion rampant of Zachariah Barnes. The Herculaneum Pottery used several marks, but not until 1822 were they always applied to bone china. At first the name HERCULANEUM might be impressed upon pieces thick enough to bear the impress without distortion. The name, printed in puce or blue, is sometimes found in an arc above a crown or carried on a garter enclosing a crown.

The firm's committee of management in 1822 decided to identify all their wares by impressing or printing upon them the words HERCULANEUM POTTERY. This mark, with or without a scroll, continued until 1833 and was sometimes accompanied by the liver bird, the heraldic device of Liverpool, with wings extended and holding a sprig of liverwort in its beak. An anchor with or without the name LIVERPOOL was sometimes impressed. Herculaneum porcelain exported to America was usually impressed with the American eagle. Jewitt records a Herculaneum mark in which the name of the pattern was wreathed and surmounted by the crest of Liverpool rising from an heraldic wreath. This is usually found in blue on blue-printed ware.

The collector of Liverpool porcelain will derive invaluable help from "The History of the Art of Pottery in Liverpool" by Joseph Mayer and "The Liverpool Potteries" by Charles T. Gatty, (*Transactions of the Historic Society of Lancashire and Cheshire*, Vols. 7 and 33). These sources have been explored, although often inadequately, by all writers on the subject.

15

TRANSLUCENT porcelain decorated with coats of arms, crests, monograms or initials surrounded by flowers and floral borders, was long believed to have originated at Lowestoft. Some authorities put forward the astonishing theory that this armorial hard-paste porcelain was manufactured in Lowestoft and sent to China for decoration. Other experts were equally emphatic that no porcelain had ever been made at Lowestoft. The battle was waged wordily until 1902.

Then some workmen laying a drain near a malt-house kiln in Morse's Brewery at Lowestoft unearthed a few moulds. It was realized that the old malt-drying kiln was in fact part of the porcelain factory closed just a century earlier. Further excavations showed that the kiln floor had been raised to a higher level with rubbish containing numerous wasters and fragments of porcelain decorated with simple oriental motifs, and various plaster moulds. Two of the moulds were found to be dated: a tea-pot mould of 1761 with garlands of leaves and Japanese chrysanthemums in relief, and a sauce-boat of 1785. Casts were taken from some of the moulds and placed in the British Museum, where they have proved of inestimable value in identifying Lowestoft porcelain.

Several pieces found in the biscuit state were decorated ready for firing. The enamels, not being fixed by the glaze, easily rubbed off, proving decoration at Lowestoft. Several nests of cups and saucers that had run together in the kiln were found, proving firing. Nothing was found suggesting that high-quality ware was made. The wasters, covering a period of more than forty years, were all of substantial body, with glazes invariably displaying a bluish tint. Soft-paste porcelains of varying quality were found, but not a single fragment of hard paste.

The significance of this find was that it proved Lowestoft to be entirely unconnected with the hard-paste armorial porcelain termed Chinese-Lowestoft or Sino-Lowestoft. It has since been proved that the so-called armorial Chinese-Lowestoft porcelain was made and glazed at Ching-tê Chên, and carried five hundred miles overland to Canton where it was decorated and re-fired. Made in western shapes from samples sent to China by the East India Company, this ware consisted chiefly of table-services.

Gillingwater's *History of Lowestoft* published in 1790 records that it was Hewlin Luson, squire of Gunton Hall, near Lowestoft in Suffolk, who discovered a deposit of local clay suitable for the manufacture of soft-paste porcelain. Sand from near-by Lynn was also used. Already delftware was being made on the Gunton Hall estate: one particularly fine dish from this pottery is decorated with a border in vivid blue and inscribed "Robert and Ann Parish in Norwich 1756".

In this year Luson erected a suitable kiln and employed a few London potters. It appears that a London competitor bribed these men to spoil Luson's porcelain deliberately, with the result that within a year production ceased. The factory was then taken over by a company managed by Robert Browne, a practical chemist who appears to have worked at Bow. His partners were John Richman, a merchant, Philip Walker, and Obadiah Aldred, a bricklayer. Early productions were intended to supply only the needs of East Anglia, and such ware continued to be the factory's main concern throughout its existence. This accounts for the fact that porcelain of a mediocre standard proved profitable until forced to compete with the finer and less expensive productions of the bone-china potters of Staffordshire and elsewhere. The consistently poor quality of most Lowestoft porcelain suggests the employment of workmen lacking wider experience.

The existence of a London warehouse in 1769, however,

indicates that for a time at least porcelain of a better quality was made to meet the competition of Bow, Chelsea and Derby. An advertisement dated March 17, 1770 announced: "Clark Durnford, Lowestoft China Warehouse, No. 4, Great Thomas The Apostle, Cheapside, London. Merchants and shopkeepers may be supplied with any quantity of said wares at usual prices. N.B. Allowance of 20 per cent for ready money."

The Lowestoft factory, which appears never to have operated more than one kiln and was also engaged in the herring industry, traded as Browne and Company. Robert Browne died in 1771 and was succeeded by his son, who continued with Philip Walker as his partner. The *Universal Dictionary* for 1795 records the firm as "Walker and Browne, China Manufactory and Curers". The great loss sustained by the firm when Napoleon seized several thousand pounds' worth of its porcelain at Rotterdam, combined with the competition of bone china, was responsible for the closing of the works in 1802.

Lowestoft porcelain was generally poorly potted and inexpensively decorated: it was made less for display than for use. Its paste, chemically approximating that of Bow, was less skilfully treated during manufacture. The result is that Lowestoft porcelain possesses marked peculiarities, differing materially from that of any other English ware. This makes identification by the collector comparatively easy. Any soft-paste porcelain of the bone-ash group is fairly opaque and of uniform translucency. At least three distinct varieties of paste appear to have been made. The first has a bluish tinge, with a bluish glaze, and is decorated in blue designs. In this the blue-and-white of Worcester was extensively imitated.

The second and most characteristic paste is of a deep creamy white tint which if held to the light shows a yellowish tinge. The thin glaze, almost invariably tinged with blue, tends to disguise the creamy whiteness of the paste. While wet the glaze had a tendency to settle more thickly in crevices of relief moulding and within the inside edge of rims and handle joints, displaying a decidedly bluish hue in such places. The glaze is usually marred by innumerable

PLATE 34

Above: Bristol hard-paste porcelain chocolate-cup, cover and saucer painted in colours with gilded rims, 1770s.

Hard-paste porcelain. *Top right:* Bristol mug with silhouette in black of Richard Champion in a laurel wreath with initials below; the sides are painted with bouquets of flowers in colours and fish-scale rim, *c.* 1775. *Below left:* Bristol tea-pot painted with flowers in colours and inscribed There is nothing covered that shall not be Revealed. Draw water out of the well of Salvation. Isaiah Chap. 12 verse 3." *Below right:* Plymouth mug painted in colours, *c.* 1768.

PLATE 35

Bristol hard-paste figures painted in enamel colours. *Top row:* (*a* and *c*) shepherd playing a bagpip and wearing a dull pink coat over a flowered white waistcoat, and striped knee breeches; and shepherdess wearing a green bodice and a white skirt decorated with coloured flowers, *c.* 1770 (*b*) Venus and Adonis with Cupid, Venus wearing yellow-lined drapery decorated with coloured sprigs and circular medallions on a bluish-green ground, Adonis in drapery decorated with gil sprays on dull crimson ground, *c.* 1770. *Lower row:* a set of four figures emblematic of the Element Earth, represented by a young husbandman; Air, a youthful winged figure in loose diapere drapery; Fire, a bearded man in the guise of Vulcan, and Water, a woman wearing a wreath c rushes and a flowered mantle.

microscopic black and blue specks, fine sand, and tiny bubbles. Sometimes the passing of years has caused it to become slightly discoloured towards the foot of a vessel.

A third variety was evidently intended to imitate superficially Chinese hard paste, as the glaze is green-tinted to correspond with oriental productions of the same character. This is a peculiar duck-egg tint: placed side by side with characteristic Lowestoft the green is very pronounced. Chinese decorations and colourings were copied on such ware.

Some authorities consider these characteristics sufficient to enable collectors to identify Lowestoft porcelain. But while the congealed glaze is less pronounced on other soft-paste porcelains it is nevertheless apparent, and sand specks are frequent in other glazes of the period.

Moulding in low relief is characteristic of Lowestoft, and often enclosed panels of painted decoration. Delicate scroll-work, wreaths of floral ornament, and beaded borders might be accentuated with touches of opaque white enamel. Among the excavated moulds were several indented with tiny flowers and feathery fringes such as appear in no other English porcelain. Wickerwork decorations in relief and ropework with rosettes at intersections were widely used. Cups with fluted sides were also made, as well as a coarse edition of the spiral fluting so popular at Worcester.

As with all early porcelain-makers, the first efforts of Lowestoft painters were entirely dominated by oriental motifs. Much of the old tea-ware was decorated in under-glaze blue, the colour having run in most remaining examples. This early blue and white was generally associated with moulding in relief. A powdered-blue ground was also used with white reserves painted in underglaze blue. Blue-and-white patterns included the oriental pine-cone, flowers, foliage, feathery scrolls and a wide variety adapted from the pattern book entitled *The Ladies Amusement or Whole Art of Japanning*. Similar patterns more artistically developed are found on contemporary Worcester.

Some transfer-printing in underglaze blue was used from about 1765, the copper plates being unskilfully engraved and the hatching amateurish. Between 1770 and 1785 table-ware might be printed with a pagoda pattern accompanied by coarse, dark flowers and fruits. Views and sporting scenes were also transfer-printed. When applied to tea services the transfers were neatly placed, but on mugs, bowls, coffee-pots, tea-canisters and jugs little care seems to have been taken.

Coloured enamels applied overglaze were first used in association with underglaze blue and appeared shortly after 1765. Chinese mandarin figures were painted in light reds verging towards brown with additional motifs in strong pink, light turquoise, blue and green. The horizontal brush lines painted below these figures are in a reddish brown. Such decoration was frequent on cylindrical mugs and might be accompanied by panels of black diaper-work. These and other oriental motifs were probably taken from drawings which, according to Gillingwater, were lent by Lady Smith to the proprietors. It must be remembered, however, that they closely resemble Worcester decoration of the same type, the Worcester enamel being richer in colour and applied more thickly. The Lowestoft version was in its turn copied at Canton on hard-paste export china. Posies of pink roses from original Lowestoft patterns were also copied.

Sprays and borders of simple flowers in polychrome enamels with green leaves were used in several more or less standard patterns, together with feathery rococo scrolls. Painted diapers were popular on hollow-ware, the trellis diaper being a favourite. Some Lowestoft diapers are not met with elsewhere, such as trellis in red or pink dappled with equidistantly spaced darker spots. Hexagonal and other cell diapers in blue were frequent and might also be in red and blue. Pink scale borders were also used.

Among the most frequent of Lowestoft decorative motifs was the rose. Some authorities are emphatic that a Lowes-toft specimen may be recognized by its lack of stalk. This is incorrect, however, for a similar rose may be found on Bristol hard paste of an earlier date. It was also used at New Hall—so frequently in fact that much from this factory has been wrongly ascribed to Lowestoft. There should be little difficulty in distinguishing between the two, for Lowestoft glaze is blue-tinted while that of New Hall is pure white.

The popularity of the rose at Lowestoft is explained by the fact that the full rose is part of the arms of the old borough. Roses with stalks found painted on excavated fragments entirely dispose of the theory that Lowestoft always painted stalkless specimens. A decorator named Thomas Rose is considered to have been responsible for many of the later roses in chocolate, red, pink and purple, with petals shaded in almost horizontal lines. His roses are invariably stemmed. The finest flower painting in the form of bouquets and sprays was done between 1773 and 1780. The French sprig, which originated in the Parisian factory of the Duc d'Angoulême, was used from about 1790.

A design of which there are several variants is known as the Redgrave pattern, being painted by the two brothers Redgrave and their sister. One version is composed of a diaper border in underglaze blue broken by small panels in red and gold. The foreground of the picture itself is painted in a fine apple-green, upon which stands a pierced rock in deep-blue underglaze, and a delicate red fence of swastika fret. From this rock rise Chinese flowers in blue and Indian red, and pink peonies touched with gilding, a decorative medium employed but sparingly at Lowestoft and never until after 1770.

Landscapes were painted in puce colour, often with local views such as that of Lowestoft Parish Church. Rococo styles of decoration lasted longer at Lowestoft than elsewhere: not until the early 1790s did the neo-classic vogue affect decoration there.

Like other porcelain factories of the period Lowestoft might be commissioned to supply table-ware decorated with coats of arms and crests. In 1784 the Founders' Company ordered "a set of six china punch bowls with the Company's Coat of Arms thereon". These varied from 10 inches to 20 inches in diameter, and each had a deep outer rim border of gold with roses below. In the British Museum is part of an armorial service made at Lowestoft in 1789 for the Rev. Robert Potter.

Inscribed examples of Lowestoft porcelain form a

numerous group and date between 1761 and 1796, appearing chiefly on inkwells, tea canisters, bowls, jugs and mugs. Such documentary pieces are usually of local significance. Punch bowls with vividly coloured exteriors and with interiors painted in an even-toned, luminous blue enamel were a Lowestoft speciality. Examples are found inscribed for hunts, weddings, farmers' celebrations and so on.

Birthday plaques and medallions were also made, inscribed with names and dates from 1765 to 1797, accompanied by scroll flourishes and neat border edges. On the reverse of such a piece was painted a sprig of forget-me-not in blue and green.

Lowestoft was responsible for a wide variety of domestic ware. Jugs of the moulded cabbage-leaf type and well-designed basket dishes with relief decorations at the trellis joints were made. The globular tea-pots were roughly finished beneath and had higher foot rings than those made elsewhere. Their lids were invariably glazed all over the flange and often possessed a finial composed of two leaves. Foot rings were often irregular, their sectional shape being that of a wide-based inverted triangle.

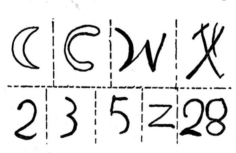

Lowestoft:
All blue; *top, second from left*, printed on blue-printed pieces, the others painted;
Top line, imitations of marks of Worcester and Meissen;
Bottom line, typical of marks placed inside foot ring.

No regular trade mark was used at Lowestoft. Poorly shaped numerals, 1 to 60, were generally inscribed in underglaze blue on the inside of foot rings. So frequently are they found in this position that such marks might almost be considered as factory marks: they are not found on porcelain made elsewhere. A curiously formed "5" is sometimes found in this position on early blue-and-white Lowestoft.

The letters H, S, R, Z, W and "R.P.", found in the same

PLATE 36

collection of Bristol hard-paste porcelain tea table-ware illustrating typical forms and decorations
sued by Richard Champion, including examples of "Cottage china" with scattered flowers, the
ose predominating. The shell-shaped salt-cellar at the bottom is by William Cookworthy, *c.* 1770.

PLATE 37

Top and middle rows: collection of New Hall hard-paste porcelain in the Victoria and Albert Museum
tea-cups and saucers, *c.* 1790; milk jug, *c.* 1800; coffee-pot with domed cover, *c.* 1800.   *Bottom row*
Rockingham bone china with well-modelled flower-encrusted figures in the Dresden style, supporting containers for flowers, late 1830s.

position, are workmen's marks. The first two refer to the modellers Hughes and Stephenson, both of whom later moved to Worcester; R. was the initial of John Redgrave the decorator, and R.P. those of Richard Phillips. The meanings of Z and W remain unknown.

The Lowestoft firm was also a prolific imitator of marks belonging to other factories, the most favoured being the Worcester crescent. Japanese characters and the crossed swords of Dresden were also copied. Examples of most of these marks were excavated from the works site.

Real Lowestoft soft-paste porcelain is comparatively scarce, reproductions being more abundant. Large quantities of reproductions have been imported from France during the present century, most of these being armorial in character; but these are of hard paste, in pursuance of the old belief that Lowestoft made such ware.

Immediately the factory was closed in 1802, Robert Allen, who had been works manager from about 1780, established an enamelling shop in Crown Street, Lowestoft. He had joined Robert Browne as a fourteen-year-old apprentice in 1758 and painted some of the early blue patterns, eventually becoming one of the more outstanding of the Lowestoft artists. Allen bought large consignments of bone china in the white from Staffordshire, Coalport and, after 1820, Rockingham. These he enamelled in the simple styles favoured by Lowestoft during the final years and fired them in a muffle furnace. An example is known signed by Allen in 1835, the year of his death at the age of ninety-one.

It is probable that some of this china bearing decoration characteristic of Allen's former work is to-day masquerading as Lowestoft, in spite of the difference in paste and the fact that a narrow iridescent halo is visible around the edge of the muffle-fired enamels. Crown Street productions might be signed "Robert Allen"; "R.A"; "Robert Allen, Lowestoft"; or inscribed "A Present from Lowestoft". Allen even painted his signature upon hard-paste oriental porcelain bought ready decorated for merchanting.

Allen also decorated in coloured enamels some fine flint-glass, examples of which still remain with the East Anglian families by whom the work was originally commissioned.

16

A BIZARRE figure in the world of English ceramics was William Billingsley (1758–1828), founder of the Nantgarw Porcelain Manufactory. Celebrated as a flower painter at Derby from the early 1780s until his resignation in 1795 (see page 106), he became a master potter ambitiously determined to produce porcelain equalling that of Sèvres. Although never commercially successful, Billingsley was responsible for some of Britain's most exquisite porcelain.

His father had been a flower painter at Chelsea until 1756, when he established himself at Derby as an enameller of porcelain and a japanner: in addition he acted as landlord of the Nottingham Arms, in Bridge Gate. This property was inherited by William Billingsley. When working as head decorator for Duesbury II he made use of the firing kilns for carrying on a long series of unobtrusive experiments in an effort to produce a fine frit porcelain. Eventually he created an extremely beautiful translucent milk-white soft-paste porcelain containing about 40 per cent of bone ash. This was given a thick, white, glassy glaze approximating that used at Derby.

Parting from Duesbury in 1795, Billingsley embarked upon the first of a series of porcelain-making ventures at Pinxton, followed by others at Mansfield and Brampton-in-Torksey. By the end of 1807, faced with bankruptcy and domestic difficulties, he disappeared, changing his name to Beeley. Within a few months he had established a small enamelling shop at Wirksworth.

By October 1808, the firm of Flight, Barr and Barr of Worcester had acquired the services of Billingsley and of

166

Samuel Walker, an able technician who had joined him at Brampton-in-Torksey, Lincolnshire, five years earlier. Experimental facilities were provided to enable them to develop a fine porcelain, but this was never made in commercial quantities. Billingsley's daughter Lavinia, in a letter to her mother, wrote that he never received more than 30*s*. a week. Still fired with the urge to be his own master, Billingsley decamped in 1813, accompanied by Walker, who had married his daughter Sarah.

Within six months, on the insufficient capital of £250, they were operating a small two-kiln porcelain factory at Nantgarw, in the Taff Valley, South Wales. The site was on the north bank of the Glamorgan Canal and is believed to have been a dwelling-house in which Billingsley lived with his two daughters and son-in-law and a housekeeper. The district was probably selected because of its remoteness, for fifty-five-year-old William Billingsley, still using the pseudonym Beeley, no doubt felt it more necessary than ever to conceal his whereabouts. Coal was plentiful and cheap, flints for the silica were close at hand, and sand from Lynn could be brought direct by coastal vessel, as were other raw materials from Cornwall and bones from Cardiff.

So fragile was the ware that distortion and cracking in the biscuit stage were extensive. This meant that the venture could not be profitable, and before the end of the year their all-too-small capital had vanished. To their aid, then, came William Weston Young, who from 1803 to 1806 had been employed as a decorator at the Cambrian Pottery, Swansea, and was now farmer, land surveyor for the County of Glamorgan, and also botanist and author. At his home near Porthcawl Young had continued his interest in ceramics, decorating Swansea pottery, using a small muffle furnace for fixing the enamels.

At first Young advanced various sums of money to Billingsley, totalling approximately £600. But so satisfied was he with the quality of the porcelain that in June 1814 he entered into partnership with Billingsley and Walker. Two months later the partners, through the medium of their local Member of Parliament, Sir John Nichol, applied to the Committee for Trade and Plantations for financial assistance, claiming their porcelain to be the best in Europe with "a combination of the Qualities of the best French Porcelain, Whiteness and transparency, with the firmness and closeness of Grain peculiar to the Saxon or Dresden Porcelain". Financial aid was refused, but Sir Joseph Banks, a member of the Committee, urged L. W. Dillwyn, proprietor of the Cambrian Pottery Works, to make further investigations into the claim.

Years later Dillwyn reported on his visit to Nantgarw: "From the great number of broken and imperfect articles which I found, it was quite plain that the porcelain could not be produced with any certainty, but I was made by the parties to believe that the defects arose entirely from the ineconomies of their little factory and was induced to build a small China work adjoining the Cambrian Pottery, that the granulated body might have a fair trial." Dillwyn also noted that the body was too clearly allied with glass to withstand the high temperature required in the kiln. He also recorded, with possible exaggeration, that nine-tenths of the contents of the kiln became wasters during firing.

Billingsley and Walker apparently convinced Dillwyn that their fine porcelain could be produced profitably, for in October 1814 they left the Nantgarw factory standing and proceeded to Swansea, faced with the task of strengthening the body of their porcelain while retaining its celebrated translucency and chalk whiteness. Two kilns were erected at a cost of £340.

Experimental work was carried out for about eighteen months in an endeavour to strengthen Billingsley's product. Then the commercially minded Dillwyn decided that the proportion of perfect pieces being made could not possibly be increased without a change of composition. He instructed the partners to replace the Lynn sand with ground flints which contained fewer impurities, and to increase the proportion of china clay. By the autumn of 1816 a porcelain more tractable in the kilns was being produced. Its greenish translucency has caused collectors to name it duck-egg porcelain.

168

A six-months' trial proved this to be a commercial failure. Soapstone was then added to the paste for strengthening purposes and in the spring of 1817 this new porcelain was being marketed, but was rejected as unsuitable by the London dealers. The entire project having proved a failure, Dillwyn ceased manufacturing porcelain in September 1817, after a costly trial lasting nearly two years.

Billingsley and Walker then returned to their idle kilns at Nantgarw, and porcelain was once more being produced before the end of 1817. A capital of £1,100 was subscribed by William Weston Young and some business associates, followed by an additional £1,000 later. The London dealers considered Nantgarw porcelain to be the finest yet made in Britain, and at once agreed to take the entire output glazed in the white.

Because of its delicate nature only symmetrical shapes could be pressed or thrown in Billingsley's porcelain. It has been estimated that flat-ware constituted more than 80 per cent of production. Firing difficulties entirely precluded the manufacture of figures and deep hollow-ware pieces. Even vases of simple form are rare.

About twenty work-people were employed during this period, including twelve children. Richard Millward, a youth working as a turner's assistant at Nantgarw at this time, has described Billingsley as "a thin man of middle height, fair with grey hair, but no beard; was a pleasant speaking man but very hot tempered. He kept a horse whip to thrash the boys and girls if they neglected their work." Unfortunately the proportion of fire-cracked and distorted pieces continued too great for the factory to be run profitably. By the end of 1819 the £2,100 had vanished, and production ceased early in 1820, when Billingsley and Walker, without even informing their benefactor Young, abandoned both the factory and their household goods and left for Coalport at the invitation of John Rose.

After their departure Young acquired the raw materials, plant and stock with the intention of operating the works himself. Faced with impending bankruptcy, however, he found this impossible. Billingsley had accumulated large quantities of stocks, mostly slightly defective with warping and firing cracks and therefore unacceptable to the London dealers. Glazed examples were flawed and pitted. Young employed Thomas Pardoe to glaze and decorate this stock between 1821 and 1823. The premises then remained un-occupied until 1835 when they were acquired by W. H. Pardoe for the manufacture of pottery and clay pipes, a trade continued by the Pardoe family until 1920.

Coalport was the final refuge of Billingsley (see page 222). His fame to-day in the sale-room rests principally upon his flower paintings, and has in consequence suffered from indiscriminate application of his name to every quality of cabbage rose painted upon porcelain. Billingsley ended his days, still known as William Beeley, in a small cottage at Kemberton, near Coalport, and died there in 1828, a bitterly disillusioned man still believing that porcelain manufactured from his costly, impractical recipe outrivalled that of Sèvres.

Porcelain made at Nantgarw and Swansea may be divided into four periods: (1) late 1813 to October 1814, at Nant-garw; (2) October 1814 to September 1817, at Swansea, during which time three kinds of paste were used; (3) November 1817 to spring 1820, at Nantgarw; (4) 1820 to 1823, Nantgarw-decorated seconds. In this total of ten years fewer than four were occupied in active production.

There was little variation in the Nantgarw body. It was always soft and very white, a notable feature being its fine translucency, slightly cloudy and with a distinct yellow tone when held against the light. It breaks with a granular-looking fracture. Dillwyn noted that the Nantgarw body was too closely allied with glass and was therefore too fusible to withstand the necessarily high kiln temperature: hence the exceptionally large proportion of wasters during firing. The thickly applied glaze, evolved by Billingsley as being ideal to use with his porcelain, was soft, pure white, smooth and glassy with a brilliantly lustrous surface, rarely disfigured by crazing.

It is believed that the Billingsley Nantgarw recipe for soft-paste porcelain was in use at Swansea for a short period, and despite claims to the contrary such ware was not impressed with the mark of Nantgarw. It probably remained unmarked and was decorated in the earthenware works.

Many variations in Swansea paste are known, indicating that two or three kilns were fired with porcelain made from each of Billingsley's experimental recipes. Then, after two years, came the "duck-egg" paste made from the autumn of 1816 to the spring of 1817 and so called because of its clear green translucency when held against the light. E. M. Nance has noted the resemblance of its composition to that of Spode's bone china, and suggested that equal quantities of china clay, china stone and bone ash were incorporated in each. Spode, however, never produced soft-paste porcelain and the standard recipe for his bone china has never varied.

The Swansea paste containing soapstone was made from the spring of 1817 until the factory closed in the following September. Known as trident porcelain because of its mark, it lacks translucency, and when held against the light reveals a smoky yellow cloudiness. Its thin, dull glaze is disfigured with pigskin pitting. A third Swansea paste— rarely found however—was made with about half the quantity of soapstone. It is very hard, extremely glassy and has a dull white surface. There is no evidence that porcelain was made at Swansea after September 1817, remaining stocks apparently being decorated at the Cambrian Pottery Works.

The paste made by Billingsley from late 1817 until early in 1820 was considered by contemporary dealers to be even more translucent than that of the earlier period. Certainly the potting was finer and the range of shapes more extensive. The biscuit was now cleaned by turning in the lathe, concentric marks caused by this process being frequent. Billingsley's original glaze was used.

Considerable stores of biscuit porcelain were left by Billingsley. The glaze applied to these during the Pardoe-Young régime differs entirely from that used by Billingsley. It is more creamy in tone and lacks high surface brilliance, and, being applied very thinly, it leaves the texture of the biscuit clearly visible.

Early Nantgarw productions consisted mainly of heavily

moulded plates and dishes made by flat-pressing on to plaster-of-Paris moulds. They are wide-rimmed and invariably low in proportion to width. The scroll moulding in relief repeated six times on the rim of a plate so closely resembles early Sèvres plate ornament that when decorated by the London enamellers it was difficult to distinguish between the two. This relief moulding appears not to have altered throughout the period. So heavily pressed was the tool that the design is clearly outlined on the underside of the rim. Many plates, of course, were smooth rimmed.

Owing to its fine quality and the exceptionally large number of wasters in manufacture Nantgarw porcelain was more expensive than competing productions, but because it could be taken for Sèvres it was in great demand by London dealers. The output, however, never exceeded twenty-five dozen plates a week. It is doubtful if any hollow-ware was made commercially during this period owing to lack of funds.

Dealers such as John Mortlock and Company and Apsley Pellatt bought in the porcelain, glazed but plain white, and issued it to professional enamellers such as Robins and Randall, Islington, and John Sims, Pimlico, for decoration. The dealer's name was often added to the Nantgarw mark.

The London enamellers heated their muffle furnaces with charcoal, giving greater depth and brilliance to their colours than did any of the china factories. Such enamelling, however, lacked hard-wearing qualities. W. D. John points out that "the London-decorated Nantgarw porcelain may be readily identified by the presence of a narrow iridescent halo around the enamel colours, and by the dentil gilding at the outer edge of the border".

Decoration consisted chiefly of conventional flower sprays painted between each border motif in relief and a central, more expansive floral bouquet. These were sometimes exact copies of early Sèvres plates, and others were in the life-size naturalistic manner of contemporary Spode and Derby. Such plates might be sold in harmonizing sets of twelve, with each motif different. Other plates were ornate cabinet pieces meticulously painted with flowers,

PLATE 38

Top left: Derby plate painted in colours by Richard Askew and gilded; mark "CD" in puce. *Top right:* New Hall cup and saucer in hard-paste porcelain, *c.* 1790. *Lower left:* New Hall hard-paste porcelain saucer painted in colours, *c.* 1790. *Lower right:* New Hall bone-china plate, the edge moulded in relief with lavender ground, and the centre painted with a basket of fruit and gilt leaves. Mark "NEW HALL" in a double circle in brown, *c.* 1815.

PLATE 39

Spode bone china. *Top left:* dessert plate with gadroon edge etched with gold, the rim decorated in bright blue enamel around a lace border and the centre painted with Dumfermline Abbey in a rich brown characteristic of Spode; marked "SPODE" painted in red. *Top right:* early openwork fruit-dish, pattern number 282; the reserves of flowers in the border of elaborate gilded patterning are in natural colours; *c.* 1798. *Lower left:* bone-china plate, the rim embossed with a wreath of flowers joined by a ribbon and showing white through a royal-blue ground. *Lower right:* bone-china plate with gadrooned edge and flowers in full colours.

birds, landscapes, elaborate figure and classical decoration covering almost the entire field. Grounds and borders were coloured in the fashionable deep green, turquoise, claret, and *bleu de roi* enamels, and the lavishly applied gilding was highly burnished.

Experts sometimes include another class of decoration painted on the stock remaining at Nantgarw when Billingsley transferred to Swansea in 1814. It is believed that this was sold to Thomas Pardoe, who decorated it at his enamelling workshop, 28 Bath Street, Bristol. There is no direct evidence of this, as Nantgarw stock was usually in the biscuit and none but Billingsley's glaze has been noted on porcelain of this period. Plates were decorated on the Nantgarw premises by Billingsley and his daughters: it is more than possible that glazed examples were bought by Pardoe.

Shapes at Swansea included a considerable amount of small hollow-ware copied or adapted from the fashionable and costly French porcelain. Less than 30 per cent of Swansea productions were enamelled in London. At Swansea Billingsley himself did a small amount of painting, mostly for copying by less experienced hands. His beautiful roses were used, and for the first time he painted stemless flowers. Insects, landscapes with floral borders, scattered sprays of flowers, as well as flowers and scrolls in low relief, decorated Swansea porcelain. A dark-green enamel of peculiar tint is a Swansea characteristic.

Decoration on Nantgarw porcelain made from 1817 was again mostly the work of London enamellers in styles resembling that of the earlier period. Among the leading artists whose work decorated Swansea and Nantgarw porcelain were Billingsley, W. W. Young, Thomas Pardoe, John Latham, James Turner, Moses Webster and William Pegg the younger.

Collectors easily distinguish Pardoe's 1821-23 decoration by the gritty texture of his red, green, yellow and blue enamels, contrasting with the smooth brilliance of London-applied enamels. All kinds of patterns came easily from his brush, lightly painted sprays of garden flowers, sprigs of foliage, birds, fruit, animals, butterflies, shells, oriental motifs and some landscapes of local interest. He used a fine, deep underglaze blue for borders, and his gilding was lavish and intricate.

The numerous plates painted by Pardoe during this period include those known as the "chocolate-edge group". Those of the biscuit seconds not considered worth the fashionable gilding with its expensive burnishing process were painted instead with a chocolate-enamel edge and simply and quickly decorated. These plates have irregular edges and most are plain rimmed, although examples are found decorated with low-relief moulding.

The notice of the auction sale which appeared in *The Cambrian* newspaper, October 28, 1822, gives some idea of the ware made at Nantgarw during 1817–20. "A large ASSORTMENT OF NANTGARW PORCELAIN, RICHLY PAINTED AND GILDED, comprising dessert and tea services, ornamental china of various descriptions; also a quantity of the same porcelain in White consisting of dishes, plates, tureens, and a variety of other table ware; also Dessert and Tea ware and a large Assortment of Ornaments. . . . The Moulds, Saggars, and other Articles used in the Trade will likewise be disposed of at the same time." This dispels the widespread belief that Billingsley sold the moulds to Rose of Coalport. Pardoe apparently bought the porcelain sold in the white and continued decorating for a further twelve months.

Nantgarw flat-ware was usually marked, with the exception of saucers which, like hollow-ware in general, were seldom marked. The mark most frequent is the name Nantgarw hand-impressed in small capitals and generally in the hyphenated form NANT-GARW. Sometimes the hyphen is omitted, and the name is sometimes found impressed as a single word. Below are the letters "C.W.", believed to mean "China Works" or "China Ware".

NANT-GARW

C.W

Nantgarw:
Impressed, sometimes not hyphenated.

Beneath these marks is sometimes also found one of the first letters of the alphabet, A, C, E or G in small capitals, B, D, or F in script, or one of the numerals 1 to 6, X, or an asterisk. As on the products of most other small factories, there are a number of rarely found marks added at the whim of decorators.

Porcelain made at Swansea from Billingsley's formula was marked with the name SWANSEA impressed. Duck-egg porcelain is marked SWANSEA impressed or printed in capitals, or written in red script, occasionally in gold. Porcelain made from the soapstone formula is impressed SWANSEA together with a single trident or crossed tridents.

Swansea:
Top left and right, impressed.
Bottom, left, in solid red or, occasionally, in another colour; *bottom right*, in red or another colour.

Reproductions of Nantgarw porcelain have been made from the early 1890s, both paste and marks being copied by the French firm of Samson. Other reproductions are hard paste and lack the clear white of the genuine porcelain, and the mark is slightly larger than the real impressed name and is enclosed within a narrow rectangle. The presence of the latter is simple indication of spurious ware.

The fakers make no attempt to imitate the styles and mannerisms of Nantgarw and Swansea artists: a study of known examples quickly enables the collector to detect copies. Many articles of a type never made at Nantgarw or Swansea have been made in France: these often bear the name Nantgarw in gold script.

The faker will sometimes add the name Nantgarw in overglaze red enamel to good-quality bone china of similar shape and decoration made during the mid-nineteenth century. Many such examples have been sold to the uninitiated, the price enhanced accordingly. Duck-egg blue with appropriate Swansea marks is widely reproduced.

175

17

FOR a brief spell in the second quarter of the nineteenth century Thomas Martin Randall (1786–1859) owned a small porcelain factory at Madeley in Shropshire. His products left the works unmarked, and to-day the names of Randall and Madeley are alike almost unknown to the porcelain collector. Yet Randall was the man responsible for one of this country's strangest tales of retrogression in manufacturing technique, and Madeley porcelain still figures, honoured because unrecognized, in innumerable collectors' cabinets.

It has been shown in previous chapters that until the last years of the eighteenth century the fashionable and beguiling porcelains of Bow and Chelsea, Worcester and Derby, even of the vastly lauded French establishment at Sèvres, were but imitations of the oriental product. They were very lovely in their gleaming translucency, velvet-rich colours, fat, creamy glazes, but they were imitations nevertheless, and when the demands of hard use were made of them, they failed. In the last years of the century their producers had the opportunity to develop the less ephemeral bone china, and the wasteful old porcelain formulæ were gladly forgotten—until the Prince Regent forced the trade to remember them. The Prince's ardent enthusiasm was for the pre-Revolution porcelain of Sèvres: the resultant nation-wide collecting vogue made the French ware so scarce that by 1815 it was almost unobtainable. After Waterloo, when the French establishment needed ready money for re-equipment, the sale of old stocks of unfinished soft-paste ware appeared an obvious source. There was no difficulty in selling to

PLATE 40

A collection of marked Spode bone china in the Victoria and Albert Museum, 1810-25.

PLATE 41

Spode table-ware in the Spode-Copeland Museum, Stoke-on-Trent. *Top:* bone-china tea-cup an saucer, tea-pot and cream-jug with embossed sprays of conventional flowers in white on lavend ground; between the sprays are painted flowers, and in the centre of each is a botanical specime the name inscribed beneath the piece; marked "SPODE" painted in red. *c.* 1820. *Centre:* ston china dish with pattern known as rising sun; marked "SPODE STONE CHINA" printed in blu *Bottom:* bone-china ice-cream pail with lining and cover, arabesque embossments on ground la crimson; painted flower groups in natural colours.

London dealers, who issued it to English enamellers for decoration in the costly styles associated with the old-Sèvres régime under the leadership of Madame de Pompadour. They had then but to add the famous double-L Sèvres monogram and such pieces would sell at fabulous profits as wholly genuine products of the mid-eighteenth century.

So profitable was this trade to the china dealers that any expedient was used to acquire Sèvres porcelain for decorating in the old style. Agents were employed in Paris to buy sparsely decorated pieces from which the enamel was removed with fluoric acid. This treatment affected the surface lustre, however, and was never wholly satisfactory, even when the new decoration was given three or more firings. It may be detected by the thinness of the underlying glaze which, through the acid treatment, became incapable of retaining the full volume of colour. Blackish-grey stains on the foot rims are also associated with the treatment received from the English decorators.

What the English dealers wanted, and long demanded in vain, was someone in England who would—and could—hark back to the previous century's methods and manufacture once again the old, impractical, long-superseded soft-paste porcelain so that it could be placed on the market as the precious antique Sèvres. Randall was the man who most nearly met their requirements: only his Quaker conscience stood between him and complete commercial triumph, for though he manufactured and decorated brilliantly in the *vieux Sèvres* manner he never completed the fraud by giving his manufactures the double-L mark. Nevertheless, those who marketed the wares had their own methods of creating an air of authenticity, and Randall's nephew John has recorded: "Indeed, they have been known to have boxes of china from Madeley sent on [by river and sea] to Dover, to be redirected as coming from France, inviting connoisseurs to come and witness them being unpacked on their arrival 'from Paris'. A little entertainment would be got up and supposing themselves to be the first whose eyes had looked upon the rich goods after they left the French capital, where it would be represented that they had been bought of the Duc de ? or of Madame Someone, after having been in the possession of royalty, they would buy freely."

Inevitably this was only a passing vogue. Even by the 1830s the fundamental excellence of the wholly English development bone china was so widely appreciated that the cult of imitation old Sèvres was becoming slightly ludicrous. Randall was glad enough to abandon manufacture by the wasteful old formulæ which had been profitable only at the enhanced prices given to antique rarities, and to accommodate himself to the current trends in manufacture. Perhaps the finest tribute to him, as a true artist-craftsman rather than a mere imitator of antiques, was the fact that as late as 1856, within three years of his death, the great Herbert Minton offered him—unsuccessfully—a partnership in return for the secret recipes that produced his wonderful ground colours.

Thomas Randall was, first and last, a decorator. As a porcelain manufacturer he almost certainly owed far more than hitherto has been realized to another and much more widely publicized, and far less commercially successful, ceramic decorator, William Billingsley. Randall was born at Broseley in Shropshire. After being apprenticed as a gilder in 1798 for a five-year term to John Rose of Caughley he was engaged as a decorator at Derby. In 1808 he moved to Pinxton where already the manufacture of a soft-paste porcelain was being attempted. This was based on a formula adapted from that used by William Billingsley during the period of his partnership there (1796–99), but Billingsley's formulæ were beautiful rather than workable, and Pinxton closed in 1812. (See Chapter 16.)

Randall and a fellow-decorator named Richard Robins thereupon established themselves in London, but as master-enamellers, not as porcelain manufacturers. They acquired the workshops formerly occupied by the celebrated enameller Thomas Hughes at Barnsbury Street, Spa Fields, Islington, and within three years were employing more than forty decorators. A large proportion of this enamelling was carried out to the commission of the leading London dealers, who supplied Randall and Robins with porcelain and china glazed in the white. Recognized specialists in the old-Sèvres style, they decorated Nantgarw and Coalport china for John Mortlock, Oxford Street; Swansea porcelain and Worcester china for John Bradley and Company, Pall Mall; imported French porcelain for the firms of Baldock and Jarman, Bond Street, and Daniel and Company, Wigmore Street. Among the better known of Randall and Robins' employees was Moses Webster, formerly of Derby, a specialist in floral groups, and celebrated for dessert services in which the decoration consisted of large flower-spray centres, surrounded by borders incorporating four small panels of fruit and birds.

Not until 1825 did Randall dissolve the partnership and establish his own small factory at Madeley in Shropshire for the manufacture of soft-paste porcelain. This was six years after Nantgarw had closed down. A considerable amount of information has recently come to light regarding the experimental efforts of William Billingsley as a maker of soft-paste porcelain and not merely as the renowned painter of rose decorations. So close was the resemblance of his paste to that of the old-Sèvres manufactory that his whole output of both Nantgarw and Swansea porcelain had been accepted eagerly by the London dealers. Now here was Randall making a last, commercially successful, attempt to recapture the eighteenth-century porcelain-masters' technique in a factory not a mile from where Billingsley was living at Kemberton.

Randall selected a canal-bank site about one mile from Coalport where a plentiful supply of experienced labour was available for all processes. Decorators he brought from London. But it seems virtually certain that his choice of site was largely governed by the opportunities of contact with Billingsley before the older man's death the following year. Experts recognize a close similarity between the soft-paste porcelain of Madeley and that formerly made by Billingsley in South Wales. Obviously, while at Pinxton Randall gained practical experience in the manufacturing methods and processes which had been prescribed by Billingsley, and there seems little reason to doubt that Billingsley was Randall's principal advisor.

Characteristic Madeley porcelain was of the Nantgarw variety, although less extremely thin and translucent than the latter. Early examples of Madeley were comparatively thick, and only dimly translucent, easily cut with a file, and possessing a glaze tinged faintly green. Moulding in relief was sometimes used. From about 1828 the paste had a mellow, creamy hue closely resembling that of old Sèvres, with a glaze thin and hard. Unlike Billingsley, Randall successfully produced large hollow-ware porcelain.

Most of the Madeley porcelain was decorated with fine ground colours, having the slightly granular appearance of powdered enamel applied over size. Flaws in the body, and there were many, such as fine hair cracks, were concealed beneath this ground colour.

Some of Britain's loveliest porcelain decoration originated at Madeley. Flowers, birds, animals, landscapes, garlands, bouquets, *chinoiserie, fêtes galantes*, portraits—every known subject belonging to the Sèvres porcelain gallery—were produced at this small factory, displayed against beautiful backgrounds of dark blue, light blue, turquoise, apple green and soft pink, always slightly deeper in hue than genuine Sèvres. The *bleu de roi* was seldom used without a delicate covering of gold tracery in patterns of network, vermicelli, and *œil de perdrix*. The latter, one of Randall's favourite grounds, consisted of circular sea-green or bright-blue spots centred with points of black. The background was white, and raised gilded moulding separated the design from the panels or reserves of more important decoration. Alternatively, little rosettes surrounded by blue and gold circles might be scattered over the surface. Gold might be used either in flat touches or in relief, made brilliant by skilful burnishing. Randall's success was immediate, and ended only when there was no longer any considerable demand for expensive copies of early Sèvres.

It is doubtful if the porcelain manufacture itself could possibly have yielded profit, so high was the percentage of distortion and wastage in the kiln. Randall succeeded because he could decorate his ware in the old-Sèvres style. The well-known decorator John Randall, nephew of the potter, in his book *The History of Madeley* has recorded that after "repeated and persevering experiments Madeley succeeded in producing a frit body with a rich glaze bearing such a close resemblance to Sèvres porcelain that connoisseurs and famous judges failed to distinguish them. Thomas Randall refused, however, from conscientious motives, to apply the Sèvres mark, the initials of Louis Louis, crossed, at the bottom". So rich were the paintings, grounds and gilding that the London dealers offered, unavailingly, to contract for Randall's entire output no matter how great, if only he would give his porcelain the Sèvres mark. His refusal led some dealers to boycott his products. No porcelain made at Madeley left the factory with a mark.

It must be noted, however, that in addition to making porcelain Randall still carried on a considerable trade as a decorator of French porcelain. This was supplied to him either in the white or so sparsely decorated that it was profitable to remove the design and redecorate it at Madeley in the most costly and elaborate style. John Randall wrote in this connection that his uncle "had less hesitation in putting the mark on what was known to be Sèvres. . . . The less scrupulous London agents, however, did not hesitate to pass it off as being really the work throughout of the Sèvres artists."

Among Randall's decorators, his nephew John painted birds in a naturalistic style which later became celebrated as "Randall's birds"; these are also found on late Rockingham, and on Coalport china from 1842. Robert Bix Gray, a fine imitator of the French style, was apprenticed to Randall in London and worked with him until 1840 when he began enamelling on his own account. He excelled in floral patterns with delicate foliage. George Gray, who painted some fine naturalistic flowers at Madeley, later became director of art at the South Kensington Museum.

Philip Ballard was the finest of the Madeley figure painters. He specialized in pastoral scenes after Watteau and Boucher, although amorini in medallions were his favourite subjects. Thomas Randall himself undertook responsibility for the ground colours, sometimes with Ballard's assistance.

Towards 1840, when the demand for Sèvres porcelain suffered through the competition of less expensive bone china, Randall produced bone china such as was being made at near-by Coalport, and decorated it in similar styles. A great deal of this was purely domestic ware and formed the staple production of the last few years.

By 1840 the demand for "old-Sèvres" had ceased, and Randall abandoned the manufacture of both porcelain and china, moving to Shelton, near Hanley. Here he continued working, but only as a decorator, using his Madeley reserve stock, imported French porcelain, and bone china made in the Potteries. When approached by Herbert Minton with a partnership proposal in 1856 he declined on the pretext of old age, retired, and three years later died.

18

JOHANN BÖTTGER at Meissen discovered in 1709 the secret of making a hard translucent porcelain equal to that imported from China. But more than half a century passed before England produced hard-paste porcelain, using methods applied in the Orient for centuries. By then, of course, soft-paste porcelain had been made at Chelsea, Derby, Worcester and elsewhere.

As early as 1712 Englishmen had known that deposits of clay suitable for the manufacture of porcelain existed in the west country. Hamilton, discussing in 1727 the porcelain clays of China, commented: "We have the same sort of Clay in Great Britain, that porcelaine is made of, but we want the warme sun to prepare it." This Cornish clay resembled the kaolin of the Chinese. It was left to William Cookworthy (1705–80), a Quaker chemist of Plymouth, to evolve a process by which it could be cleaned of impurities. Cookworthy, too, discovered native deposits of petuntse, the fluxing element essential in the manufacture of hard-paste porcelain.

Soon after the death of his father in 1718, William Cookworthy was apprenticed, through the Society of Friends, to Sylvanus Bevan, a London druggist of No. 2 Plough Court, Lombard Street. He continued employment with Bevan until about 1730, taking every opportunity of improving his education, becoming fluent in French and a Latin scholar. He then established himself at Plymouth as a wholesale druggist, trading in Notte Street, his establishment being styled Bevan and Cookworthy. Five years later he married, but his wife died in 1745. At this time, having repaid the advances made by Bevan, he took his brother into partnership, styling the business William Cookworthy and Company.

While studying in London he had been immensely interested by Réamur's scientific treatise describing experiments in porcelain-making which he had carried out on a consignment of Chinese kaolin and petuntse. This material had been sent to Réamur, together with a detailed report on manufacturing methods, by Père d'Entrecolles, a Jesuit missionary from Ching-tê Chên, one of the largest porcelain factories in China.

Treatise and report greatly impressed Cookworthy, and when the report was fully transcribed in Du Halde's *History of China* (1738) he determined to introduce the manufacture of hard porcelain into England, and spent half his lifetime in this endeavour. Samples of "china earth" from Virginia were brought to London by Andrew Duché in 1744. This was the unaker mentioned by Thomas Frye of Bow in his first patent (see Chapter 7). Duché was already making hard porcelain in America, specimens of which were inspected by Cookworthy early in 1745 and pronounced by him as "equal to the Asiatic". In a letter to Richard Hingston at this time Cookworthy wrote: ". . . having read Du Halde, he [Duché] discovered both the *Petuntse* and *Kaolin*. He is gone for a cargo of it."

As mentioned in Chapter 10, Cookworthy had samples of unaker sent to him, and, inspired by the success of Duché in America, endeavoured to match it with the clays of Cornwall. In his search for suitable materials he appears to have become aware of the Cornish soapstone deposits. In a memorandum written by Cookworthy in about 1775 and published by his grandson in 1852 he noted that d'Entrecolles "observed the Chinese have two sorts of bodies for porcelain; one prepared with petunse and caulin, the other with petunse and *wha she* or soapy rock." As already described in Chapter 10, it is reasonably conjectured that Cookworthy, in association with Benjamin Lund and William Miller, established a factory at Bristol for making soapstone porcelain. This operated from 1748 to 1752 and was then transferred to Worcester.

Cookworthy continued his search for the materials from which hard porcelain could be made. Among his friends he counted John Nancarrow, superintendent of the St. Austell tin mines, an engineer celebrated for his improvements to steam engines. Nancarrow drew Cookworthy's attention to a clay capable of withstanding intense heat without disintegrating. Known locally as "moor stone" it was used for repairing engine furnaces and fireplaces. This, when freed from mica and other impurities, was found to match the American unaker. It is commonly regarded as kaolin, although differing in several respects from the Chinese variety, and comes from deposits of granite rocks from which various alkalis have decomposed, leaving a clay consisting mainly of felspar. Its presence is recognized by a depression in the ground surface of peat beneath which it is found at depths varying from 3 to 80 feet.

Many years elapsed before Cookworthy evolved a satisfactory method of purifying the clay. So important was this process that it was incorporated in the patent granted to him in 1768. "The clay is prepared by diluting it with water until the mixture is rendered sufficiently thin for the gravell and micae to subside, the white water containing the clay is then poured or left to run off from the subsided micae and gravell into proper vessels or reservoirs, and after it has settled a day or two, the clear water above it is to be then poured or drawn off, and the clay or earth reduced to a proper consistency by the common methods of exposing it to the sun and air or laying it on chalk. This earth or clay gives the ware its whiteness and infusibility as the stone doth its transparence and mellowness." Cookworthy's method of preparing clay, still in use, was monopolized until 1796 by an extension of the patent, delaying until that year the use of china-clay by other makers of porcelain, although it was legally used for earthenware.

The fluxing element of porcelain had long been known in Cornwall as "growan-stone". It remained for Cookworthy to recognize this as the petuntse of the Chinese. In 1753 *Chambers' Cyclopedia* described growan as "a coarse, gritty stone which the miners of Cornwall are usually obliged to dig through before they come to the veins of ore". Now known as china-stone, it is a partially kaolinized felsitic granite consisting of felspar crystals together with white mica and other impurities. It is found 6 to 20 feet below loose earth and gravel. Cookworthy recorded that he found deposits of growan-stone on Tregonning Hill in the parish of Germo. This was possibly in 1756, but not later than 1758.

With Cornish kaolin and petuntse at his disposal Cookworthy was all set to pioneer the manufacture of true porcelain in England. After several experimental years developing a technique of manufacture essentially different from that used by the makers of soft-paste porcelain, he established a small factory at Bristol, where skilled potters were available. Hugh Owen[1] illustrates an experimental bowl in hard porcelain inscribed "Francis Brittain, Jan 9, 1762", decorated in blue under an imperfect glaze. The factory was operating at the time of Cookworthy's first meeting with Richard Champion in January 1764. A company was then formed with fourteen £15 or £20 shares, of which William Cookworthy held three, his brother Philip one, Richard Champion one. This pioneer hard-paste porcelain was of poor quality and kiln distortions were so numerous that the venture was regarded as unprofitable and abandoned early in 1766.

That the factory actually operated is proved by a letter from Richard Champion to Lord Hyndford in 1766: "I therefore had it tried at a manufactory set up here some time ago, on the principle of the Chinese Porcelain, but not being successful is given up. . . . The Proprietors of the work in Bristol imagined they had discovered in Cornwall all the materials similar to the Chinese; but though they burnt the body part tolerably well, yet there were impurities in the Glaze or Stone which were insurmountable." He added that "the body is perfectly white within but not without which is always smoky".

Within a short time Cookworthy established a pottery at Coxside, Plymouth, a waterside site enabling materials to be delivered direct by sea. In the British Museum is a mug of hard paste porcelain, flawed with many black specks and

[1] *Two Centuries of Ceramic Art in Bristol*, 1873.

decorated with the arms of Plymouth in a pale and blackish underglaze blue, and inscribed "Plymouth Manufactory". Beneath is the date "March 14 1768 C.F.", three days before Cookworthy enrolled his patent specification. The initials are assumed to stand for "Cookworthy *fecit*". On July 14 Cookworthy was granted the sole rights of making and vending for fourteen years a "kind of Porcelain newly Invented by Me". The firm was then styled "The Plymouth New Invented Patent Porcelain Company".

The financier was Thomas Pitt of Boconnoc, later created Lord Camelford, upon whose land suitable china-clay had been found. He granted Cookworthy a 99-years' lease. Lord Camelford in 1790 wrote an account of his association with Cookworthy: "With regard to the porcelain manufactory that was attempted to be established some years ago and which was afterwards transferred to Bristol, where it failed, it was undertaken by Mr. Cookworthy upon a friend of his having discovered on an estate of mine, in the Parish of St. Stephens, a certain white saponacious clay and close by it a species of moor stone, white with greenish spots, which he immediately perceived to be the two materials described by d'Entrecolles as the constituent parts of the Chinese porcelain; the one giving whiteness and body to the paste, the other vitrification and transparency. The difficulties found in proportioning these materials so as to give exactly the right degree of vitrification and no more, and other niceties with regard to the manipulation, discouraged us from proceeding in this concern, after we had procured a patent for the use of our materials and expended on it between two and three thousand pounds. We then sold our interest to Mr. Champion of Bristol."

The transfer of plant and materials to Bristol during the summer of 1770 was the direct consequence of the fact that the Plymouth manufactory, although employing between fifty and sixty workers, failed to attract experienced hands from the older potteries. This despite advertising, such as appeared in *Berrows Worcester Journal*, February 22, 1770: "China Ware Painters wanted for the Plymouth New Invented Manufactory. A number of sober, ingenious artists capable of painting in enamel or blue, may hear of constant employment by sending their proposals to Thomas Frank, Castle St., Bristol." It should be noted that the Bristol factory operated as William Cookworthy and Company.

There appears to have been little difference between Cookworthy's Plymouth and Bristol productions, although a small group of finer artists was employed at Bristol. Financial losses continued, too. Greater technical knowledge was required to prevent the porcelain emerging from the kiln tinged by smoke, and competition was intensified by improvements in the rival soft-paste porcelain. In 1773 William Cookworthy, then "a tall venerable man", assigned factory and patent to Richard Champion.

The hard-paste porcelain made by Cookworthy has the merit of withstanding boiling water. His paste was of two main types. At Plymouth he used materials from Thomas Pitt's estate at St. Stephens. This estate yielded a deposit of china-clay and china-stone already mixed by nature and, according to Cookworthy, "it burned to a degree of transparency without the addition of petuntse, making a body much whiter than the Asiatic, and, I think, full as white as the ancient China ware or that of Dresden." He appears to have deceived himself somewhat as to its high quality, and Champion noted its unreliability in the kiln. Losses from distortions and cracks more than counterbalanced the saving in using ready-mixed clay delivered by sea to the factory quay-side at Plymouth.

Its white body has a slight tendency towards grey, and translucency varies from a faintly yellowish green to a greyness likened by William Turner to sodden snow. It breaks with a granular fracture. Fire-cracks, warping, pin-holes and other flaws are frequent.

Minute bubbles, or pigskin pitting, visible on the surface of Plymouth porcelain were caused by imperfect "wedging" —that is, slapping two pieces of clay together until all the air is removed. Cookworthy's potters failed to do this skilfully and in the kiln the air bubbles expanded and disfigured the surface.

In the experimental period 1763–66 at Bristol the composition of the paste, according to Cookworthy himself, had been "generally about equal parts of washed moor stone and growan stone brought from Tregonning Hill". The same formula was probably used in Cookworthy's Bristol period 1770–73, but the raw materials came from the St. Stephens estate of Thomas Pitt. The resulting porcelain is milky white with the surface glow of polished ivory. Translucency is faintly greyish and fractures show a smooth surface. Fire-cracks are frequent. There are seldom any surface defects, apart from occasional dark-brown spots with black centres brought about by the presence of iron specks in the clay. Such marks are rarely seen on soft-paste porcelain.

A characteristic of the hard-paste porcelain from both Plymouth and Bristol is the spiral ridging or wreathing found on both interior and exterior of some hollow-ware. This is clearly visible when the porcelain is held at an angle against the light. Several incorrect theories, such as un-skilful throwing, have been put forward to account for this feature. These almost invisible spiral wreathings were, how-ever, purposeful. Because Cookworthy's and Champion's paste softened at one period during the firing, the ware tended to collapse beneath its own weight. The slight variation in thickness provided by wreathing was sufficient to prevent this. This wreathing is not present on the German-made Plymouth- and Bristol-marked forgeries of about eighty years ago.

At first Cookworthy endeavoured to follow the Chinese system of glazing by covering the dried, unbaked ware with glaze. The technical difficulties involved caused him quickly to abandon this method which had the advantage of needing but one firing. At both Plymouth and Bristol he used a standard glaze of the frit variety consisting almost entirely of china-stone: one part quicklime and two parts of fern ashes were fritted and one part of the frit added to fifteen of china-stone. The glaze, brilliant and thin, incorporated with the body made the porcelain appear dense and semi-opaque, and possessed the peculiar smoothness of surface found on true oriental porcelain.

Cookworthy always used wood fuel and never seems to have overcome the smoky appearance characteristic of his porcelain caused by "those tinging vapours", which gave a faintly brownish hue to the surface of the biscuit. Few pieces were produced without this defect. On early blue-and-white porcelain the glaze was thickly applied, and imperfect fusion caused uneven patches. Where the glaze collected in crevices it displays a tint varying from pale greenish yellow to a faint cobalt blue.

Blue-painted underglaze on the white was the earliest decoration used by Cookworthy. At first the colour was dull and often over-fired to a greyish tone or a brownish black. At Plymouth the colour was improved to a deep blue-black, so plentifully applied that it often ran and appears streaky. Cookworthy was the first chemist to produce cobalt blue from English ore: the result was apparently poor. Naïve oriental flowers and landscapes were the most frequent motifs, following very closely the Chinese originals. The ware itself was far from perfect and blue painting seldom of a high standard, some of it being done by Cookworthy himself.

Binns and other authorities consider that Cookworthy might have acquired the services of one or more modellers formerly employed at Bow, for among the early blue-and-white porcelain are dessert stands in the form of an escallop resting on a conglomeration of other shells. These were copied from Bow, which in turn had borrowed the design from the Capo Di Monte factory at Venice. Some well-fired Plymouth vases so closely resemble Bow blue-and-white that it is difficult to distinguish between unmarked pieces without testing the paste. Mugs, cups, jugs, sauce-boats following contemporary silver patterns, and shells were issued in blue-and-white. Leaf plates are fairly frequent in underglaze blue, sometimes with outlining in overglaze red.

Soon after the establishment of the Plymouth factory bright enamel colours were being used in Chinese figures and foliage, standing out sharply against the brilliant glaze. Enamels, however, were difficult to fix to the thin, hard glaze, sometimes appearing to be quite dry owing to a portion of the flux having been lost to the glaze without apparently softening into it. This has sometimes caused the colour to flake away, leaving merely a rough surface to the glaze. When well fired the colours are bright and glossy, but so frequently did over-firing occur that many colour schemes were entirely ruined.

Enamel painting was usually in the form of such motifs as floral sprays, birds and butterflies. Decoration on vases followed the fashion of the day, with exotic birds of brilliant plumage. Landscapes were sometimes painted, and gilding is frequent. No artists of distinction were employed at Plymouth, although tradition has it that Henry Bone, R.A., the celebrated miniaturist in enamels, was apprenticed there.

Sets of cider-mugs were made, both bell-shaped and straight-sided, some painted with bright flowers, others with flamboyant birds in floral settings. Tea services found a ready sale. William Chapple, a contemporary of Cookworthy, complained that tea was ousting Devonshire cider: "the dispiriting Infusion of an Asiatic Shrub ... is preferred to the exhilarating Beverage derived from the red-streak Apple-tree or the Barley Mow, the capacious Tankard being rejected for a complete Set of Tea-Tackle and a Sugar-Loaf". The tea- and coffee-pots of Plymouth in double-curved profile were given handles flattened on the inside and longitudinally ribbed outside.

Two advertisements inserted in *Felix Farley's Bristol Journal* give an insight into the Bristol productions. On March 30, 1771, Cookworthy advertised "beautiful Dessert Services, ornamental Figures, Candlesticks, and many other valuable articles". An advertisement printed November 28, 1772, announced: "At the Manufactory in Castle Green, Bristol, are sold various kinds of True Porcelain ... wholly free from the Imperfections in Wearing, which the English China usually has, and that its composition is equal in Fineness to the East India, and will wear as well. The enamell'd ware which is rendered nearly as cheap as the English Blue and White, comes very near, and in some Pieces equal to the Dresden, which this work more particularly imitates."

Decorations at Bristol until 1773 followed those of Plymouth, but artists were more experienced. Garniture sets of three, five, or seven were made closely resembling the Chinese in shape, elaborate examples being decorated with festoons of modelled flowers. Some simple, well-designed tea- and coffee-pots with highly domed lids were enriched with polychrome enamels in the Chinese style; others were given marbled grounds of claret or blue. Japanese kakiemon patterns and certain *famille verte* designs were issued in great variety. Collectors will note that quality of decoration varies and that the same hands that painted Worcester and other ware worked on Cookworthy's hard-paste porcelain. This was brought about by potters selling porcelain in the white to dealers who sent it out to established enamellers for decoration to their customers' requirements.

Most of Cookworthy's figures were enamelled, their scroll bases in the rococo style being touched in a brownish crimson or red. The majority were clumsily executed, the clothing being decorated with small motifs widely spaced. Well-modelled *bocages* and bird models were made at Bristol. Some figures appear to have been made from certain of the Longton Hall moulds sold at Salisbury in 1760 (see Chapter 8). The Cookworthy version of "The Four Continents" from Longton Hall achieved considerable popularity. "Boys with a Goat", "Seated Musicians" and figures of birds and animals were other Longton Hall models. Busts of George II, Woodward the actor, and Kitty Clive, first modelled at Bow, were reproduced at Plymouth.

Cookworthy's porcelain was seldom marked. At the early Bristol factory an "X" in blue under the glaze was used; on rare occasions it might be incised.

The mark applied to the best of Plymouth productions was the zodiacal symbol for the planet Jupiter and the chemist's symbol for tin, resembling the arabic numerals 2 and 4 conjoined. This is found in five colours, blue underglaze on blue-and-white porcelain, blue enamel, red, reddish brown, and gold. Rarely it is found incised. Examples inscribed on the base in red "Mr. Wm. Cookworthy's

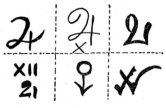

Plymouth and Bristol:
Top left and right, Plymouth; *top centre*, Bristol. *Bottom*, Plymouth in blue underglaze or brown, blue, red or gold overglaze.

PLATE 42

Top: Nantgarw porcelain plates, their rims having shaped edges moulded in relief with gilt scroll-work forming panels containing flower, fruit and bird motifs. Mark: "NANT-GARW C.W." impressed. Probably decorated in London. *c.* 1815. *Middle:* Nantgarw porcelain plates probably decorated in London. Mark: "NANT-GARW C.W." impressed. (*a*) with shaped edge, and centre painted with currants, cherries, plums and an apple with foliage, *c.* 1815; (*b*) with four rim panels, two containing Chinese figures and two with miniature Chinese pavilions among trees, *c.* 1815. *Bottom:* two Swansea plates; a pen-tray impressed "NANT-GARW C.W." *c.* 1815, and a Pinxton rummer painted with panels of flowers, impressed "G" beneath.

PLATE 43

Top: Swansea porcelain dish painted with basket of flowers in colours and roses on the rim, *c.* 1820.
Lower left: Nantgarw porcelain plate with gilded border and a basket of flowers painted in London
by James Turner of Derby, *c.* 1815. *Lower right:* Swansea porcelain cabinet plate painted in full
colours, rim with panels of roses and gilding, *c.* 1820.

Factory, Plymo, 1770" are thought to be the porcelain from the last kiln fired at Plymouth.

When Plymouth had closed and the plant was transferred to Bristol the two marks were amalgamated into a single trade mark, the cross being placed below the tin symbol. Champion abandoned the tin symbol when he assumed control in 1773, retaining only the early Bristol "X". Cookworthy's imitation Meissen was marked with the Meissen crossed swords painted in blue under the glaze: additionally a number might be inscribed in enamel over the glaze.

19

IT has been seen that the fundamental step towards the production in England of hard-paste porcelain—the application of native materials—had been achieved by the Plymouth Quaker, William Cookworthy. It was a fellow Quaker, Richard Champion (1743-91), member of a well-to-do Bristol family, who continued the venture.

Inheriting a modest fortune when he came of age, Champion launched into business as a general merchant trading with America. His undoubted success in this capacity and his flair for politics might have placed him high among the influential men of his day had not chance brought him into contact with Cookworthy, with the result that he experienced ruin, exile and an early death.

Champion displayed intense interest in Cookworthy's process of converting raw Cornish clay and china-stone into materials suitable for the manufacture of hard-paste porcelain, which he referred to as china "on the principle of Chinese Porcelain". Experimental kilns capable of producing an even temperature higher than was required for soft-paste porcelain or earthenware had already been erected at Bristol at Cookworthy's expense. Champion, with others, became a partner with a one-fourteenth share, but it was soon evident that the venture could not be commercially profitable. As described in the previous chapter, Cookworthy's next establishment was at Plymouth. But when, in the summer of 1770, he transferred plant and material from the unprofitable Plymouth factory to 15 Castle Green, Bristol, it was no doubt with the knowledge that Champion would join him, which he did in September.

The firm continued trading as the Plymouth New Invented Porcelain Company, the proprietors being William Cookworthy and Company. By then the aging Cookworthy was feeling the strain of running two businesses, as manufacturing druggist and porcelain-maker, and in 1773 he conveyed his interest in the firm to Champion.

The firm was then styled Richard Champion and Company, although the legal transfer was delayed until May of the following year. The assignment was made on condition that Champion granted Cookworthy an annual payment equal to the royalties paid to owners of the land upon which the raw materials were found. This greatly increased his production costs for the Cornish china-clay and china-stone. At this period Champion raised money by selling his house in Bristol Old Market, where he had spent the winter months, and living entirely at Henbury.

Champion, owning the exclusive rights of manufacturing hard-paste porcelain from English materials, envisaged vast profits by forceful development of the industry: a royalty of £100,000 per annum was foreshadowed for Thomas Pitt, owner of the mining rights and highly influential in the political world. In a letter to his friend Edmund Burke, Champion outlined his hopes of being granted a state subsidy such as the Meissen, Sèvres and Vienna porcelain factories received from their governments. At the same time he realized that the quality of his hard-paste porcelain left much to be desired, and that the patent so far had been a source of considerable loss to all associated with it. He decided therefore, early in 1775, to apply for an extension of the patent for a period of 14 years beyond its expiry date of 1782. Consent to such an application could only be secured by an Act of Parliament, and this Champion believed would be passed unopposed. In this he was mistaken, however, for Josiah Wedgwood, leading a group of eminent Staffordshire potters, strenuously contested what was really a monopoly of these materials, contending that the benefits of Cookworthy's efforts in the clay-pits of Cornwall should be enjoyed freely by all.

Following several months of costly wrangling in the Commons and finally in the Lords, the Bill, with amendments but still substantially in Champion's favour, became law on September 12, 1775. An extended patent was then granted, giving Champion the sole and exclusive rights to use china-clay and china-stone in the manufacture of translucent porcelain, but allowing their free use to makers of opaque pottery. Thus a monopoly was created in these essential materials, effectively preventing the development of the hard-porcelain and bone-china industry in England until the close of 1796.

Champion's Bill was wider in scope than is generally realized for it contained a clause placing a tariff of 150 per cent on imported porcelain. This caused Horace Walpole, when writing to Lady Ossory in October 1775, to complain "I did not know that the Act to favour the Bristol Manufacturers laid a duty of 150 per cent on French China, and I paid at Dover seven guineas and a half for a common set of Coffee things that had cost me but five."

The costs of the case had been heavy, but Champion's resources were not unduly pressed, for in addition to the china works he owned a prosperous general merchanting house operating a small fleet of sailing vessels that traded with the American Colonies. But ruin was not far distant, for on December 23 of the same year the government, at war with the American Colonies, prohibited English merchants from trading with them. Almost overnight Champion's merchanting business became an entire loss. Quaker friends came to the rescue, several investing money in the porcelain business in the mistaken belief that they would also share in profits which might accrue from the patent rights acquired personally by Champion.

Champion had relied upon the now-lost American market to take a great proportion of the Bristol output. Production costs continued high and sales to home buyers failed to reach expectations in spite of various technical improvements and occasional advertisements proclaiming the popular virtues of the ware. *Felix Farley's Bristol Journal*, March 2, 1776, published one such advertisement: "Established by Act of Parliament. The Bristol China Manufactory in Castle Green". This emphasized that the texture of the ware "is fine and its strength so great that water may be boiled in it". This feature had been a claim exclusive to soapstone porcelain and fine stoneware and was dreaded by Wedgwood as competing with his cream ware. The advertisement went on to decry the soft-paste porcelain made elsewhere as "being composed of a Number of Ingredients mix'd together the principal part being glass occasions it to soon get dirty in the wear, renders it continually liable to Accidents and in every respect only an Imitation and therefore is stiled by Chemists, a false porcelain".

Two years later further disaster overtook Champion: his ships were captured by the French. This completed his financial dissolution, and on August 24, 1778, he "assigned his property to trustees for the benefit of his creditors". On the same day Josiah Wedgwood wrote jubilantly to his partner Bentley: "Poor Champion, you may have heard, is quite demolished. It was never likely to be otherwise, as he had neither the professional knowledge, sufficient capital, nor scarcely any real acquaintance with the materials he was working upon. I suppose we might buy some Growan stone and Growan clay now upon easy terms, for they prepared a large quantity this last year."

No public failure was deemed necessary and all liabilities were later fully discharged. Active manufacturing appears to have been suspended even if it did not cease at once, but the large accumulated stocks of biscuit were decorated and sold. These must have been considerable, for Champion's London warehouse, 17 Salisbury Court, Fleet Street, remained open until May 1782, when the remaining stock at Bristol was sold by auction.

The sale was advertised in *Felix Farley's Bristol Journal* dated April 27, 1782: "CHINA. To be sold by Hand on 29th of April Instant, at the late Manufactory in Castle-Green, the remaining stock of Enamel, Blue and White, and white BRISTOL CHINA. The Manufactory being removed into the North—The Time of Sale is each Day from Ten till One, and from Two till Six." The sale was postponed, however, until the end of May, about a month after Champion's return from Newcastle under Lyme, where he had stayed since the previous November after assigning his patent to a company of six Staffordshire potters who proposed operating from Tunstall with Champion in a managerial capacity. The advertisement suggests that plant and material were acquired by the Staffordshire group.

The Marquess of Rockingham at this time appointed Edmund Burke to the £4,000-a-year post of Paymaster-General to H.M. Forces. Burke in his turn, grateful for a decade of political services from Champion, offered him the position of Deputy Paymaster-General at £500 a year, with apartments in Chelsea hospital. Champion accepted and at once resigned from the porcelain company. Two other partners withdrew in consequence, leaving the remaining four to form "The New Hall Company" (see Chapter 20). Unfortunately for Champion the Rockingham ministry fell a few months later, leaving him unemployed. In 1784 he emigrated to America where he was later elected to a seat in the Assembly.

The hard porcelain made by Richard Champion was substantially the same as that made by Cookworthy. Like all hard-paste porcelain it is very durable: many pieces passed undamaged through the fierce fire at Alexandra Palace which reduced all examples of English soft-paste porcelain into shapeless masses. The paste is white faintly tinged with grey, and is often disfigured with fire-cracks and warping.

As with other eighteenth-century porcelains its translucency varies as the result of inaccurate blendings and difference in the raw materials. Outwardly, however, the appearance is fairly constant.

If held to the light, the tint seen varies from a cold grey tone to a faint yellowish green. Small tears, reminiscent of Chelsea moons, are frequent. The surface is liable to be flawed with brownish specks, and grit is often present in the foot ring. The body of hollow-ware possesses to a more marked degree than Plymouth the deliberate spirallings or wreathings referred to in the previous chapter.

Sir Arthur Church[1] describes fractures in Bristol porcelain as "sub-conchoidal, slightly flaky, lustre of fractured surface something between greasy and vitreous: apparently compact and homogeneous".

1 Sir Arthur H. Church, *English Porcelain*.

A. Brongniart,[1] on the authority of John Rose, stated that "soft china" was made by Champion in 1776. It is extremely unlikely that this was so in view of Champion's opinion of soft paste published in that year. Soft paste may have been produced in Bristol experimentally, however, after the closing of the hard-paste porcelain works. Little is known concerning Champion's operations during the years 1779–81. It has been suggested by Mr. George Eyre Stringer in *New Hall Porcelain* that "John Turner (of Lane End) became interested in the manufactory on the Castle Green at Bristol, the manufacture of hard paste was abandoned and that a soft paste took its place—a soft paste porcelain with a process similar to that which Staffordshire was using in the manufacture of its cream-coloured earthenware, a process in which the biscuit fire was harder than the glost. In my opinion the porcelain which Turner and Champion evolved developed its translucency at the temperature of the biscuit oven of the day, which would probably be in the region of 1,150 degrees Centigrade."

Hugh Owen[2] refers to a pair of coffee-cups of very soft paste marked with the Bristol cross. Professor Church examined one and reported "the cup is thick in substance, but very translucent; some of the flowers on it are painted with that peculiar lilac grey enamel which was occasionally used by both Plymouth and Bristol. The paste is rather easily abraded by the file—the glaze with greater difficulty; the latter is full of air bubbles and perhaps has a felspathic base."

On better-quality Bristol-produced ware under Champion's management the glaze is thin and faint, colour of paste and glaze being almost identical. Such glaze is always hard enough to withstand wear and stains. Enamels did not sink into this glaze but stood up above the surface and therefore were in danger of peeling off with use. On less expensive polychrome ware, and on blue-and-white ware, a much softer glaze was used, lustrous and with a bluish tint.

Bristol glaze is always brilliant, clear and even-surfaced

[1] Alexandre Brongniart, *Traité des Arts Céramiques.*
[2] Hugh Owen, *Two Centuries of Ceramic Art in Bristol.*

apart from occasional pinholes caused by the bursting of tiny bubbles of carbonic gas escaping from the interior during the process of vitrification and leaving tiny depressions in the surface. Very seldom has crazing occurred.

Some Bristol porcelain was "dipped raw", that is, the article was made, dried, dipped in the glaze and then fired. When biscuiting and glazing were thus carried out with a single firing, as in the Orient, the result was a lower proportion of kiln distortions.

The greater part of Champion's output consisted of teaware for which the heat-resisting hard-paste porcelain was eminently suited. A forty-three-piece set of tea-china consisting of lidded coffee-pot and stand, lidded tea-pot and stand, slop-basin, sugar-box and cover, milk-pot and cover, bread-and-butter plate, twelve tea-cups and saucers, six coffee-cups and a spoon-tray, was sold at 2 guineas.

A three-day sale of Bristol porcelain was held at Christie and Ansell's sale rooms, Pall Mall, in February 1780. The priced catalogue printed by Nightingale gives a brief glimpse of Bristol productions, which included tea, dessert, breakfast, chocolate, and coffee sets, but no dinner services. Some tea services were: 37-piece green festoon, £1 16s. od.; 48-piece green festoon with gold edge, £5 2s. 6d.; 48-piece enamelled French, £6; 31-piece green and white with brown edge, £1 9s. od.; 50-piece blue, £6 17s. 6d.; 48-piece Dresden pencilled, £17 5s. 6d.; 32-piece crimson band, £4 6s. od.; 48-piece rich blue ribbon, £4 10s. od.; 32-piece Dresden sprigged, £3 16s. od.; 57-piece green husks and pink pattern, £7 5s. od.

Among the dessert services were several of "Dresden pattern festoon flowers" consisting of 17 compotiers and 18 plates at prices varying from 10 to 12 guineas; 38-piece ribbon pattern with festoons of flowers, £15 4s. 6d.; enamelled festoon consisting of 15 compotiers and 18 plates, £11 os. 6d.

The three hundred lots included blue-and-gold egg cups, embossed chocolate cups and saucers, barrel-shaped cups, caudle cups with covers and stands, coffee-cups with a green lock border, blue-and-white chocolate-cups and saucers decorated Chantilly pattern, ivy-sprig cups, and an assortment of "medallions of curious China Flowers accurately model'd and highly finished".

Champion's version of the fashionable globular tea-pot had straighter sides than was usual; some were slightly ogee shaped. Sometimes the handle design consisted of a large loop longitudinally ribbed and flattened only on the inner side, while the knob on the lid might resemble a small fir cone touched with gilding. The spout rose more vertically than in other contemporary designs. Tea-cups were often in ogee outline; others were fluted, plainly curved or cylindrical. The twig with tiny buds was a characteristic handle.

Dishes, large plates, and other flat-ware liable to sink and warp during firing were supported underneath with strengthening ribs. On an oval dish this resembled a raised pot-hook down the centre of the base. A circular plate was given a supporting ring. Such a strengthener was slightly shallower than the outer rim. So troublesome did Champion find the production of dishes and plates true and flat that few, if any, dinner services were issued.

Champion at first found difficulty in decorating domestic ware with blue underglaze owing to the hardness of the Bristol body. This he eventually overcame by introducing an expert from the Continent whose decorations in the Chinese manner, such as river scenes, floral sprays and diaper borders, may be recognized by their deep rich blue.

At first Champion's polychrome decorations followed the rococo styles favoured by Cookworthy: with change of management came the influence of Sèvres. Champion's principal pattern on domestic ware consisted of looped-up swags of laurel painted in green enamel shaded in brown or black. The green is found in two distinct shades, one showing more blue and the other more yellow. They were used in conjunction with excellent effect, particularly when associated with festoons and small crimson berries.

The laurel sometimes appears hanging from gold rosettes in the form of Tudor roses, or festooned from gold encircling bands, and tied with ribbon in the Sèvres style. Wreaths and festoons on tea services might be interspersed with individual roses or small sprays of skilfully painted flowers in brilliant colours including, among many others, tulip, nasturtium, poppy and convolvulus. Such flower decoration varies from the meticulously correct to the slovenly and conventional, according to cost. Laurel and husk designs, known to some collectors as the mignonette pattern, were frequent, and the grey *camaieu* painting of Sèvres was also copied. Ground colours on table-ware are infrequent, but examples occur in pink, canary yellow, maroon, blue and chocolate.

Gilding is bright and peculiarly rich and solid in appearance. The areas to be gilded were first thickly coloured with vermilion enamel fluxed with liquid glaze. This slightly raised the foundation of the gilding, greatly enhancing its effect. In place of gilt borders, the rims of cups, saucers, basins and tea-pot covers were sometimes enamelled in brown, which might have a tinge of pink in its composition.

Experiments—they can be regarded as nothing more—were carried out in transfer-printing, then in its infancy. The style of the transfers themselves suggests the hand of Robert Hancock, who supplied transfers to the trade after leaving Worcester in 1774. Champion made little commercial use of the process, however, as the hard glaze was not sufficiently fusible to take such decoration. Overglaze transfers in outline were washed over in polychrome: blue-underglaze examples bear some resemblance to contemporary Caughley work.

Like other porcelain-manufacturers of the period Champion made many finely decorated vases. The most elaborate of these were hexagonal and fitted with high-domed covers to match. Covers were usually finished with well-modelled knobs in the form of inverted bunches of grapes and vine leaves. Necks might be plain or perforated with open trelliswork. There were also shorter, coverless hexagonal vases with everted mouth rims and a series of baluster-shaped vases with high-domed covers.

Characteristic applied ornament in high relief included female masks, festoons of flowers, acanthus leaves at each angle of the base, and well-modelled rustic handles with flowers and foliage at the body junctions. Panels might be decorated with exotic birds of brilliant plumage against landscapes notable for their tall, delicately pencilled trees. Chinese subjects, birds and insects in medallions on sha-green or blue salmon-scale grounds were featured. Some-times all six panels of a hexagonal vase were painted in a matching style: others alternated polychrome-patterns with designs *en camaïeu*. No marked vase has yet been noted.

In spite of technical shortcomings Bristol figures, usually in pairs or sets of four, were among the finest made in Georgian England, carefully modelled and coloured with restraint. Considerable numbers appear to have been made. Many were inspired by Dresden, a few being direct copies but smaller than the originals, shrinkage approximating one-quarter. Early examples have scrolled bases, but Champion quickly changed this style for the less elaborate rockwork fashionable in France at that period. Such bases were decorated in high relief with ferns and leaves, to which might be added motifs associated with the individual figures.

A glimpse into Champion's managerial methods is found in a letter dated February 27, 1772, which he wrote to the modeller of the four "Elements", Earth, Air, Fire and Water. These are among the most distinguished figures made at Bristol. "I have seen the four Elements which are made at Derby, they are very Beautifull, the dress easy, the forms fine, two in particular Air and Water are charming figures. I apprehend that you make the models & therefore hope that from your Execution the following fancies will not look amiss." Champion then described at length and in minute detail exactly how he wished the models to appear.

Many examples of the four "Elements" have the mark "T°" impressed, said to be that of the well-known Tebo, indicating that he asembled the pieces after they left the moulds. It appears more likely, however, that this mark, found on the porcelain of a number of factories, had nothing to do with Tebo, or Thibaud, for Champion himself has recorded that this man did not work at Castle Green, but modelled for other factories: he is known to have been employed by Wedgwood in 1775.

Characteristic of decoration on Bristol figures was the tendency to decorate dress with tiny posies in a manner reminiscent of those found on Dresden shepherdesses. Unlike other manufacturers of porcelain figures, Champion, with Quaker restraint, refused to allow his specimens to be dressed in fantastic splendour. Ground colours on dress included vermilion, bluish green, pink, and pale yellow.

The biscuit plaques of Bristol are renowned for their design and fine finish and are unique in the world of English ceramics. The delicacy of the raised flowers is fascinating, especially when touched with gilding and when the piece is enclosed in its original black and gold frame with convex glass. The actual trade cost of such a plaque exceeded £5, and with the exception of the floral type they were presentation pieces made by Champion for his friends.

Four main types were made, and examples in each class might be oval (6 inches by 4 inches), or circular (3½ inches diameter), with portrait, armorial, monogram or floral decoration. The portrait plaques display profile busts in biscuit on oval foundations, usually blue or chocolate coloured and plain-surfaced. Some, however, are surrounded by wreaths of raised leaves in thick matt gold with details burnished, and outer borders of flowers exquisitely modelled in biscuit. Each motif was hand-built, petal by petal and leaf by leaf, with infinite care and patience, the result being a wreath in high relief sharply and minutely modelled.

In the late 1840s a series of similar plaques was made at Bristol by Edward Raby. These are of softer paste, and the ground may be surface-stained blue. In Champion's blue plaques the paste was stained before firing. Champion's plaques are recognized by a slight gloss or smear glaze.

A series of inexpensive cups, saucers and sugar basins, known to collectors as "cottage china", was issued for sale at fairs and markets from early in 1777. Had this line been marketed efficiently there is little doubt that the approaching dissolution of the Bristol factory might have been prevented. Some descriptive information concerning this ware was contributed to Owen's *Two Centuries of Ceramic Art in Bristol* by Dr. H. P. Blackmore. "The white ground is relieved by scattered flowers or small groups of flowers at irregular distances, the rose predominating and, in a bunch

PLATE 44

Top: front and back views of flower-encrusted candelabrum in Derby bone china, with figure of shepherdess playing lute, and sheep at her side; painted in colours and gilded. *Below:* Rockingham pastille burners in bone china, *c.* 1830, (left) castle in lilac ground with gilt edges and encrusted flowers; (right) summer house with lilac ground, white pillars and painted flowers.

PLATE 45

Collection of Rockingham bone china in the Victoria and Albert Museum. *Top row:* jug, *c.* 1840; plate with moulded rim, *c.* 1825; sugar basin, cover and stand 1830s. *Middle row:* two pairs of spill vases and a fruit dish, 1830s. *Bottom row:* inkstand with movable fittings, vase and cover, cup and saucer, 1830s.

of flowers, occupying the place of honour in the middle. To these flowers is generally added a border of ribbons in festoons, often festooned in bows at regular intervals round the cup, or having small bunches of flowers hanging perpendicularly at these points. The border round the saucer is repeated round the inside of the cup, but not on the outside. The tea-cups have no handles, and no coffee-cups are met with. The painting on all these pieces is done without much finish, the colour being roughly laid on with a coarse brush." The colours were few: a bright translucent green, pale blue, a wet-looking red, pink and lilac; gilding was not used.

The majority of Champion's Bristol porcelain appears to have been marked, with the notable exception of the figures. But even unmarked pieces are not difficult to

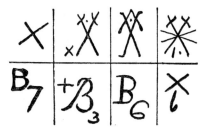

Champion's Bristol:
Second from left, top line, in blue enamel and underglaze blue; remainder in blue enamel.

recognize, so essentially different are paste and glaze from any other English porcelain, and also from the Meissen which it set out to imitate.

Four main marks were used at Bristol, the principal one being a cross, impressed or painted in blue-enamel over-glaze. On blue-underglaze ware the cross is also in under-glaze. An occasional gilt cross has been noted. A letter "B" in blue-enamel overglaze is sometimes found. On copies of Meissen the crossed swords, often with a dot between the hilts, might be used in underglaze blue. This mark might be accompanied by a cross, the letter "B" or the painter's name, all in overglaze.

Such marks were almost invariably placed centrally on

the base and might be accompanied by a numeral from 1 to 24 with 13 omitted, placed at random. All numerals appear to have been applied by the same hand in blue enamel or gold and are believed to be the decorator's reference numbers.

Reproductions of Bristol porcelain in hard paste and marked with a cross came from Germany in the years following 1874. So closely resembling the originals were paste, glaze and decoration that experts are still deceived by such pieces. More recently reproductions, particularly figures, have been made in England and France.

20

ALTHOUGH England's wealth spectacularly increased during the later part of the eighteenth century, the only firms making porcelain in considerable quantity between 1781 and the end of the century were at Derby, Liverpool, Lowestoft, Worcester, Caughley and New Hall. The hard-paste porcelain made by Hollins, Warburton, Daniel and Company at the New Hall China Manufactory, Shelton, Staffordshire, was the direct descendant of Bristol. Richard Champion in 1781 sold his patent, and, according to an advertisement in *Felix Farley's Bristol Journal* of April 27, 1782, the manufacturing plant also, to a group of six Staffordshire potters, Samuel Hollins of Shelton, Jacob Warburton of Hot Lane, who had witnessed the failure of Littler at Longton Hall, John Turner of Lane End, Charles Bagnall of Shelton, William Clowes of Port Hill, and Anthony Keeling of Tunstall, with Champion himself as the managing partner. The group established themselves at Tunstall.

Champion resigned from the venture after a few months upon his appointment by his friend Edmund Burke to the office of Deputy Paymaster-General. It is thought that his departure was followed by some disagreement between the remaining partners, resulting in the withdrawal of John Turner and Anthony Keeling, John Daniel being nomi-nated managing partner. The business was transferred to Shelton when they converted a mansion, known as New Hall, into a pottery, styled on their bill heads as "Hollins, Warburton, Daniel and Company, manufacturers of real porcelain". The firm also made earthenware, and like most other potteries of importance operated its own grinding mills.

Alfred Searle confirms that "the earliest New Hall ware was precisely similar in body and glaze to that of Bristol, to which it bears a marked resemblance in ornamentation". This hard-paste porcelain, greyish white in hue, has a thin transparent glaze, free from pinholes, clear and brilliant although tinged faintly blue and green. Seldom is an example found in which the glaze has crazed. This ware continued in production until about 1810, almost the entire output being confined to tea-pots, tea-sets, and dessert services. It appears that New Hall, like Champion at Bristol, experienced difficulty in producing the flat-ware for dinner services.

New Hall hard-paste porcelain was tough, standing up to any amount of hard wear without chipping or breaking. Nearly every one of the many thousands of remaining pieces is almost as perfect to-day as when made, with the exception of tea-pots, in which regular use, with constant alternations of heat and cold, has produced cracks. When Doctor James Aikin visited New Hall in the early 1790s (*Description of the Country from thirty to forty miles around Manchester*, 1795), he reported that "the china made at New Hall is very little, if at all inferior, especially in colours, to that of the East Indies".

The firm of Hollins, Warburton, Daniel and Company was probably the first of the Staffordshire potters to establish its own enamelling department. Wedgwood's enamelling until about 1783 was carried out at studios in Chelsea, directed by his partner Bentley until the latter's death in 1780. Enamelling at this period was usually the work of specialist decorators working in their own homes. New Hall appears to have started with a full palette of enamels, excellent in quality and some of them extremely costly, applied over the glaze: Jacob Warburton's mother was a fully experienced enameller skilled in the preparation and application of the enamels. A change of policy occurred in 1790, for a letter written late in that year by Fidele Duvivier, the celebrated enameller, to Duesbury II records the ending of his engagement with the New Hall firm as a

PLATE 46

Rockingham bone china. *Top left:* pastille burner in form of a gabled house encrusted with creepers and flowers. *Top right:* tea-pot with crown finial to the lid, from a tea- and coffee-service, with gilded decoration, in which the saucers are marked with a griffin painted in purple. *Centre:* poodle with hair composed of fine china threads. *Below:* pair of chimney ornaments in form of dog with puppies and cat with kittens, in baskets.

PLATE 47

Top: part of a Wedgwood tea-set in bone china, hand-painted with English scenes in colours and with gold line decoration, 1815; plate, Brockenhurst, Hampshire; tea-pot, Paddington, Middlesex, and Ullswater, Cumberland; sugar-box, Brookhill, Nottinghamshire, and Sultram, Devonshire; cup, Langley Park, Kent; saucer, Nottingham Castle; cream-jug, Aldervally, Derbyshire. *Below:* part of Derby dessert service in soft-paste porcelain painted with English scenes by Zachariah Boreman, *c.* 1790.

result of the proprietors' decision to cease decorating their ware with fine paintings.

G. Eyre Stringer in his book *New Hall Porcelain* (Art Trade Press, London, 1949) records that almost a thousand patterns decorated New Hall hard-paste porcelain between their establishment in 1781 and the change-over to bone china in about 1810. Each pattern was numbered consecutively as issued, the highest so far noted on hard paste being N940. The pattern numbers on New Hall bone china range from 1040 to 1669. The old patterns were continued in the new medium under their original numbers. Several authorities have stated that Bristol designs continued on early New Hall porcelain. This is very probable, for a potter's pattern books are included as "plant".

The well-known "silver-shape tea-pot" always associated with New Hall, although made in lesser quantities at Liverpool and elsewhere, was the most popular tea-pot of its period. The shape was adapted from the fashionable neo-classical design, oval or polygonal on plan, made by the silversmiths from the early 1760s. In porcelain the sides of the oval body, rising vertically from a broad flat base, were widely fluted on each side of the spout and handle. Lacking a foot-ring, such a tea-pot was necessarily accompanied by a low stand of similar outline with four balls or rosettes beneath to lift it above the table. Tea-pot and stand were ornamented to match in overglaze enamels. From about 1800, again following a silver prototype, stands were discarded and the four feet applied direct to the flat base of the tea-pot itself. New Hall tea-pots were cast in four-part moulds, and a deep vertical gallery encircled the lid opening. Another New Hall characteristic was the position of the vent-hole in the lid: this was bored down the axis of the knob instead of being drilled to the side. New Hall made these tea-pots in three sizes, but the middle and small sizes are rare.

New Hall hard-paste porcelain quickly became known as a reliable ware capable of withstanding the everyday stress caused by hot liquids. The firm became celebrated for its tea sets, and for tea and coffee sets composed of twelve tea-cups, six or twelve coffee-cups, twelve saucers, tea-pot and stand, slop-basin, sugar-dish and cream-ewer. Some early New Hall cups were, surprisingly, handleless, and saucers were made without wells for the cups until about 1810.

Eighteenth-century New Hall was decorated entirely by hand, and included simple flower motifs, often in a claret red, festoon borders, and small baskets of flowers as central motifs. From about 1790 colours tended to be gaudy, and inexpensive enamels were used, thus drastically reducing the palette. Landscapes and classic figures were painted and these now rare examples possibly pre-date 1790. A feature of New Hall decoration was a pair of back-to-back roses, without stalks, one pink and the other mauve. Transferred outlines for decorations were first used in about 1800: earlier, hand-applied outlines in black had been filled in with coloured enamels.

It is somewhat surprising, perhaps, that the firm in whom the monopoly of china-clay was vested for fifteen years should be a laggard as regards the manufacture of bone china. It has shown that lack of this essential ingredient prevented the establishment of the trade in bone china until after the lapse of the patent in 1796: no record has yet come to light suggesting that the New Hall firm sold china-clay on licence to other porcelain-makers. It was used, of course, without restriction by earthenware-makers and others making non-translucent wares.

Whether because of the success of their hard-paste porcelain or because they were involved in an attempt to compete more successfully with their rivals by turning to soft paste, the fact remains that apparently it was about 1810 before they turned their attention to bone china.

The body of New Hall bone china, more translucent than the hard-paste porcelain, is pure white with a glittering glaze noticeably increasing the brilliance of the enamel decoration. Many of the hard-paste patterns continued in use, but another 629 designs more in harmony with the Regency and the reign of George IV were added to the pattern books, some of these being adapted from other ware. Gilding was now used in conformity with the popular demand for colour and brilliance in table-ware.

Raised floral and leaf decoration is found on New Hall bone china. Bone china was made at New Hall until 1830, when, facing such formidable competitors as Spode, Minton, Derby and Coalport, the company went into liquidation. The premises were later acquired by William Ratcliffe, who manufactured inexpensive earthenware, white and printed.

New Hall hard-paste porcelain was in the main unmarked until 1790 except for the pattern number painted usually in pink, occasionally in mauve or blue, over the glaze of some large pieces. Then an incised cursive, freehand "N" might precede the painted number which at this period might also be applied to small pieces. Bone-china tea and dessert services were impressed or printed over the glaze with the name New Hall in two concentric circles. In late examples this mark is found under glaze.

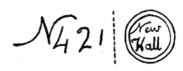

New Hall:

Left: in pink or crimson 1782 to about 1810;

Right: in red about 1810 to 1825.

Some authorities, such as G. Eyre Stringer,[1] are inclined to dispute the fact that New Hall worked the patent for hard-paste porcelain after the transfer of the plant from Bristol. The New Hall enthusiast will find this fully and factually discussed in his book.

1 *New Hall Porcelain.*

21

EXCELLENCE of modelling combined with the colourful vitality of its decoration on a paste of notable whiteness and translucency have long since carried Spode china into collectors' cabinets. When Josiah Spode (1733–97) at the age of sixteen was apprenticed to Thomas Whieldon of Fenton his engagement was recorded in the memorandum book: "Hired Siah Spode to give him from this time to Martelmas 2/3 or 2/6 if he deserves it." So began a genius of courage and energy whose first achievement was to produce colourful earthenware decoration for the dressers and tables of small homes. Succeeding in this, and aware that the tables of the rapidly growing middle class required something more ambitious, he evolved the bone china that revolutionized the pottery industry and made the name of Spode world-famous.

At the age of twenty-nine Spode was appointed manager at the pottery of Turner and Banks, Stoke-upon-Trent, and when Turner died in 1770 Spode acquired the business on mortgage. Here he continued making sporting jugs with relief decoration, toby jugs, and inexpensive earthenware. The year 1776 saw him sole proprietor of a prosperous factory trading under his own name.

Spode's importance in the world of ceramics rests largely upon his purposeful pioneer work. Like other master potters of his period he continually experimented with new bodies, glazes, methods and styles of decoration, and was always willing to employ specialists from rival establishments. Soon he developed a white domestic earthenware decorated with simple all-over designs in blue transfer-printing over the glaze, an art evolved by Thomas Turner of Caughley. Spode improved the process by inventing and carrying to perfection a method of blue-underglaze transfer-printing.

Thomas Lucas, an engraver, and James Richards, a printer, came to Spode from Caughley bringing their incomplete technique with them. Notable improvements made by Spode in transfer-printing affected the whole course of English china decoration and eventually brought great prosperity to the Potteries. He introduced stipple engraving and still further developed the idea of using outline transfer as a means towards colour display.

The development of this process is to be traced in the old Spode pattern books. In early work the sharp black of the transfer outlines showed through the brush-applied enamel colours, but in about 1805 Josiah Spode II introduced printed outlines in tints harmonizing with the enamels. The transfer-printed scaffolding was thus concealed when the guide-lines were filled in with colours. In a later phase, entire portions of the transfer-print were left without any hand colouring, the painters concentrating on outstanding features of the pattern. Transfer-printing made it possible to issue inexpensive lines of pleasant-looking bone china.

From his productions in blue-underglaze printing Spode reaped rich rewards in both home and overseas markets. It was in order to improve the selling arrangements for his table-ware that in 1785 he established a London warehouse in Fore Street, Cripplegate. Under the management of William Copeland, a Staffordshire-born tea-merchant of London, this venture proved an immediate success.

Josiah Spode's achievements in potting fine-quality earthenware inevitably encouraged him to consider seriously the problem of making porcelain. Derby with its heritage of Chelsea and Bow traditions was at that time his only formidable rival in embarking on such a venture. Derby, together with Worcester, Caughley, New Hall, Liverpool and Lowestoft, comprised the entire British porcelain industry. Spode was already using Cornish clay and stone in the manufacture of earthenware, and had an active interest in one of the Cornish mines. The existence of Cookworthy's patent, however, prohibited the use of these materials in the manufacture of porcelain for sale until after the expiry date in July 1796. With the materials available for experimental purposes Spode evolved a method of incorporating them with bone ash while dispensing with the frit. By the 1790s he had achieved technical mastery over his new paste. The original Spode pattern books prove conclusively that bone china of an advanced type was being made from china-clay and china-stone, either imported or obtained from Hollins, Warburton, Daniel and Company, proprietors of Cookworthy's fast-expiring patent.

Again Spode met with notable success: all the merchants and dealers placed vast orders for the new china. Copeland in London found a more spacious warehouse essential and bought No. 5 Portugal Street, Lincoln's Inn Fields, formerly the Theatre Royal.

In 1796 Spode embarked upon extensive improvements in the plant, new kilns and ovens being erected by John Pepper. These greatly reduced fuel consumption and produced more equal diffusion and regularity of heat. The profits of the year exceeded £13,000, of which William Copeland received £1,000 as a gift, at the same time becoming a partner in the firm which was styled Spode, Son and Copeland. A year later Josiah Spode died.

The pottery now came under the direction of Josiah Spode II, William Copeland being responsible for the commercial side of the business. While continuing the production of bone china according to his father's splendid formula, Spode experimented with pastes in which felspar was added to give greater hardness, durability and transparency. Among the most notable of his achievements was the invention in 1805 of a felspathic earthenware known as "stone china". The Prince of Wales visited the factory in 1806 and appointed Spode his potter.

Spode was regarded as a leader in mechanization. In 1802 the Trevithick steam-driven beam engine, which had driven Spode's grinding mills since the late 1770s, was replaced by a Watt steam engine, and this in turn was superseded in 1810 by a more up-to-date 36-h.p. steam engine. The Factory Inspector found it worthy of comment to report that Spode's engine operated the throwers' and turners' lathes as well as the grinding pans for flint, clay and colour.

William Copeland died in 1826 and Josiah Spode II a year later. Both were succeeded by their sons, William Taylor Copeland and Josiah Spode III. Within two years the latter had died and W. T. Copeland, Lord Mayor of London in 1835, became sole proprietor. Under his progressive guidance output rose to tremendous proportions and rivalry with the Minton firm was intense. If Minton's glaze one season was more brilliant than Copeland's, then the chances were that the latter's white paste was more perfectly white, and immediately one discovered an outstanding modeller the other produced an equally brilliant painter. In 1833, just a century after the birth of Josiah Spode, Copeland took into partnership Thomas Garrett, the firm trading as Copeland and Garrett until 1847. Since then the name of Copeland has stood alone, the firm being controlled by direct descendants to the present day.

Spode's bone china, known at first as "English Cornish china" and from about 1810 as "Stoke porcelain", united many of the best qualities of hard- and soft-paste porcelains and affected the whole subsequent history of England's ceramic industry. The formula consisted chiefly of the basic materials of hard porcelain—4 parts china-stone and $3\frac{1}{2}$ parts china-clay—together with 6 parts bone ash. This is a standard that has remained unaltered, and so effectively did this new porcelain body supersede all that had been used before, that it occupies a unique position in porcelain technology.

Without entering into technicalities as to exactly how Spode's compound of bone-ash differed from those of soft porcelains, it is sufficient to say that Spode's composition achieved whiteness of paste and evenness of translucency. Furthermore it was less liable than the earlier soft pastes to be flawed in the process of firing, and the glaze was fusible enough to allow the enamel colours to sink well into it. In the matter of fashioning and finish the china itself was beyond criticism.

While continuing to develop the quality of the bone china, Josiah Spode II introduced a variant of the paste by including a quantity of felspar into its composition and reducing the proportion of china-stone. This enabled the body to withstand firing at a higher temperature, thus increasing hardness and durability. In 1822 pure felspar was used, probably from newly discovered deposits in Montgomeryshire, producing a harder paste, as translucent as anything that came out of China; it was also less brittle and less liable to fracture. This was extensively used for dessert services, the richness of texture and glaze being suitable for coloured grounds and painted centres. Although output was rich and varied felspar china never displaced or superseded bone china. The manufacture of this felspar china was discontinued in about 1833.

Stone china was also pioneered by Josiah Spode II, being displayed in the shops from about 1805. Although closely resembling china, this was an extremely hard felspathic earthenware with a fine dense body of faintly bluish-grey tint. Lightly tapped it produces a clear ringing note.

Polychrome enamelling on Spode bone china was always carefully and neatly painted, with gilding rich and solid. In the matter of style, the rapidly changing tastes of the age were reflected, but at the same time the firm's designers made their own individual contributions to passing fashions and helped to shape contemporary taste in china-ware.

The appeal of *chinoiserie*, never long dormant in England whatever the fashionable mode might be, asserted itself in the blue-and-white ware that always retained its hold on popular affection; and the china with oriental decorations in polychrome was equally entrenched in favour. Josiah Spode I fully recognized the position of Chinese designs in the ceramic world.

Spode pattern books covering the period, from the simple blue-and-white of the 1770s to the present day, still exist, priceless records of English ceramic decoration. These show that with the introduction of his bone china Josiah Spode departed from the traditional circular plate and oval dish, and made domestic ware in unusual shapes. On these he might enamel Chinese emblems and trophies, usually in bright yellow and two shades of blue.

Evidence of the dated pattern books proves that decorations in the Imari style with their deep, velvety royal blues, bold patches of intense scarlet and rich gilding, long pre-dated the flood of Japanese designs issued by Derby, Worcester, Davenport and others. Although such designs are now termed by collectors "Crown Derby patterns", Spode Imari patterns were in general of superior quality to those painted elsewhere. When closely analysed it will be found that Spode oriental decorations are more essentially Chinese than Japanese, although their superficial resemblance to Imari has led to their general classification as Japanese. Less numerous, but equally characteristic, are Spode's decorations of the Kakiemon type. His "Shanghai" pattern was of Chinese inspiration, and, like other Chinese designs, the motifs had an underlying meaning.

The peacock pattern, with its delicate mesh-work background and brilliant yellow, constitutes one of the most attractive forms of decoration on Spode's china. On this a peacock and peahen stand before a huge pink peony unfolding in gorgeous bloom over a fence. Four garlands of bright flowers encircle the rim. The parrot, peacock and peony patterns, derived from *famille rose* porcelain also decorated stone china.

Even when Josiah Spode II was attempting to depart from the oriental motifs, the Chinese influence was often distinctly evident, while many vases suggest Moorish characteristics in the richly gilded arabesque patterns which are added to the *bleu de roi* ground, invariably appearing on those splendid pieces displaying landscape panels painted in natural colours.

Spode's main themes were oriental and rural English. Some of his western decorations were adapted from the best of those issued by English, French and German competitors, and included floral subjects, birds, fruit, and painted and transfer-printed landscapes. Motifs might be used either in conjunction with ground colours or on white porcelain. The most usual ground colours were dark and scale blues, apple green, deep yellow, grey, turquoise, marbled brown, crimson, marbled blue, salmon, yellow-green, lavender, canary yellow and cane-colour. Such ware was also distinguished by the profusion of gold applied as a decorative feature, Spode's use of gold being influenced by the splendid effect it achieved by candlelight. Burnished gold patterns slightly raised above the china were the work of Henry Daniel, a Spode gilder and enameller from 1802. There were also solid gold grounds in either bright or matt gold; dotted or stippled gold grounds; and grounds of gold scale on blue.

Sets of three vases sumptuously decorated with brilliant enamels and glittering gold were produced by Josiah Spode II. Such sets usually consist of a tall central vase and a pair of *pot-pourri* vessels. The daring colour combinations are such that only master artists could use them successfully in so small a space and avoid garishness.

Spode, like John Rose at Coalport, issued a considerable amount of ware in the style of eighteenth-century porcelains. Perhaps his most ambitious attempt was the claret ground with bird decoration in gold associated with Chelsea: the ground colour, however, fails to achieve the Chelsea splendour. Spode's Meissen reproductions may be difficult to distinguish from the genuine ware, but the paste is far softer. It was, however, in his efforts to reproduce early Worcester that Spode was most successful. Although Spode *gros bleu* is a perfect reproduction, the blue in the salmon-scale decoration is livelier than that of Dr. Wall. Reproductions invariably bore the Spode trade mark: these have sometimes been ground off at a later date.

Marks on Spode china are always plain and unmistakable, and no unmarked pieces were issued after about 1800. Though frequently altered with changing managements they are never cryptic and in no way resemble the marks of any other pottery.

On the earlier productions the name SPODE is usually impressed, although in some instances it is painted in minute letters.

Between about 1800 and 1833 the felspar ware was marked SPODE FELSPAR PORCELAIN printed in blue: alternatively it was marked with a wreath of roses, thistle and shamrock enclosing the words SPODE FELSPAR PORCELAIN printed in puce.

Marks on stone china from 1805 to 1810 consisted of a

SPODE

Printed in Blue
(1784-1789)

Spode

Printed in Blue
(1790-1800)

Printed, Blue Ground
(1795-1805)

SPODE

Stone-China

Printed in Blue
(c. 1805)

SPODE
Stone China

Printed in Blue
(c. 1805)

SPODES NEW STONE

Impressed
(1810-1815)

Printed in Puce
(1800-1833)

S P O D E
Felspar Porcelain

Printed in Blue
(1800-1833)

Spode's Imperial

Printed in Blue
(From 1810)

SPODE & COPELAND,

Printed in Blue
(First used in 1815)

Printed in Blue
(1833-1846)

Printed in Blue
(1833-1846)

COPELAND & GARRETT

Impressed
(1833-1846)

Printed in Blue
(1833-1846)

Copeland
Late Spode.

Printed in Blue
(1847-1867)

Copeland late Spode

Impressed
(1847-1867)

Printed in Green
or Blue

COPELAND
Printed in Green
Late 19th Century

Impressed

**SPODE
COPELANDS CHINA
ENGLAND**

Modern Mark
Printed in Green

Copeland
Stone China

Printed in Blue

COPELAND

SPODE

ENGLAND

Modern Marks, Printed in Various Colours

COPELAND
Printed in Green
Late 19th Century

COPELAND

SPODE

ENGLAND
New Stone

Spode and Copeland trade marks, with their dates.

pseudo-Chinese seal with SPODE overprinted in a panel and
STONE CHINA below, printed in blue. During the period
1810–1815 such ware was impressed SPODES NEW STONE.

From then the original printed mark was used with the words SPODES NEW STONE.

During the proprietorship of W. T. Copeland COPELAND LATE SPODE was impressed or printed in blue, and during the Copeland-Garrett régime there were several devices containing the names of the partners.

22

A NOTHER of England's most successful china factories owed its commercial distinction to the vision and energy of its founder, John Rose (1762-1828). Like Thomas Minton, Rose served his apprenticeship under Thomas Turner at Caughley, and in 1785 he established a small pottery in the near-by village of Jackfield.

Ten years later he moved a mile farther down the Severn to more convenient premises at Coalport on the bank of the newly cut canal, which enabled water-borne china-clay and china-stone to be delivered direct to his wharf from the Cornish coast. These materials were about to be freed from the monopoly created by Cookworthy's patent of 1768 and its subsequent extension to 1796. Rose realized early that the porcelain industry would be transformed when potters were permitted to use Cornish materials hitherto denied them, and planned accordingly. On the opposite side of the canal stood a small pottery operated until 1803 by his brother Thomas, from whom he then acquired it.

Supplies of china-clay were obtained for experimental purposes, so that immediately Cookworthy's patent expired John Rose was in a position to produce china on an ever-increasing scale. Like Spode, he considered bone ash one of the essential ingredients. The new china, although not as purely white as that of Spode, was an immediate success. While Rose's trade prospered the demand for Turner's steatitic porcelain declined, and in 1799 Rose became master of the factory at which he had received his training. He operated both factories until 1814 when the Caughley plant was transferred to Coalport. These premises were then enlarged with building materials obtained from the demolition of the Caughley factory.

Until 1830 Coalport was largely engaged in supplying white glazed china to London dealers and provincial enamellers. The Victoria and Albert Museum possesses a water-colour painted in 1810 by Thomas Baxter showing the interior of his father's decorating shop at No. 1 Goldsmith Street, London. Fixed to the wall is to be seen a notice headed "New Price List. Coalport White China". Displayed on the benches are pieces of china recognized as belonging to the Coalport-Caughley period. Some are painted with blue decoration, and others are about to be gilded (see Frontispiece).

John Mortlock of Oxford Street, London's leading china-dealer and Rose's agent for decorated ware, bought a considerable amount of Coalport china in the white for painting and gilding by outside enamellers. Much of this decoration was in the current French style. Occasionally the name Mortlock was added in gold script to the Coalport mark. Daniel and Company, Wigmore Street, bought a considerable amount of Coalport for decoration in the Sèvres style.

Outside enamellers, seldom employing more than a dozen artists and gilders, produced polychrome ornament, delicate ground colours and gilding superficially more handsome than factory work, but unfortunately lacking the long-wearing qualities of kiln-fired decoration. From about 1830, however, English potters developed the employment of women copyists inside their factories. As a result, finely decorated china was sold at prices far lower than those asked for the work of outside enamellers who thus gradually became displaced.

During the late Regency years the translucent soft-paste porcelain made by Billingsley at Nantgarw adversely affected the sales of Coalport productions so far as the London dealers and enamellers were concerned. They gave Billingsley an open order for all the porcelain he could produce in the white. Interested in this rival product, Rose in 1820 invited Billingsley and his son-in-law Samuel Walker to join him at Coalport on a seven-year agreement. The intention was to develop the Nantgarw porcelain formulæ, but this proved unnecessary for when the Nantgarw ware was no longer available Rose's improved felspar china won back the lost London trade and was the immediate reason for many new markets being developed successfully. The story that John Rose bought the Nantgarw plant and moulds is now entirely discredited: they were sold by auction at Nantgarw in 1822 at a time when Coalport had no need for such acquisitions.

John Rose died in 1828. He was succeeded by his son who died in 1841, the business then being continued by his nephew, W. F. Rose.

Rose's pioneer efforts at making bone china produced a ware without any distinction of character, the surface flawed with black spots, possessing little translucency, but nevertheless whiter, stronger and far cheaper than soft-paste porcelain. Technical improvements were gradually made, and shortly after 1810 Coalport china was distinguished by its soft white tone, a clear surface and a creamy translucency. By 1825 Rose's bone china had become more purely white, finer textured, with a high white translucency.

Felspar china, hard and brilliantly white, was produced at Coalport from about 1822 until the mid-century. Felspar china had been made by Josiah Spode II from the early years of the century. In about 1818 deposits of pure felspar were found in the near-by Briedden Hills, near Welshpool in Montgomeryshire, and acquired by John Rose. The introduction of this pure felspar into a mixture of Cornish clay and china-stone enabled Rose to produce in 1822 one of the most translucent ceramics ever made in England. It was less liable to fracture than oriental hard-paste porcelain. Fired at a higher temperature than either soft-paste or bone china, the resulting ware was harder than either, free from surface flaws and not subject to such a high percentage of distortions in the kiln.

The glaze on Coalport china was soft and smooth until 1820 when Rose evolved his famous hard, white, highly lustrous leadless glaze. The presence of lead and arsenic in glaze was a health hazard to the workers concerned—glaze dippers invariably died at an early age after contracting paralysis; the lead also affected enamel colours, particularly delicate tints, and those prepared with gold or chrome. Rose's leadless glaze also had the advantage of fusing at a lower temperature without specks or other flaws, and the enamels, as when applied to lead glazes, incorporated solidly with it, while retaining brilliancy. The Society of Arts reported this to be the finest glaze that had ever come under their observation, and awarded Rose the Isis gold medal.

The principal ingredient was felspar ground to a fine powder. The published recipe, which was not patented and remained free to all, was "27 felspar, 18 borax, 4 Lynn sand, 3 nitre, 3 soda, 3 Cornwall china clay. This is melted to a frit, ground to a fine powder and 3 parts of calcined borax added before grinding." In expensive and elaborate decorations, requiring repeated firings, the absence of lead in the glaze permitted more radiant results to be achieved.

During the Coalport-Caughley period decoration was confined chiefly to painting and printing in underglaze blue. A small amount of polychrome work was carried out. From about 1805 the outstanding motifs of transfer-printed designs in pink or purple outline were filled in with brush-work, portions of the transfer remaining undecorated. Blue printing included the all-over Caughley designs of blue willow and blue dragon.

Decorative motifs were always more sparsely applied on Coalport domestic table-ware than on competing productions, and such ware always constituted the greater proportion of output. Flower painting was mannered and gilding usually light in colour. Similar ware from Rockingham may be distinguished by its copper-hued gilding. Although gilding was lavish it did not so completely cover the surface as on the work of Spode and Derby. In 1821 Samuel Walker introduced a maroon ground which became a Coalport characteristic.

After perfection of the felspar body in about 1820, Coalport output became richer and more varied. Splendid dinner, dessert and tea services decorated with brilliant colours and burnished gilding were created during the reign of George IV. So exquisite did Rose II consider the felspar body that he copied the more magnificent Sèvres,

Meissen and Chelsea shapes, reproducing colours, decorations and marks used in the eighteenth century. These handsome pieces, made consistently for nearly twenty years, are now frequently presented as genuine products of the famous continental factories, although paste and glaze differ entirely, and the thinly applied, burnished gilding of Coalport bears little resemblance to the dull gold used on the originals.

Great expense was involved in experimental work to emulate rich ground colours in imitation of Sèvres, particularly turquoise blue. Coalport used a pale, feeble imitation known as *celeste* until 1840 when an improved version was evolved, but even this never equalled the old Sèvres colour. The claret of Chelsea and the deep velvety mazarine of Derby were among the successful efforts in ground colour decoration. So accurately were these colours reproduced that it is difficult to distinguish them from their originals. From Worcester, Derby and Staffordshire Rose attracted experienced artists capable of reproducing the stylish colours and patterns introduced by his competitors. The Registration of Designs Act of 1842 prevented a continuance of this practice.

Coalport made every style of china admired during the period, and by the time of William IV the establishment was recognized as one of the most important potteries in the kingdom. Decorative ware such as vases, clock cases, ink stands, pastille burners and night lights in the form of cottages might be overlaid with masses of tiny flowers modelled in the round, and on fine work often enclosing painted landscape panels. The largest of such flowers, representing carnations, sweet peas and ranunculus, were Coalport characteristics. These flower-encrusted pieces are usually referred to by collectors as "Colebrook Dale china", from the name given to the works in 1828 by John Rose II because of Coalport's proximity to the celebrated Coalbrookdale ironworks.

There is no typical Coalport style of decoration, although unmarked pieces may be recognized by their characteristically clean painting in light, fresh colouring. A series of wide-mouthed jugs in various sizes, often painted with

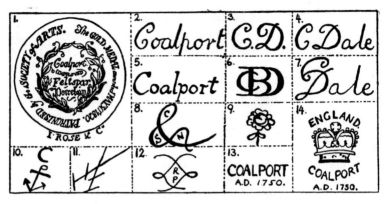

Marks used by the Coalport firm:

1.   From 1820 onwards, printed in red.
2.   1815–28, painted in blue script.
3–7.   "Coalport" and various shortenings of "Colebrook Dale" used 1828 to *c*. 1850; No. 6 possibly to 1861.
8.   1861–75, the letters standing for factories which they claimed to have incorporated—Caughley, Swansea, Nantgarw.
9.   Rare—for John or W. Rose.
10–12.   Adaptations of other firms' marks—Chelsea, Meissen, Sèvres.
13.   1875–81. This mark shows the introduction of the date 1750 which the firm claimed as its date of foundation.
14.   A later specimen, used from 1894, when the word "England" was required by law.

large pink roses and inscribed beneath the lip, were a Coalport speciality of 1828–40, but are often assumed to be much earlier. From about 1840 flat slabs of china decorated with naturalistic groups of flowers and fruits had a considerable vogue. Coalport made particularly handsome examples in the form of trays, wall pictures with burnished gilt frames, and furniture and fireplace decorations. Eggshell china of paper-thinness was made from 1845.

Coalport was the first English pottery to obtain the famous *rose pompadour* colour for which a gold medal was awarded at the Great Exhibition, the Jury describing it "a particularly remarkable rose ground, not only being the nearest approach seen to the famous colour which it is designed to imitate, but also commended for the excellence of the flower-painting, gilding and other decorations, and in hardness and transparency of the glaze".

Collectors should note that a vast quantity of biscuit china, the accumulation of half a century, was taken from stock in 1875 and decorated in mid-Victorian style, although paste qualities and forms were those of earlier periods. Such pieces are marked COALPORT A.D. 1750.

Early Coalport china was unmarked, but examples of Caughley-Coalport might be marked with "C", "S", or various disguised numerals, in blue underglaze. From 1815 to 1828 the name "Coalport" was painted in blue script on bone china.

Felspar china, made from 1820, might be marked J. R. F. S. CO. printed in red, indicating perhaps that Rose formed a separate company for its development. More usually the mark is a circle 2 inches in diameter inscribed "Coalport (Improved) Feltspar Porcelain" within a laurel wreath encircled with the words "Patronised by the Society of Arts. The Gold Medal awarded May 30th 1820." This was printed in red and the inscription might include the name "J. Rose & Co.".

Marks on bone china from 1828 until about 1850 include: JOHN ROSE & CO.; COLEBROOK DALE; C.D.; C. DALE; C. B. D., in blue script of various forms. A monogram "CBD" in blue or gold marked china made at the time of the Great Exhibition and possibly until 1861. From then until 1875 a "C" was combined with an "S" scroll to form three loops containing the letters "CSN": this was used in gold, occasionally in red or blue enamel. The letters enclosed in the loops are the initials of Caughley, Swansea and Nant-garw, factories which the firm claimed to have incorporated. Between 1875 and 1881 the mark was COALPORT A.D. 1750; from 1881 to 1894 the same with the addition of a crown; from 1894 with the addition of the word ENGLAND. Late marks are all printed in dark green. The Coalport factory is still in operation.

23

THE name Minton immediately calls to mind a wealth of beautiful china decorated in the manner of Sèvres with flowers, birds, animals, landscapes, garlands, bouquets and *fêtes galantes*, framed in radiant backgrounds of blue, canary yellow, apple green, soft pink and turquoise. The man particularly associated with these glories was Herbert Minton (1793–1858), a keen business man, enterprising, indefatigable, dignified, kindly. But it was his father, Thomas Minton (1765–1836), who founded the pottery which later won world renown. Thomas Minton was born at Wyle Cop in Shrewsbury and in due course was apprenticed to Thomas Turner of Caughley as a transfer-print engraver. This craft was then in its infancy. Minton's original copper plate of the willow pattern is a treasured relic now in the British Museum.

Soon after becoming a journeyman in 1786 Minton found employment with Josiah Spode at his London ware-house where he was provided with a private workshop to ensure secrecy for his work of transfer-printing in blue under the glaze. Here he engraved copper-plates adapted from oriental originals. So delighted was Spode with the work that he commissioned James Northcote, R.A., to paint Minton's portrait.

On New Year's Day 1789 Minton married Sarah Webb of Bruton Street, and almost immediately moved to Stoke where he set up as a master engraver. From his workshops in a block known as Bridge House, erected by Thomas Whieldon, he designed and engraved copper plates for printing in blue underglaze, at the same time supplying stock transfers to small potters. Assisted by Henry Doncaster of Penkhull, Minton designed and engraved an adaptation of the blue willow for Spode. Among his pupils was W. Greatbach, father of the eminent engraver, and later chief engraver with Spode and Copeland.

In 1793 Minton built a house and works on the banks of the Trent at Stoke and began the manufacture of printed earthenware on a small scale. A contemporary records that "to start with there was one 'Bisque' and one 'Glost' oven with a slip house for preparing the clays, and only such other buildings and appliance as were necessary to make a good working commencement".

Well established by 1796, Minton soon turned his attention to the new bone china being produced so successfully by Spode, its manufacture made possible by the expiration in that year of Cookworthy's extended patent. Minton secured the co-operation of Joseph and Samuel Poulson who were making earthenware in an adjacent pottery. Joseph, formerly Spode's manager, was a highly skilled practical potter; Samuel a clever mould-maker and modeller. Their technical knowledge, combined with Minton's skill as an organizer and decorator, enabled them to produce and market successfully a wide range of table-ware in bone china decorated with blue transfers in imitation of painted Nankin. Orders had become so heavy by 1798 that financial assistance was secured from William Pownall, a Liverpool merchant. At the same time Joseph Poulson became a partner, the firm trading as "Minton, Poulson and Pownall".

So tremendous became the demand in the Potteries for Cornish china-clay and china-stone that in 1799 Minton bought suitable deposits at St. Denis and formed the Hendra Company to work them. His associates were several master potters including Wedgwood, and the New Hall firm of Hollins, Warburton, Daniel and Company, owners of the Cookworthy patent from 1781 until 1796. The Hendra Company operated profitably until the 1850s.

Minton became sole proprietor of the pottery in 1808 following the death of Poulson and again traded under his own name. John Turner, who had joined Minton after the failure of his own business in 1803, now became managing potter and was responsible for remarkable improvements in earthenware bodies and glazes. About fifty workers were employed at this time. When Minton took his sons Thomas and Herbert into partnership in 1817 the firm was styled "Thomas Minton and Sons". Thomas resigned in 1821 to join the Church. Herbert Minton remained and it was chiefly owing to his unbounded energies that by the time of his father's death in 1836 the factory was among the most influential in the country.

Herbert Minton at once entered into partnership with John Boyle, the firm trading as Minton and Boyle. After five years Boyle resigned and joined the Wedgwood establishment. Michael Hollins, a nephew of Minton's first wife, and Colin Minton-Campbell were later taken into the firm: Minton was married three times, but there were no children. At the time of his death in 1858 more than 1500 workers were employed. The firm has continued to the present day.

Early Minton bone china had a faintly greyish tint and was inclined to be flawed with black specks. Gradually the paste became purer and whiter of body and by 1815 equalled that of any competitor. Borax to a considerable extent replaced lead in the glaze from about 1830. By 1825 the firm was priding itself upon a bone china whiter and more translucent than that made elsewhere, with highly lustrous glaze. In the museum at Sèvres are some fine examples of Minton china bought in 1826: alongside are others of about 1840 showing further remarkable progress in body and colour brilliance.

Decoration until about 1820 was simple. In addition to blue-printed underglaze patterns in the Nankin style, there were transfer-printed shell and seaweed patterns in dark brown: some excellent stipple printing belongs to the Regency years. Polychrome decoration consisted chiefly of painted flower motifs. Slight landscapes painted in black, red or blue monochrome without gilding were also issued.

A number of skilled artists joined Minton from Derby during the early 1820s, introducing decorations in the style of contemporary Derby but painted with considerably greater clarity. Ground colours of exceptional purity were now produced including carmine, purple, *bleu turquoise, rose du Barry, bleu de Vincennes, gros bleu* and *pomme verte*, effects all secured by combining gold with salts of ammonia and various other chemicals. Outstanding among Minton's artists in fruit and flowers from this period were Steele, Bancroft and Hancock. John Simpson was the principal enameller of figures and fine-quality ware from 1837 to 1847 when he went to London to take charge of enamel painting on porcelain at the school of industrial design established at Marlborough House. Samuel Bourne was the chief designer until 1848 when the growing importance of pupils from schools of design influenced a change in favour of decoration in the French style.

Bourne was succeeded by Leon Arnoux, already internationally known as being "more profoundly versed in the mysteries of ceramic manufacture than any other savant in France". Decoration now followed the style of old-Sèvres, and the production of cabinet pieces never intended for utilitarian service became important.

Herbert Minton, by economizing on the various manufacturing processes and without affecting appearance, succeeded in converting formerly expensive table services into everyday commercial wares. Labour costs on such ware never exceeded 30 per cent of total production outlay: on ornamental and cabinet-ware these seldom represented less than 60 per cent. Like other great potters of the 1840s Minton issued blue-printed ware.

From about the mid-nineteenth century, the firm was renowned for the now scarce reproductions of faience, Palissy ware, Della Robbia ware and majolica. The faience gives an effect of intricate inlay, its pure white clay body being covered with interlacing arabesques whose spaces are filled with vari-coloured pastes. Palissy, majolica and Della Robbia ware display very distinct characteristics, but all were made from a calcareous clay body covered with opaque white enamel composed of sand, tin and lead. Enamel glazes supplied the colour decoration.

The exquisite *pâte-sur-pâte* decoration developed by Sèvres was made from about 1870. This took the form of ornamental motifs and figure subjects on a bone-china background coloured black, green, blue or dark grey. A thin wash of the slip gave a translucent film so that by washing on successive layers where required gradations of tint were produced. Figure designs were built up by methods reminiscent of Wedgwood's Georgian jasper. Other potters made this ware, but not with the meticulous care exercised by the Minton establishment.

Minton marks are neither complicated nor numerous. The early mark consisted of the crossed L's of Sèvres, somewhat modified, with the addition of the letter "M". The mark was usually in blue enamel and a number might be added. A Roman "M" belongs to the same period. From 1836 to 1841, with the admission of John Boyle into partnership, the mark consisted of an elaborate cartouche containing the name of the pattern and the initials "M. & B." This was printed in blue. From 1842 symbols were used to indicate the year of manufacture: a list of these appears in *Nineteenth Century English Pottery and Porcelain* by Geoffrey Bemrose.

From 1851 a filled-in trefoil or ermine mark with three dots above might be impressed or printed. The name Minton impressed was first used in 1865. The globe with the name Minton inscribed across it appeared in 1868 and was printed on all later productions. Design registration stamps were also used from 1842 to 1883.

24

THE white brilliance of Rockingham china, radiant with glowing colour and sumptuous gilding, made it the choice of William IV when he selected a dessert service to grace the table of his coronation banquet. This magnificent 200-piece service, now displayed intact in the household breakfast-room at Buckingham Palace, was made to the command of the king at a price not to exceed £5,000. Yet so lavish was its ornate decoration and so thick the burnished gold, that factory cost was immeasurably higher.

The 144 plates bear the royal arms in full colour in the centre, with a border of oak leaves. The other pieces are enriched with views of English country homes.

This utter disregard for expense was adequately compensated for by a seven-year flow of orders for richly decorated table services from the English nobility and foreign royalty. A Rockingham dessert service became essential to the ambitious hostess, and a vogue was also created for the firm's less expensive china.

While the products of the generally accepted Rockingham period 1820–42 are widely appreciated in spite of what now appears often to be tasteless design, and while attribution of much fine unmarked Staffordshire bone china is made to this firm, comparatively few collectors know the full story of Rockingham. Few appear even to be aware that china manufacture was continued by a member of the firm after the closing of the original works. Fewer still, perhaps, associate the name with earthenware production in the reign of George II.

Earthenware was already being manufactured on the

estate of the Marquess of Rockingham at Swinton, near Rotherham in Yorkshire, when Edward Butler discovered a bed of fine clay near Swinton Common. Here, in about 1745, he established a small pottery, and it was this that was developed during the reigns of George IV and William IV by the Brameld family into the celebrated Rockingham Works. Butler made nothing more than common brown domestic earthenware, and upon his death in 1765 production continued uneventfully under Thomas Malpass.

When Thomas Bingley became proprietor in 1778 he modernized and enlarged the works, increasing the scope of production to include white earthenware, both painted and printed in blue. It was Bingley who first won repute for the name of Rockingham by originating the celebrated tea and coffee services, brown-glazed, chocolate-coloured and mottled, and often richly gilded with oriental and floral designs. Although for long advertised as "Rockingham china", they were actually a hard earthenware covered with a rich-brown glaze. This so-called "Rockingham china" has been responsible for the legend that Rockingham bone china dates to the eighteenth century, when in fact it dates no earlier than 1821. Jugs in this brown-glazed earthenware were issued in tens of thousands in all shapes and sizes. The Bingley versions of the toby jug continued in demand for more than half a century: especially popular was his model of a snuff-taking squire.

Green, Bingley and Company, who operated the Rockingham pottery from 1790 until 1807, were associated with the Leeds Pottery, their printed price lists being identical apart from their headings. This firm made a fine cream-ware and open basket-ware superficially resembling that made at Leeds. They also manufactured a lustrous black-ware resembling that of Jackfield in Shropshire. The factory was acquired in 1807 by John and William Brameld (d. 1819 and 1813).

Rockingham earthenware was sometimes marked. Eighteenth-century examples might bear the name "Rockingham" in a bold cursive script: from 1790 impressed Roman capitals were used. The name "Brameld Brameld and Co" impressed in Roman capitals belongs to the period 1807–19.

Upon the death of John Brameld in 1819 the works passed into the possession of his three nephews, Thomas, George Frederick and John Wager Brameld. These men introduced the manufacture of bone china to Rockingham and brought to the factory its brief spell of lavish splendour. Thomas, the technician of the family, was also the most influential, and was described by Jewitt as "a man of exquisite taste intent on making art-advances in his manufactory". He was soon engaged in experiments which resulted in the establishment of the Bramelds as manufacturers of fine bone china, with John Wager Brameld in charge of the decoration. In 1821 appeared a small amount of the ornamental ware for which the Bramelds became celebrated.

The Bramelds searched England for suitable materials, selecting only the finest from Cornwall, Devon, Sussex and Kent. Calcined bones were used to give strength and whiteness, and the hard glaze was in effect a transparent glass. Experienced craftsmen and decorators of bone china were attracted from Staffordshire and Derby by offers of higher wages and eventually there was a considerable interchange of workmen and artists between the three areas.

While their competitors were governed by production costs the Bramelds entirely ignored such considerations in their determination to achieve technical perfection in what was then a comparatively new medium. The resulting china in its most luxurious forms displays more advanced potting technique and more beautiful glazing, enamelling and gilding than any comparable contemporary work. Form and superabundant decoration were in the execrable florid rococo taste of the period, an after-war reaction against the severe empire and classical styles.

So costly were Brameld productions that financial resources, dependent upon profits from the earthenware which they still made, proved unequal to the strain. Instead of bankruptcy, however, they had the good fortune to attract the interest of Earl Fitzwilliam, who came to their aid in 1826. The further extent of his patronage and that of his successor from 1833 is still to be established, but it is significant that the Fitzwilliam griffin was introduced as a trade mark in 1826 and the undertaking re-named "The Rockingham Works". It is assumed that the Earls Fitzwilliam subsidized the Bramelds until about 1840.

The range of colours used at Rockingham was unrivalled during the 1830s: particularly gorgeous were many of the ground colours. Among these the thick, smooth opaque apple green is the most celebrated and is peculiar to Rockingham: the somewhat harder shade of green sometimes noticed was brought about by the use of an impure metallic oxide. Rockingham blue grounds, which include a deep *gros bleu* verging towards violet, are notable for their rich shadings and variations of tone, the mazarine and *bleu de ciel* being particularly soft and attractive. Reds vary from a deep pink to a maroon closely resembling that used by Chelsea more than half a century earlier. Derby's canary yellow was copied, but the Rockingham version is considerably darker. The delicate peach tint of Rockingham is very rare. A pink ground enriched with a gilded diaper pattern was a favourite decoration. Tea, dinner and dessert services were ornamented with these ground colours, edges of plates, dishes and cups frequently being in raised designs of moulding heavily gilded.

In an effort to outshine their rivals the Brameld brothers turned to the lavish application of gilding, often in delicate lace patterns never made elsewhere, but usually in areas of solid gold highly burnished. Wide gilt borders with heavy gilt knobs and gilt animals for handles and cover finials are characteristic. With the passing of years Rockingham gilding has tended to acquire a faint coppery tinge.

Dessert services were characterized by relief-moulded edges usually enriched with delicate gilt scrollwork and handles in the form of moulded leaves in which the veins were picked out in gold. Dinner services adapted from late Georgian silver and enriched with delicate sprays of flowers in natural colours, often against a yellowish background, were issued in considerable numbers, as was a wide variety of ornamental ware encrusted with exquisitely modelled flowers in high relief. Baskets constructed of bone-china straws were handsomely enriched with such flowers.

Some experts believe a light feather touch in the details of painted flower decoration on bone china to be exclusively a Rockingham feature, particularly in table-ware. These tiny sprays, however, were the work of Edwin Steele who worked also at Derby and in Staffordshire. Tea-cup interiors might be painted with well-composed views, the outsides being ornamented with patterns of gilding. Rockingham originated the resplendent style of painting tray or dish centres in gilded cartouches, with a skilfully executed miniature in each corner. Rockingham vases, although excellently modelled, display little originality in form or decoration, many of them obviously inspired by Derby and Worcester.

The few Rockingham artists whose names have been recorded include Edwin Steele, son of a notable enameller at Derby; F. Bailey the principal butterfly decorator; C. Speight the heraldic decorator; Collinson who enamelled plates and dishes with flower sprays, writing the botanical name in red on the back; and Isaac Baguley the flower decorator who continued this work for ten years after Rockingham closed, renting a portion of the old works for decorating china and earthenware bought in the white from Staffordshire.

Rockingham figures and statuettes are sometimes as gracefully elegant as anything comparable in English ceramics. Unfortunately, however, they are coarsely enamelled with broad washes of semi-translucent colour. A Rockingham figure may usually be identified by a gold-inscribed title on the plinth. Small shepherdesses, dancers and similar minor figures were made in a somewhat chalky biscuit, and may easily be mistaken for unmarked Derby work.

Rockingham animals are world-famed, but none surpassed the fine craftsmanship of the poodle series. These were excellently modelled, the curly hair being suggested with miraculously fine china threads. Although they were widely copied elsewhere no other firm succeeded in producing more than a matted effect.

After the death of William IV the patronage of the peerage was transferred to potters favoured by the new monarch. The Bramelds refused to lower the high standard of their decorations, a policy which quickly resulted in financial disaster and closure of the works in 1842. It must be emphasized, however, that the manufacture of Rocking-ham ware was continued at Coburg Place, Bayswater, London, by John Wager Brameld who used the original paste and glaze. He specialized in finely decorated cabinet-ware as splendidly enamelled and as lavishly gilded as before. There was, too, a considerable output of domestic ware decorated with loosely grouped flowers. Among

Brameld's display at the Great Exhibition 1851 was tableware ornamented with flowers, rose, shamrock and thistle in brilliantly coloured enamels.

The Bramelds did not consistently mark their bone china: in fact the majority was issued unmarked. Until 1826 an applied medallion might be used bearing the word "Brameld" in relief surrounded by a wreath of national floral emblems. On less costly ware the name only was impressed, or printed in red or purple.

The griffin crest of Earl Fitzwilliam was used from 1826 on Rockingham ware. The applied medallion bearing Brameld's name was a rare early mark.

Marks were always printed after 1826, when the griffin passant was placed above the inscription "Rockingham Works Brameld" in copper-plate script. This was printed in red, brown or purple. In 1830 the griffin was surmounted by a royal crown, and the inscription "Manufacturer to the King" was added below the factory name. After 1837 the word "King" was changed to "Queen". The royal crown surmounting the script legend "Royal Rock^m Works Brameld"—without the griffin—is sometimes noted on bone china made during the period 1830–40. There is no record that the firm actually made any ware to the commission of Queen Victoria and late in 1840 marks bearing royal references were discontinued, the firm reverting to the mark used between 1826 and 1830. John Wager Brameld printed the griffin with the name "Brameld" on his London-made china which dates from 1844 to 1854.

25

DAVENPORT, WEDGWOOD AND OTHER BONE CHINA MANUFACTURERS

THE revolutionary change from soft porcelain to bone china that marked the beginning of the nineteenth century affected practically all the English porcelain-makers. The resultant developments by Spode, Minton, Coalport, Derby, Liverpool, Rockingham and New Hall have already been described in the chapters on these firms. But to-day's collector is soon made aware that many other potters produced this china.

John Davenport (1765–1848), of Unicorn Bank, Longport, made some exceptionally fine bone china, but the majority of his domestic ware was intended for the low-priced market, and in consequence quality was not equal to that of Spode, Minton, Derby and others. He established himself as a master potter in 1793 specializing in fine-quality blue-and-white transfer-printed earthenware, great success being achieved with openwork rims on plates. Before the end of the century he had fully realized the potential of the bone-china trade, and by 1810 he was producing a wide range of colourful domestic ware as well as vases and a few figures. His reputation stood high as a potter in this medium.

Long experienced potters in bone china have declared that the texture, glaze and decoration of Davenport's ware was finer than anything produced by his contemporaries at this period. This, however, applied only to those magnificent services made to the commission of royalty and the gentry. He made the massive service used by William IV at his coronation banquet in 1830. As a token of royal pleasure

Some of the principal marks used by the firm of Davenport, of Longport, near Burslem, operating between 1793 and 1882.

Davenport was granted the privilege of including the royal crown in his trade mark. At this time Davenport employed more than 1400 workers, most of them producing inexpensive bone china. He now retired with a princely fortune and was elected M.P. for Stoke-on-Trent from 1832 to 1841. His sons continued the business until they closed it in 1882.

Flower and fruit decorations on the now collected Davenport bone china were enamelled in naturalistic colours of exceptional brilliance on a white, translucent paste, as opposed to the distinctly grey tint of the firm's less costly ware. From the early 1830s they made great use of ground colours, favouring a characteristic apple green. In tea services, which from the late 1830s often had coloured grounds of *rose du Barry*, cups might have sunken panels and gilded feet. Gold was lavishly used from the mid-1820s, vases having handles, borders, rims and feet heavily gilded and finely burnished. Borders of encrusted flowers might enclose a painted landscape.

Davenport's earliest work was unmarked. The first mark was the name DAVENPORT painted in red with three small irregular circles beneath. Early in the nineteenth century the name was lettered in an arc shape above an anchor, and from about 1810 this was transfer-printed. After 1806 the mark DAVENPORT LONGPORT STAFFORDSHIRE in three lines might be transfer-printed in red surmounted by an anchor. After 1830 the anchor was replaced by a royal crown. A mark used from about 1850 was the name DAVENPORT in a semi-circular ribbon enclosing an anchor. A small flower with six petals is a rare mark of early Davenport.

240

The success of fine bone-china domestic ware in the hands of such potters as Josiah Spode II, Herbert Minton and John Davenport so adversely affected the Wedgwood firm that they entered this field of the ceramic industry in 1812. Thomas Byerley, a partner from 1796, wrote shortly before his death in 1810: "Every day we are asked for China Tea Ware—our sales would be immense if we had any— Earthenware Teaware is quite out of fashion—and while we omit making China Teaware we are giving opportunity to other manufacturers."

Quality in Wedgwood's early bone china proved to be very uneven and the paste was often dense in texture. On the other hand some rare examples are of a quality which even Spode must have envied. Production ceased in 1822 in favour of stone china.

Decorations were mainly in the Regency style, but other patterns repeated those so successfully used on queen's ware for more than forty years. This was an unfortunate psychological error, for other firms were issuing more colourful modern designs. The first Wedgwood bone china issued is believed to have been blue-printed with a Chinese willow-style landscape. Wolf Mankowitz in his book on Wedgwood has listed twenty-seven designs from the Wedgwood illustrated pattern books where they are specifically scheduled for decorating bone china. The first of these, numbered 512, is described as "Chinese flowers, green ground, gold edge, and foot line and handles". The last, No 676, is noted as "Botanical flowers, with a green edge".

Many pieces were ornamented with birds and flowers adapted from Pillement's book of designs, in outline transfers overpainted in colours. Others were speedily painted by John Cutts with English and Irish landscapes. The embossed vine designs were modelled by William Hackwood. Tea sets were sold at prices ranging between 3 and 4 guineas each: dinner, dessert and coffee sets and a range of small pieces were also made. Wedgwood bone china is normally marked WEDGWOOD in red over the glaze, also in blue on blue-printed ware, and, rarely, in black or gold.

No fewer than twenty lesser-known Staffordshire potters

were listed as manufacturers of bone china in *Parsons' and Bradshaw's Directory* for 1818:

Goldenhill, Tunstall, etc.: Marsh and Haywood, Brownhills; W. S. and T. Rathbone, Tunstall.

Longport, Burslem, Cobridge, Hot Lane: Philip Brookes and Company, Sitch; Machen and Company, Holehouse: J. and R. Riley, Hill Works; Wood and Caldwell, Fountain Place.

Hanley and Shelton: Hicks and Meigh, Shelton; Reuben Johnson, Miles Bank; Frederick Peover, High Street, Hanley; Hollins, Warburton, Daniel and Company, Shelton.

Stoke: Poulson and Dale, Dale Street.

Fenton (or Lower Lane), Lane Delph and Lane End: Thomas Baggaley, Lane Delph; Charles Bourne, Foley Pottery; Thomas Drury and Son, Daisy Bank; Hilditch and Martin, Lane End; George and Charles Mason, Lane Delph; Mathers and Ball, Lane End; Mayer and Newbould, Market Place; William Nutt, Lane End; Simkin and Waller, Lane End.

Very little of the bone china issued by these potters was marked. Some collectors, therefore, are inclined to class such china collectively and without justification as Rockingham, and thus acquire for it the value of that establishment's flamboyant reputation. Alternatively, since these Staffordshire potters in bone china issued a considerable amount of ware in the style of eighteenth-century porcelains, some of this now masquerades as soft porcelain in many collections. From about 1820, however, new forms and styles of decoration were continually being evolved. So diverse were these, and so slight the variations in the pastes apart from progressive improvement, that it has as yet proved impossible to classify them on the lines of the eighteenth-century soft-paste porcelain.

The general tendency was for design to be overcrowded, colours brilliant, gilding lavish: on the other hand a great amount of table-ware was made in which decoration was limited to simple borders and painted or transferred posy centres. The parrot pattern, with its delicate mesh-work background in brilliant yellow, was among the most attractive decorations of this period. Japanese designs in the

Imari manner, with their deep velvety blues, bold patches of Indian red and rich gilding, such as were first issued by Spode, were followed by a flood of similar decorations from Derby, so that they have become known to collectors as "Crown Derby Japan". Industrial designs were freely pirated until the operation of the Registration of Designs Act, 1842.

Ground laying dates from about 1830, although the process was introduced by Henry Daniell of Shelton in 1826. The colours most frequently used on bone china were dark blue, apple green, deep yellow, canary yellow, grey, turquoise, crimson, salmon, rich yellow-green, lavender, biscuit or cane colour, striped red and gold, marbled brown and marbled blue. Ground laying or colour dusting was carried out with colours less fusible than those used by the painters and fired at a higher temperature to give a level glassy surface. This meant that they were unaffected by the firings required for the subsequent decoration.

SHORT BIBLIOGRAPHY

GENERAL

History of the Staffordshire Potters: *Simeon Shaw. 1829.*
Ceramic Art of Great Britain: *Llewellyn Jewitt. London, 1878.*
Contributions towards the History of Early English Porcelain:
J. E. Nightingale. Salisbury, 1881.
English Porcelain: *Sir Arthur Church. London, 1885.*
Handbook to the Collection of British Pottery and Porcelain:
Museum of Practical Geology. London, 1893.
Catalogue of the Willett Collection: *Brighton Museum. 1899.*
History and Description of English Porcelain: *William Burton.
London, 1902.*
Old English Porcelain: *M. L. Solon. London, 1903.*
Porcelain: *Frances Dillon. London, 1904.*
Catalogue of English Porcelain in the British Museum: *R. L.
Hobson. London, 1905.*
Chats on Old English China: *Arthur Hayden. London, 1906.*
First Century of English Porcelain: *W. Moore Binns. London, 1906.*
Transfer Printing on Enamels, Porcelain and Pottery: *William
Turner. London, 1907.*
Artificial Soft Paste Porcelain: *E. Atlee Barber. U.S.A., 1907.*
Ceramic Literature: *M. L. Solon. London, 1910.*
The Journal of Lady Charlotte Schreiber: *2 Vols. London, 1911.*
English Porcelain of the 18th Century: *Sir Arthur H. Church.
London, 1911.*
Catalogue of the Herbert Allen Collection: *Bernard Rackham.
Victoria and Albert Museum, 1917 and 1923.*
English Pottery and Porcelain: *Downman and Gunn. London, 1918.*
The China Collector: *H. W. Lewer. London, n.d., about 1920.*
General History of Porcelain: *William Burton. London, 1921.*

Analysed Specimens of English Porcelain: *Herbert Eccles and Bernard Rackham. H.M. Stationery Office. 1922.*

Guide to English Pottery and Porcelain: *British Museum. London, 1923.*

Picture Book of English Porcelain Figures: *Victoria and Albert Museum, 1925.*

Pottery and Porcelain: *Frederick Litchfield. London, 1925.*

English Porcelain Figures of the 18th Century: *William King. London, 1925.*

How to Identify Old China: *Mrs. Willoughby Hodgson. 1928.*

Transactions of the English Ceramic Circle: *London, from 1928.*

Old English Porcelain: *W. B. Honey. London, 4th ed., 1949.*

Catalogue of the Schreiber Collection of English Porcelain, Enamels and Glass: *Bernard Rackham. Victoria and Albert Museum, 1920.*

Some Thoughts on 18th Century English Porcelain: *Dykes. London, 1931.*

Catalogue of the Lady Ludlow Collection of English Porcelain: *London, 1932.*

English Pottery and Porcelain: *W. B. Honey. London, 1933.*

Catalogue of the Glaisher Collection: *Fitzwilliam Museum, Cambridge. Bernard Rackham. 1934.*

English Blue and White Porcelain of the 18th Century: *Stanley W. Fisher. London, 1947.*

Pottery and Ceramics: *Ernst Rosenthal. London, 1949.*

Traité des Arts Céramiques: *Alexandre Brongniart.*

Marks and Monograms on Pottery and Porcelain: *William Chaffers. Various editions.*

English Porcelain of the 18th Century: *J. L. Dixon. London, 1951.*

Nineteenth Century English Pottery and Porcelain: *Geoffrey Bemrose. London, 1952.*

The Decoration of English Porcelain: *Stanley W. Fisher. London, 1954.*

BOW

A Chronograph of the Bow, Chelsea, and Derby China Factories: *F. W. T. Tiffin. Salisbury, 1875.*

245

Bow, Chelsea and Derby Porcelain: *William Bemrose. London, 1898.*
Old Bow China: *Egan Mew. London, 1909.*
Bow Porcelain Early Figures: *H. W. Lewer. London, 1919.*
Bow Porcelain: *Frank Hurlbutt. London, 1926.*

BRISTOL

Two Centuries of Ceramic Art in Bristol: *Hugh Owen. London, 1873.*
Catalogue of Collection of Bristol and Plymouth Porcelain in the Trapnel Collection: *London, 1912.*
Old Bristol Potteries: *W. J. Pountney. Bristol, 1920.*
Bristol Porcelain: *Frank Hurlbutt. London, 1928.*
Champion's Bristol Porcelain: *F. Severne Mackenna. Leigh-on-Sea, 1947.*

CHELSEA

A Reprint of the Original Catalogue of one year's Curious Productions of the Chelsea Porcelain Manufactory: *Raphael W. Read. London, 1880.*
Chelsea Porcelain: *William King. London, 1922.*
Cheyne Book of Chelsea China: *Edited by Reginald Blunt. London, 1924.*
Chelsea Porcelain Toys: *G. E. Bryant. London, 1925.*
Chelsea China: *Frank Hurlbutt. London, 1937.*
Chelsea Porcelain: The Triangle and Raised Anchor Wares: *F. Severne Mackenna. Leigh-on-Sea, 1945.*

DERBY

Old Derby China Factory: *John Haslem. London, 1875.*
History and Classification of Derby Porcelain: *F. Williamson. 1924.*
Old Derby Porcelain and its Artist Workmen: *Frank Hurlbutt. London, 1925.*
Early Derby Ceramic Artists: *Major W. H. Tapp. London, 1925.*
Early Period of Derby Porcelain: *E. E. Hyam. London, 1926.*
The Derby Pot Manufactory known as Cockpit Hall, Derby: *F. Williamson. Derby, 1931.*
Derby Porcelain: *F. Brayshaw Gillespie. 1950.*

BIBLIOGRAPHY

LIVERPOOL

History of the Art of Pottery in Liverpool: *Joseph Mayer. Liverpool, 1885.*

Liverpool Potteries: *C. T. Gatty. Liverpool, 1882.*

Catalogue of Liverpool Pottery and Porcelain: *P. Entwistle. 1907.*

Liverpool and her Potters: *H. Boswell Lancaster. London, 1936.*

LONGTON HALL

Longton Hall Porcelain: *William Bemrose. London, 1906.*

LOWESTOFT

Lowestoft China: *W. W. R. Spelman. London and Norwich, 1905.*

Lowestoft China Factory: *F. A. Crisp. 1907.*

Lowestoft China: *A. G. Murton. Lowestoft, 1932.*

NANTGARW

The Ceramics of Swansea and Nantgarw: *William Turner. London, 1897.*

Pottery and Porcelain of Swansea and Nantgarw: *E. Morton Nance. London, 1942.*

Nantgarw Porcelain: *W. D. John. Cardiff, 1948.*

NEW HALL

New Hall Porcelain: *George Eyre Stringer. London, 1949.*

PLYMOUTH

Cookworthy's Plymouth and Bristol Porcelain: *F. Severne Mackenna. 1946.*

SPODE

Spode and His Successors: *Arthur Hayden. London, 1925.*

Antique Blue and White Spode: *Sydney B. Williams. London, 1943.*

The Story of Spode: *G. Bernard Hughes. London, 1950.*

247

SWANSEA

The Ceramics of Swansea and Nantgarw: *William Turner. London, 1897.*

A Guide to the Collection of Welsh Porcelain in the National Museum of Wales: *Isaac J. Williams. Cardiff, 1931.*

Pottery and Porcelain of Swansea and Nantgarw: *E. Morton Nance. 1942.*

WEDGWOOD

Wedgwood: *Wolf Mankowitz. London, 1953.*

Wedgwood Ware: *W. B. Honey. London, 1948.*

WORCESTER

A Century of Pottery in the City of Worcester: *Richard William Binns. Worcester, 1877.*

Catalogue of the Collection of Worcester Porcelain in the Royal Porcelain Works: *1882.*

Worcester China, *1852–1897: Richard Willian Binns. Worcester, 1897.*

Worcester Porcelain: *R. L. Hobson. London, 1910.*

Catalogue of Worcester Porcelain: *Drane. 1922.*

Catalogue of the Frank Lloyd Collection of Worcester Porcelain of the Wall Period in the British Museum: *R. L. Hobson. London, 1923.*

Worcester Porcelain: *F. A. Barrett. London, 1953.*

INDEX

(pl. *indicates plate number.*)

249